H
C
C
S

Harvard Contemporary China Series, 15

The Harvard Contemporary China Series is designed to present new research that deals with present-day issues against the background of Chinese history and society. The focus is on interdisciplinary research intended to convey the significance of the rapidly changing Chinese scene.

Popular Protest in China

Edited by

Kevin J. O'Brien

Harvard University Press

Cambridge, Massachusetts

London, England   2008

Library of Congress Cataloging-in-Publication Data

Popular protest in China / edited by Kevin J. O'Brien.
    p. cm. — (Harvard contemporary China series ; 15)
   Includes bibliographical references and index.
   ISBN 978-0-674-03060-2 (cloth : alk. paper)
   ISBN 978-0-674-03061-9 (pbk. : alk. paper)
   1. Social movements—China.   2. Political participation—China.
I. O'Brien, Kevin J., 1957–
   HN737.P65 2008
   303.48'40951—dc22

                                        2008013946

For Lianjiang, Betsy, and Molly

Contents

Acknowledgments

This volume derives from a conference held at the University of California, Berkeley, in October 2006. The impetus for the conference was a realization that work on protest in contemporary China had reached a critical mass, and it was high time to see what a group of China scholars could contribute to the wider study of contentious politics. The contributors were asked to consider how their research, old or new, used or challenged concepts and theories drawn from the literature on social movements. I was open to contributions on any social group and anything related to the unfolding or consequences of protest, so long as theoretical implications were explored whenever feasible.

To help us on our way, I invited David Meyer and Sidney Tarrow—experts on contention elsewhere—to serve as discussants. Both took to their task with rate-busting dedication, arriving in Berkeley ready to comment on all the contributions, not only the ones they had been assigned. To David and Sid, I am grateful for launching our discussions and pointing out implications we had missed. Two China scholars, Rachel Stern and Tom Gold, also offered insightful commentary on the contributions, knitting together close-to-the-ground empirics with the larger issues at hand.

Our conference would not have been possible without the generous support of the Institute of East Asian Studies, the Center for Chinese Studies, and the Travers Department of Political Science at the University of California, Berkeley. Nor would the weekend have proceeded so smoothly without the efforts of Elinor Levine. That she is the only staff member mentioned here, and that she ran three other large conferences that semester, says what needs to be said about her abilities.

Finally, I would like to thank Elizabeth Perry, both for her leadership in studies of Chinese protest (even when the topic was far less fashionable) and for encouraging me to seek publication in the Harvard Contemporary China Series. Although Liz was not able to attend the Berkeley conference, she volunteered to write a conclusion highlighting historical themes that are often downplayed in the current burst of research on Chinese contention. Like Sid Tarrow, who stepped up to provide a substantial prologue, I know that Liz joins me in welcoming the up-and-coming voices spotlighted in this volume, the careful fieldwork they have carried out, and their efforts to reach a broad audience with their writings.

SIDNEY TARROW

Prologue: The New Contentious Politics in China: Poor and Blank or Rich and Complex?

Apart from their other characteristics, the outstanding thing about China's 600 million people is that they are "poor and blank." This may seem a bad thing, but in reality it is a good thing. Poverty gives rise to the desire for changes[,] the desire for action and the desire for revolution. On a blank sheet of paper free from any mark, the freshest and most beautiful characters can be written; the freshest and most beautiful pictures can be painted.

—Mao Zedong, "Introducing a Co-operative" (1958)

The fifty years since these words were written have produced much evidence that Mao's "beautiful pictures" could be wiped away more easily than he supposed. Not only has China emerged as a "capitalist-road" powerhouse, but a new contentious politics has emerged to challenge the structure of political power he created and the new power centers that emerged after his passing. Yet aspects of the regime he created remain: the cellular structure of Communist power; the antipathy of the regime to dissidence; the availability of opportunities to petition for redress alongside practical inhibitions for such petitions' success; and a legal system that seems aimed at perfecting "rule through law" rather than the rule of law. China has changed in so many ways since Mao penned his painterly metaphor that its leaders' resistance to dissent stands out even more starkly than it did a generation ago.

Yet evidence continues to accumulate for the growing intensity of Chinese contention. In the state-owned factories of northeast China and the fields of Hengyang County in the central agricultural belt; in the throbbing metropolises of the coast and starkly poor inland villages; in the growing use of legal channels by an increasingly skilled legal profession and grassroots campaigns mounted by expropriated village and neighborhood dwellers; and in old forms of tax rebellion and new episodes of rural protest against China's one-child policy, China's panoply of contentious politics is expanding in step with its booming economic growth.

And here is something really new: a generation of younger China scholars—both Chinese and foreign—is beginning to explore the richness of China's emerging culture of contention with new analytic tools. Of course, they are not the first: culturally oriented and historically trained China scholars have long drawn on cultural and historical approaches familiar from the comparative literature on contentious politics. But this book is the first to self-consciously adapt the "political process model" to the Chinese case.

This trend is long overdue and should be welcomed by China scholars. A few years ago, animated by the rapid growth of the Chinese economy and its "peaceful invasion" of the West, a new subfield of Chinese political economy opened up. Intraparty politics, local politics, the politics of law and administration, and political protest all took a back seat to the issues of privatization, foreign direct investment, and industrial conversion, among others. It even seemed at times as if political scientists' studies of China would settle into a sinicized version of political economy—much like what happened to the study of Japan a generation ago.

Many of the lacunae are now being filled, with studies of urban and rural protest, industrial workers' collective action, use of collective petitions, disruptive protests, and religious heterodoxy. In a very short time, as this book shows, the study of contentious politics in China has become both rich and complex. Its achievements can best be understood when we recall, first, where the study of Chinese contention was a generation ago, and second, how rapidly it has been changing.

From the beginning of the Communist period until well into the 1980s, the study of Chinese contention had three main characteristics. *It was largely historical*—because scholars faced heavy political obstacles to studying current protest. *It focused primarily on "big" social revolutions and rural rebellions*—because Chinese history was full of such events. And *it had a largely structuralist rooting*, and most scholars of Chinese contention were heavily inflenced by this tradition.

This was no "little tradition" sealed off from the wider world of scholarship. Studies of Chinese rebellions and revolutions were avidly read outside the sinological community, and Lucien Bianco, Elizabeth Perry, Mark Selden, and other authors brought China to the center of the growing field of comparative social revolutions.[1] The historical sociologist Barrington Moore Jr., the anthropologist Eric Wolf, the comparativists Jack Goldstone and Theda Skocpol, and others building theories of social revolution drew on the original research of China scholars.[2]

But there were several gaps. Scholarship's historical bent (and the difficulty of gathering data on contemporary protest) meant that the event-based methods pioneered in the 1970s by Tilly, Gurr, and other Western scholars remained largely unknown to students of Chinese contention.[3] The focus on big revolutions left China scholars largely outside the new field of social movement studies that developed in the West after the 1960s. And the China scholars' structuralist rooting left them less attuned to the individual and organizational correlates of contention than their colleagues in the West.

But the Chinese tradition had major strengths that laid a positive foundation for the new generation of students of Chinese contention. The historical bent gave them a healthy respect for archival research and for precedents laid down by China's repertoire of rebellion and revolution. The focus on big revolutions connected the study of history to the study of the Chinese state and of changes in state structure and dynamics. That meant that China scholars would be in little danger (unlike some in the West) of isolating the study of social movements from contemporary politics. And the structuralist tradition made it natural for them to put Chinese revolutions and rebellion into a broad comparative framework.[4]

These virtues are all visible in the work of the generation of scholars whose work appears here. They are inspired by the historical tradition, but they also use methods that the earlier practitioners of that tradition could not, as they draw on approaches developed in Western social movement studies—especially the political process approach described by O'Brien and Stern in the Introduction.

A Laboratory for Contentious Change

This new generation of scholarship also bears witness to the great variety and increasing intensity of contentious politics in contemporary China. Consider these examples:

> From 1993 to 2005, *official* reports of acts of contentious politics increased from 8,700 to 87,000, many of them involving disruptive tactics or even violence.
>
> The Chinese repertoire of contention still draws on traditional forms of resistance like tax protest, but it has expanded to involve new forms, like internet-based mobilization.
>
> There is increasing use of legal procedures to advance claims that the legal system purports to guarantee, and a small cadre is developing of skilled legal practitioners who are pushing the margins of the legal system to respond to rights claims.[5]
>
> Alongside contentious forms of protest, there has been a widespread development of nongovernmental organizations (NGOs) nationwide; whereas, just a few years ago, scholars were wondering whether a "civil society" was even possible.

As this book shows, researchers are effectively using China's internal diversity for analytical leverage. Scholars are using regional differences in economic structure between the industrial Northeast and the booming central coast to highlight how different groups of workers frame contention. They are also exploring a wide range of social actors. Alongside peasants, workers, and heterodox religious groups—all well covered in traditional studies of Chinese contention—we find in this book Protestants, cyberprotesters, environmentalists, and taxi drivers.

The new generation is also experimenting with a wide range of Western methods, including event analysis, surveys, and frame analysis. But they have not forgotten the ethnographic tradition of village and neighborhood studies that root the examination of Chinese contention in the politics of everyday life. A diverse and changing society is producing a rich and complex panoply of studies of contentious politics.

Yet there are thorny questions that need to be addressed in a country as complex and difficult to study as contemporary China. Without attempting to survey the contributions to this book systematically, I will use them to raise three sets of questions: a first methodological, a second substantive, and a third theoretical.

Methodological Issues

When the new tradition of social movement studies developed in the 1960s, scholars had available a variety of tools: traditional historical methods and case studies, surveys of activists and event histories, organizational studies, analyses of discourse, and network and comparative analysis. Surveys have been employed in China, too, but for many subjects they require a far more open society than China's to be fully exploited. At the other methodological pole, local studies have a long tradition in China, but they are carefully monitored by local officials and are difficult to generalize from. Between these two poles, this book substantially expands the repertoire of methods available to scholars of Chinese contention.

Cultural methods are of course well established in studies of this topic, but *new* cultural approaches—like discourse and frame analysis—are not yet widely known. Chen and Hurst experiment here with these concepts and show how strongly the symbols of past episodes of contention mark Chinese experience today. Event histories of protest—when properly contextualized—can be fruitfully employed to study collective protest, as Cai's analysis of seventy-six cases of disruptive protest shows. Network and organizational analyses are also promising methods in China's expanding organizational universe, as Vala and O'Brien, Sun and Zhao, and Wright demonstrate. Finally, media analyses are still in their infancy in China, but Yang and Thornton show how they can be used to illuminate new forms of mobilization.

If I could have my wish for a methodological expansion of this book, it would be for more work placing Chinese contention in a comparative framework, as Teresa Wright so effectively does in her chapter. Three kinds of comparison should emerge from this book: regional comparisons within Asia; comparisons with other semiauthoritarian systems (it is striking that Russia appears only in passing here); and global comparisons based on middle-range issues.

Substantive Questions

Of the many raised throughout this book, four substantive issues seem particularly pertinent to China's future:

1. Aggregation and scale shift. In a 2005 article based on fieldwork in Hengyang County, O'Brien and Li pointed out that the area has a long tradition of resistance to local authority.[6] But until recently, constrained by the "cellularization" of rural China under Communist rule, farmers limited their claims making to local complaint bureaus or expressed their grievances in frustrated rage against official wrongdoers. But in the 1990s, O'Brien and Li began to observe a shift in the scale of mobilization. "Activists in Hunan province," they observed, "increasingly speak of a common cause and identify themselves as members of a larger community of aggrieved rural people."

What explains this shift in scale of O'Brien and Li's protesters to higher levels, and how widespread is it? We know that there is a disjunction between the regime's tolerance of local protest and its reluctance to countenance a shift in contention to higher levels of the polity. Is the traditional "cellularization" of the Chinese state giving way to trends that facilitate greater aggregation of contention? What role do institutional changes, like the "institutional conversion" Xi Chen finds in the *xinfang* (letters and visits) system, play in toleration of a shift in scale? And what are the limitations—both in protesters' repertoires and in the regime's still fearsome repressive capacity—for scale shift to eventually produce supralocal social movements? This seems to me a promising future direction for research on Chinese contention.

2. Economics and contention. A striking disjunction in the new literature on China is the gap between most studies of political economy and studies of contentious politics.[7] Are there patterns of causality linking economic development or economic inequality and protest? Many of the episodes examined here are associated with economic hardship—like the protests by laid-off workers studied by Hurst and Feng Chen.[8] Other protests are more closely linked to development, like the environmental campaigns studied by Sun and Zhao. Still others are not directly related to economic growth but are facilitated by China's technological development, like the cybermobilizations studied by Yang and Thornton.[9]

The studies in this book go far to link proximate causal factors—such as political opportunities, framing, and tactical organizing—to contentious politics. However, with the exception of Yang, they generally do not attempt to link these outcomes to broader structural trends in the Chinese political economy. How does economic growth influence Chinese people's propensity to engage in contentious politics? Does economic deprivation or economic growth produce more—and more challenging—episodes of protest? Do the economic and technological resources produced by development satisfy people's demands or offer them organizational and personal resources with which to engage in protest activities, or both? These are questions the next wave of studies of Chinese contention will need to confront. And one more has yet to be raised because China's contemporary economy has not yet undergone a serious recession: how will an economic downturn, when it comes, affect the magnitude and the methods of contentious politics?

3. *Policy responses to contentious politics.* Scholars of Western social movements have struggled long and hard to understand the outcomes of contentious politics.[10] When Chinese politics was both highly centralized and rigidly authoritarian, such questions seldom came up. But now that the country has become both less centralized and more difficult to control, scholars are beginning to think about the kinds of contention and the sorts of issues that are likely to receive positive policy responses. It seems clear that a good deal of local protest is tolerated and sometimes leads to such responses, whereas the aggregation of such protests into broader patterns of contention is vigorously repressed. Cai's analysis of disruptive protests shows that central or provincial governments are more likely to intervene in cases that involve casualties and are disclosed by the media—a finding recent media reports tend to support. In contrast, repression seems to be most likely when organizers attempt to organize across geographic boundaries. But apart from these precious findings, scholars of Chinese contention have not yet systematically examined the relations between protest and policy response.

4. *Transnational contention.* An important development in the field of contentious politics is the growth of transnational social movements. China's well-insulated state borders, and the difficulty transnational activists have in penetrating China's language and politics,

have slowed attention to this global trend. Yet as Thornton reminds us, China's large overseas communities are beginning to become active within China, and to offer Chinese nationals outlets for taking Chinese claims abroad, if only through online means. Foreign trade unions and international labor confederations are beginning to expose the working conditions of Chinese proletarians internationally. And Chinese environmentalists concerned about the country's galloping pollution are reaching out to the international environmental movement. It may not be long before China's isolation from transnational politics is a thing of the past.

Three factors make this eventuality a reasonably good bet. First, overseas Chinese are increasingly active within China. Second, China's growing involvement in international institutions, treaties, and regimes may eventually allow Chinese nationals to interact with activists from other countries and find a sounding board for framing Chinese internal problems.[11] Third, the activities of foreign foundations and NGOs within China are producing opportunities for both the "replication" and the "hybridization" of movements from the West.[12]

Two Theoretical Issues

Finally, this book engages two big theoretical issues: the relationship of contention to institutions and how contention advances or retards the democratization of authoritarian regimes.

Of the several international traditions of contentious politics research, this book is most directly inspired by the "political process" approach that dates to the work of Frances Fox Piven, Richard Cloward, and Charles Tilly, among others.[13] For the last two decades, this research tradition developed largely in the West. That meant that conceptual standbys of the tradition—for example, political opportunity structure, resource mobilization, and framing—were largely specified in ways that were easiest to operationalize in the liberal democracies of the West. This culture-boundedness made it too easy for scholars of the global South to dismiss the political process approach as "Western oriented."

This book is the first to systematically adapt key parts of the political process approach to China. The concepts of political opportunity structure, resource mobilization and framing, and innovations in how claims are made, recur throughout the book. Clearly, it has taken some conceptual abstraction and recontextualization to adapt the model to a country with China's scope conditions, which is as it should be. For example, Hurst and Feng Chen use the concept of framing but correctly specify it from within the Chinese experience; Cai's and Wright's studies of opportunity structure proceed from careful examinations of the opportunities and constraints protesters encounter in China. In adopting concepts from the political process model but specifying them in terms that fit the Chinese context, these efforts seem to me to have the best chance of bringing China into the international debate on contentious politics without ignoring China's distinctive heritage and politics.

I will not try to predict how sinologists will respond to these attempts to build conceptual bridges between the Western tradition and China. It is possible that—faced by the strong historical traditions of China scholarship—such innovations will be resisted by some. Even so, the blending of sinological and international traditions of social movement study is sure to take firmer root as China's internal politics evolves.

1. The relationship of contention to institutions. Traditional approaches to social movements in the West began from the assumption that social movements operated outside of politics, attacked political institutions, and followed different mechanisms and processes than did institutionalized groups.[14] A major innovation of the political process model was to specify contention in relation to political institutions, even when the actors involved were challenging the polity. This of course did not mean that movements and other contentious actors behaved like institutional actors; but it did imply that the boundary between conventional and contentious politics was porous and that contentious actors could be understood in terms of the same mechanisms or processes as institutional ones.[15]

These arguments are not unfamiliar, but they are specified in fine detail in this book. Consider, for example, with Xi Chen, the interaction between the process of "institutional conversion" and popular mobilization: "When ordinary people challenge authorities or a political system, ironically, they often turn to their targets for resources." Now think of the traditional institution of the *xinfang* system. As a mechanism for controlled participation, "it largely worked as designed before the mid-1990s. . . . After the mid-1990s, however, this system began to create strong incentives for collective action, to exert tremendous pressure on local officials to promptly deal with protest and to increase the costs of repression."

2. *Contention and authoritarian regimes.* That contention and institutional politics converge and interact is not news to students of Western social movements. Nor will limited changes in such regime stalwarts as the *xinfang* system on their own produce a system of representative politics. But if popular mobilization and institutional change intersect in other ways as well, we may eventually see fundamental changes in the current regime.

The history of Western contention is full of examples of institutional conversion *within* a regime leading to changes *in the nature of* the regime. Think of the evolution of the petition in eighteenth-century England. The petition was originally an individual's plea for redress from a powerful patron or a local justice of the peace. With the invention of the cheap penny press and the growth of named associations, petitions became a weapon of collective mobilization, both rooted in the tradition of patrimonial politics and implicitly undermining understandings about the personalistic nature of politics. Along with boycotting sugar and using the popular press to publicize the horrors of slavery, Britain's antislavery movement sent thousands of such petitions to Parliament. Eventually, that campaign produced not only an end to the slave trade but a change in how claims were made in Britain's modernizing autocracy.

We should not be overly optimistic: China's authoritarian system will not be transformed by such capillary changes alone, and modern authoritarianism has more robust tools to suppress dissent than England's eighteenth-century polity had. But such incremental changes and the unintended responses to them can often be more effective in bringing about regime change than more open challenges that question the bases of political legitimacy.

These are the kinds of changes the approaches and findings adopted in this book promise to help us understand.

KEVIN J. O'BRIEN
RACHEL E. STERN

Introduction:
Studying Contention in
Contemporary China

Do ideas drawn from the social movement literature travel
well once we leave the democratic West? In recent years,
there has been a chorus of calls to look beyond the United
States and western Europe to explore how popular contention unfolds in places where freedom of speech and assembly are tightly controlled.[1] But research on the staples
of contentious politics—for example, "political opportunity" and "framing"—remains more suggestive than comprehensive, both in illiberal states[2] and in Asia.[3]

The essays in this volume were all written by students of
Chinese politics and society. Each contributor, however,
has taken up the challenge to reach out to people interested in other regions and regime types. In so doing, the
contributors are part of a trend that has been apparent for
some years, as changes in academia have encouraged area
specialists to speak to their home disciplines and changes
in China have made it more comparable. On topics as distinct as political economy, law and society, and nationalism, sinologists have ventured provocative comparisons,
engaged colleagues who work on other countries, and
done their best to deexoticize China.

Among observers of contentious politics, the events
surrounding June 4, 1989, generated an outpouring of
analysis by longtime China hands[4] and social movement
theorists.[5] With worldwide attention riveted on unrest in

China in a way that it had not been since the Cultural Revolution, China experts and newcomers alike weighed in with fine-grained analyses of what transpired as well as what it meant for contentious politics. By the mid-1990s, it was clear that protest in China—or at least the events of 1989—had theoretical as well as historical significance.

With the exception of Falun Gong's rise and suppression in 1999–2000, popular action in China has seldom garnered the international attention it did in 1989. Still, unrest has grown of late.[6] In 1993, official Chinese statistics counted 8,700 "collective incidents" *(quntixing shijian)* (i.e., protests, demonstrations, marches, sit-ins, group complaints, and so on). A dozen years later, the number of such incidents had, by government measures, surged to over 87,000—nearly 250 per day. And China scholars have continued to quietly chronicle clashes over pensions, layoffs, corruption, land seizures, taxes, elections, and environmental degradation. By 2005, it had become easy to offer a semester-long course on collective action in contemporary China.[7]

Recent studies of China often touch on concepts from the contentious politics literature. Over the last decade, Thornton, Chen, and Mertha have discussed protest frames.[8] Wright has examined opportunities.[9] Zhao and Cai have looked at mobilizing structures.[10] Chen and Perry have considered repertoires of contention and their historical roots.[11] Others have examined a range of concepts.[12] Still others have given voice to notable "silences" in the literature.[13] These include emotions, grievances, and leadership.[14] Explicitly (or more often implicitly), these authors have all questioned the assumption of Chinese uniqueness, and instead suggested that ideas inspired by the movements of the 1960s could also help explain collective action in China and make it more legible to others.

Research on China, however, remains far from fully integrated into the study of popular protest. Much of the work mentioned above has only engaged social movement theory in passing. For a person interested in, for example, the outcomes of contention, searching for the wider implications of rich, on-the-ground findings has turned into more of a mind-reading exercise than it has needed to be. Moreover, most analyses of Chinese collective action have appeared in area studies journals or books pitched to a China audience, leaving read-

ers of journals such as *Mobilization* (or other contentious politics fa-
vorites) largely unaware of what has been happening in China, let
alone its broader significance.

This suggests an opportunity, particularly at a time when the study
of contentious politics has opened up to those who do not study industrialized democracies. Debates between the structurally inclined
pioneers of the field and more culturally minded critics have led to
an effort to recast concepts and mechanisms in less context-specific
ways.[15] This has created more room to consider culture, history, biography, and ideas—all daily fare for China specialists, out in the field,
grappling with the transformation of grievances into collective action. Staying attuned to these factors has also cleared the way to inter-
rogate the usefulness of established concepts in a country with a
vastly different heritage and history of class and state formation than
the capitalist West (Perry, chapter 10).[16]

With these thoughts in mind, this book aims to nudge the study of
contentious politics and China a step closer together. In October
2006, the Center for Chinese Studies and the Institute of East Asian
Studies at the University of California, Berkeley, hosted a conference
on popular contention in China. Participants were asked to link their
findings with concepts and theories drawn from the literature on
contentious politics, and two leading figures from that field (David
Meyer and Sidney Tarrow) were on hand to help us stay on course.
Presenters could discuss any social group and anything related to the
origins, dynamics, or results of contention, so long as they pursued
theoretical implications wherever possible. The goal was not only to
apply familiar concepts to China, but to modify or question ideas that
do not square with the reality of an authoritarian, non-Western state.
This volume, the product of that conference, thus showcases a group
of China specialists who are not only speaking to the contentious politics literature, but deploying old concepts and theories in fresh ways.

Political Opportunity

Above all, research on China demonstrates that "political opportunity"—external factors that facilitate or impede claims making—
must be disaggregated. There is not one unitary, national opportunity
structure, but multiple, crosscutting openings and obstacles to mobi-

lization. This diversity points to a natural advantage that all sinologists enjoy: China's size and internal variation. Instead of falling into whole-nation bias, China scholars are ideally situated to explain how opportunities vary across group, space, and issue.[17] The essays in this volume show that political opportunity in China depends (at a minimum) on the identity of the participants, the region, the grievance at hand, and the level of government engaged.

The most obvious way to unpack opportunity is by social group. A firmly established history of student protest, for example, affords Chinese students great latitude for complaint. Students, in Jeffrey Wasserstrom's words, have "have long served as a klaxon on public issues."[18] Even after the 1989 protest movement, "dissenting workers generally were treated more harshly than dissenting intellectuals" (Wright, chapter 1). Protests launched in the name of subsistence have also always had a certain legitimacy, which partly explains why aggrieved workers and peasants often receive a more measured response than groups like Falun Gong.[19]

Opportunity also varies by region and issue. As William Hurst points out, how local elites view workers' contention depends on a region's political economy. Officials in the Stalinist rust belt empathize with workers' clams much more than their counterparts in booming Shanghai. Guobin Yang also suggests that government attitudes toward popular action depend on the issue. Less sensitive themes, including anti-Japanese nationalism, the rights of the vulnerable, and local corruption, enjoy a degree of tolerance or, at least, indifference.

Another way to unpack opportunity is by level of government. O'Brien and Li's "rightful resistance" hinges on protesters locating support at higher levels for their efforts to check local misconduct. The Chinese state, in their words, is not a "monolith" but a "hodgepodge of disparate actors," an "attractive, multidimensional target."[20] Opportunities arise in part from "the central-local divide," as activists use the threat of (further) disruption to "increase the possibility of intervention from above" (Cai, chapter 8). Along these lines, Zhao and Sun's account of environmental contention also uncovers fissures between support for environmental protection by the central government and concerns with growth at the local level. Environmental NGOs, aware of this tension, cultivate highly placed allies in the State Environmental Protection Agency and urge them to put pressure on grassroots officials. This strategy sometimes works, provided that environmentalists do not become ensnarled in local politics and limit their challenges to low-level adversaries.

Still, sinologists and other students of contentious politics could undertake a more thorough "anthropology of the state."[21] From the commanding heights to the humblest field office, where exactly do openings lie? Shi and Cai suggest that a fragmented state, combined with differing priorities throughout the government hierarchy, provides multiple openings for resistance, especially for activists whose social networks include upper-level officials and contacts in the media.[22] Sun and Zhao's essay takes this argument a step further, noting that county and prefectural leaders are less formidable opponents than provincial officials, at least on environmental issues. Others have observed that rural activists frequently find townships to be tenacious opponents, whereas counties are often "paper tigers."[23] Much more research is needed to discover how cohesive authoritarian systems are, and what features of otherwise impressive edifices of power encourage activists to "venue shop," as they search for pressure points where elite unity crumbles.[24]

Collective action in China also offers insight into how openings arise and disappear in nondemocratic states. Students of contentious politics commonly advocate a dynamic approach to opportunity, where openings emerge, fade, and re-form over time.[25] The literature suggests several sources of change. In democracies, elections periodically alter the political landscape. The ascendancy of labor-friendly parties in the 1930s, for example, led to industrial insurgency in France and the United States, even as British and German labor remained quiescent.[26] In this way of thinking, openings, like a stretchy fabric, are slow to close. Success, especially for iconic challenges like the American civil rights movement, legitimizes claims and tactics for successors.[27] In illiberal polities, new openings typically stem from either regime liberalization or state weakness. Liberalization, such as Gorbachev's glasnost policy, can lead to an explosion of public critique and demonstration.[28] Signs of frailty, in an authoritarian state, can likewise embolden challengers or revolutionaries.[29]

Useful as they are, none of these ideas explains how opportunity has changed in contemporary China. China lacks a system of meaningful elections or any recent memory of a successful social movement. The state is strong, and the top leadership is not inclined toward political liberalization. If anything, Hu Jintao and Wen Jiabao's early years at the top have shown them to be less tolerant of dissent than their predecessors. Without significant political reform or elections, how do opportunities shift enough to enable widespread protest to occur?

Whereas none of the essays in this volume addresses this question head on, three touch on how opportunities can change, at least on a modest scale, without major political realignments. Xi Chen looks at the connection between "institutional conversion" and changes in opportunity. He argues that the decline of the work unit *(danwei)* and newly built coalitions between petitioners and higher authorities has encouraged the growth of collective petitions. Unrelated reforms and savvy complainants, in other words, has led to a change in one dimension of political opportunity—the extent to which the regime facilitates or represses collective claims making.[30] The implication here is that researchers should plumb how activists exploit (and sometimes urge along) beneficial institutional change. How are other organizations, such as courts or the police, adapting to and being transformed by contentious bargaining and pressures to take on participatory as well as control functions?

Guobin Yang's essay illuminates how the internet has generated new opportunities. Keen to promote economic growth, the Chinese government allows and even encourages internet use. Yet just as the internet facilitates business and diverts gamers, it also creates new openings for political actors—another dimension of political opportunity—and so promotes collective claims making.[31] At times, as the case of a murdered Beijing University student shows, water-cooler grumbling can escalate into powerful, collective demands. "Internet contention," to use Yang's term, can create a cadre of anonymous netizens whose posts both demand and receive government response.[32]

Patricia Thornton's essay examines how transnational ties influence political opportunities. Transnational activism was once an understudied backwater of contentious politics.[33] But researchers are now quite interested in what happens when domestic activists "go external."[34] In China, as elsewhere, globalization offers new access to influential, international allies. Exiled leaders possess resources that enable them to provide financial and spiritual support to their followers. Movement media outlets, for example Falun Gong's *Epoch Times,* organize popular action from afar. Just as American and Mexican labor organizers coordinated strikes and media blitzes against unscrupulous practices in border factories, the *Epoch Times* sought to orchestrate a mass resignation from the Chinese Communist Party (CCP).[35] Engineering such events from abroad can produce a boomerang of transnational support and help manufacture dissent, though high-profile activities may also backfire, if scandals or negative press tarnish the reputations of domestic activists and their international backers.

Teresa Wright's essay reminds us that after acknowledging that opportunities are crosscutting and evolving, opportunity structures in different systems can be compared. Wright explores how specific features of two illiberal regimes, including their propensity for repression and control over information, led to fear and distrust among protesters in China and Taiwan. Fear and distrust, in turn, affected the willingness of student leaders to compromise and made broad-based mobilization nearly impossible.[36] Different types of authoritarianism influenced relations between participants and each movement's reach, affecting not only the volume of mobilization but the form that it took.

Mobilizing Structures

Mobilizing structures—the ties that connect individuals to groups that organize action—come in many forms. NGOs, community associations, and work or friendship can bring people together to make claims. In democracies, social movement organizations, often run by professional activists, do much of the coordinating. When a state limits association, however, enterprising activists need to find different ways to inspire and organize contention. A sizable body of research shows that preexisting social networks nurture critical thinking and incubate resistance in illiberal regimes.[37] In difficult circumstances, prior ties take the place of more formal structures and reduce barriers to participation "by opening channels for uncensored materials to circulate, diffusing the risks of association, and, most broadly, substituting for a public sphere" (Vala and O'Brien, chapter 5). Social bonds also enhance solidarity and offer leaders opportunities to apply subtle forms of pressure on followers ("If you go, I'll go, too").

Several chapters examine the importance of personal ties while offering new perspectives on how social networks, and the trust they are built on, come into play. Trust, a touchstone for organizers, need not be synonymous with long-standing association or friendship. At times, as in the 1989 student movement, activists recruited only friends because they feared infiltration by state agents. But there are many ways to increase trust without relying on one's intimates. Vala and O'Brien show that strangers can be drawn to a movement and bonds can develop over time. Common identities, facilitated by shared background and constructed (or discovered) affinities, can build trust quickly and substitute for friendship. When risks are not too high (as they were during the 1989 student movement), "homophily" (using like to mobilize like) and recruitment techniques that rapidly create a sense of community may simply be different ways to create trust.[38] Shared experiences, like being laid off with virtually all your coworkers (Hurst, chapter 3), can enhance trust among acquaintances and strangers alike, and thereby aid organizing. The many paths to trust deserve more attention in studies of mobilizing structures.[39]

In this day and age, mobilization need not rely on physical proximity. Guobin Yang shows how internet chat rooms and popular websites create hubs of information that foster solidarity and aggregate claims, even though users never meet in person. Virtual contention can spill over into the media, influence public opinion, and affect policies. Even exile is ineffective when, as in Thornton's essay (chapter 9), organizers use cyberspace to reach across the Pacific Ocean to stage-manage spectacles arranged by devoted followers.

Space affects mobilizing structures in other ways. Physical environments play a crucial role in shaping mobilization.[40] The layout of Beijing University, for example, eased organization for students in 1989. Protest leaders only needed to "put several posters at the Triangle, write down the time, location of gathering, and purposes of the demonstration and slogans to be used" and wait for their classmates to show up.[41] Sometimes, however, finding a place to approach participants requires more effort. Vala and O'Brien suggest that by contacting targets in the ordinary flow of life and fashioning appeals using resonant language, Protestant evangelists have become adept at creating or appropriating "safe-enough spaces" in the creases of a corroding Leninist regime. Proselytizers take advantage of an increasingly porous state and exploit public and private spaces that are at least temporarily shielded from state control.[42] But Vala and O'Brien leave other questions unanswered. How safe do safe-enough spaces need to be? What, in an authoritarian context, makes a space "safe-enough"? What intrinsic limits on policing allow "havens" to emerge, even in repressive states?[43]

Like political opportunity, mobilizing structures take a distinct shape in illiberal circumstances, as activists adapt to a shifting and often unforgiving environment. Institutions as different as letters and visits bureaus (Chen, chapter 2), social networks, (Vala and O'Brien, chapter 5), and environmental NGOs (Sun and Zhao, chapter 7) can serve as proxies for social movement organizations, insofar as they help people attribute blame and suggest solutions.[44] Authoritarian settings offer insight into just how varied both opportunities and organizational forms can be.

Framing

In China, real (and potential) surveillance renders the usual business of framing particularly fraught. How are collective action frames—shared understandings of a problem and a possible solution—negotiated when freedom of speech and assembly are limited? When the marketplace for ideas is sparse and state-monitored, how can activists gauge whether frames strike a chord?

William Hurst's "mass frames" offer an explanation of frame resonance that goes beyond the common-sense understanding that effective frames somehow tap into the zeitgeist. Mass frames, by definition, are compelling because they dovetail with collective life experiences of social groups. Northeastern rust belt workers yearn for the security of Maoism, whereas their Shanghai counterparts tend to blame themselves for their troubles.[45] Individuals are not amenable to any picture of reality, but have coherent, structurally rooted worldviews that sometimes precipitate action. At other times, shared dispositions, shaped by the local environment, leave the disgruntled content to keep their heads down and muddle through.

If frames resonate because of the broader social arena, activists have limited leeway to fashion new frames out of whole cloth.[46]

Indeed, in Feng Chen's essay, organizers draw heavily on the rhetoric of Maoism and class struggle to frame grievances. Still, for Chen, leaders play a much more active role than they do for Hurst. Framing is a stirring up process that must be undertaken by agents. Even if mass frames explain the persistence of certain leitmotifs, contention requires agitators to articulate, adapt, and market frames. These two studies taken together remind us that discussions of framing must always keep one eye on leaders who voice claims and the other on participants who are moved to action.

The contrast between Hurst and Chen's essays also suggests that, like political opportunity, stirring up may vary from place to place. Northeastern workers, driven by deep proletarian disappointment, may not need as much prodding as central coast workers. But when mass frames promote complacency, how can activists inspire people to take to the streets? Much as James Scott's "hidden transcripts" are often more telling than what is heard in public, there may sometimes be a gap between frames that publicly reaffirm state power and ideas that privately induce the aggrieved to act up.[47] Organizers, at least in insecure states, often need "innocuous frames that support regime interests or power" if they are to secure elite allies.[48] As one worker's poster put it, "only the Communist Party can save China!" (Chen, chapter 4). Sometimes, participants truly hold such views. At other times, however, mobilization may rest on a different, private rationale. As Vala and O'Brien's essay suggests, sub-rosa conversations can be seductive. Protestant evangelists in urban China often rely on the appeal of Western culture—hardly an approved theme in a proud, socialist state—to spark initial interest. Once again, authoritarianism and a tightly controlled public sphere are sources of creativity, as activists work the system and repackage claims for different audiences.

Future Directions

The essays in this book are all designed to provide a springboard for new research. An extension of William Hurst's chapter, for example, might look at when mass frames are most salient and how they change. Or, building on Guobin Yang's study, when does internet contention move offline and into the streets? Or, following Yongshun Cai's lead, which of the three factors he isolates—number of participants, media exposure, or casualties—are most important for producing results, and do his findings about the effectiveness of disruption apply equally to all social groups and perhaps other authoritarian regimes?

As a whole, however, this volume suggests three gaps in the study of Chinese collective action and places where future research can make a contribution to understandings of contentious politics: (1) activism and the upwardly-mobile, (2) international influences, and (3) repression.

Activism and the Upwardly Mobile

So far, research on Chinese contention has zeroed in on the down-and-out: dislocated peasants, laid-off workers, unpaid pensioners, and tax-burdened farmers. These are the weak and disadvantaged left behind by China's economic boom. President Hu Jintao's vision of a "harmonious society" *(hexie shehui)* tacitly acknowledges that the authorities need to play a role in lifting them up. But where, with the exception of Sun and Zhao's environmental activists, is the upwardly mobile middle class? Are China's better-off content with their lot or, more likely, do they act up in ways different than the down-and-out?[49]

Social class should influence thinking about which tactics offer the best chance of success. Greater access to the internet and news from the outside world may, for example, affect the repertoire of contention for urban cosmopolitans. Some of the disgruntled may find that disruption pays off, as Cai describes, whereas others—perhaps those with more resources—may stick to polite, more institutionalized types of contention. Deciding among contained, transgressive, or boundary-spanning forms of claims making is always crucial.[50] What leads the aggrieved to turn to the courts or the streets is just one issue that research on China's upwardly mobile people is well suited to address.

Class may also offer insights into new types of grievances that are coming into view. To date, most contention in China has centered on material loss. For suburban farmers, this might mean fighting land expropriation. For homeowners, this might involve not-in-my-backyard efforts to protect property values endangered by a new highway.[51] However, is postmaterial protest creeping onto the agenda in China, and if so, what issues attract attention? Are a good number of academics, journalists, and crusading lawyers pushing causes like environmentalism and AIDS prevention, or are most too busy getting ahead and looking out for their own interests?[52]

Along these lines, the recent emergence of a "rights protection" (weiquan) movement, a loosely connected collection of lawyers and public intellectuals who use the law in defense of social and political rights, is starting to attract attention.[53] In a legal system with weak courts and little tradition of public interest litigation, it is not yet clear why attorneys and others have deployed the "weapon of the law" to protect citizens and push for change. Nor do we know when this strategy produces results or when it simply lands an activist in jail. Moving forward, researchers will want to unpack "rights protection"— a broad, ambiguous term—in search of a more nuanced treatment of how rights protectors with different agendas operate. Much more work is also needed on why their actions are sometimes tolerated and why, more often, they are not.

International Influences

China scholars are just beginning to consider international influences on contention. Like Thornton and Sun and Zhao here, future researchers will want to examine how external allies supply activists with resources and pressure opponents for change. But beyond this "boomerang effect," in what other ways do the aggrieved and their overseas backers find each other and work together?[54]

In China, one underresearched type of transnational activism is democracy promotion. Since Deng Xiaoping's "Southern Tour" rejuvenated economic reform in 1992, China has attracted unprecedented attention from NGOs, foundations, and foreign governments anxious to foster democratization or—given the realities of a one-party state—values like transparency, public participation, and respect for rights.[55] These days, everyone from the U.S. Department of State to George Soros's Open Society Institute is funding programs in China, many of which are aimed at developing Chinese civil society.[56] The international community, in other words, has taken to heart the notion that civil society, characterized by vibrant associations (a la Alexis de Tocqueville) and a large middle class (a la

Barrington Moore), will lay the foundation for democratic change. Thanks to the size and number of these programs, China offers an unusual opportunity to examine the relationship between funding and contention. Is international aid amplifying domestic calls for liberalization and boosting democratic consciousness? Or, as in the states descended from the Soviet Union, are overseas organizations supporting a few iconoclasts who struggle to find a following?[57] The sheer amount of cash that is up for grabs calls for close attention to power dynamics between funders and funded.[58] This is sometimes a blind spot in the literature on transnational activism.[59]

China's heterogeneity also offers an opportunity to pinpoint how international support affects contention in different regions and among different groups. Just as Africa is divided into "mineral-extraction enclaves" and "humanitarian hinterlands" reliant on NGO assistance, there are multiple Chinas, connected to the outside world in many ways.[60] Frames and tactics, for instance, may look different to Yang's technology-literate, Google-searching complainants and Chen's and Hurst's workers, most of whom are isolated from the international labor movement. Globalization, even in post–World Trade Organization China, is lumpy, uneven, and contingent. The challenge is to begin asking where, if at all, transnational influences—anything from collective viewing of the film *Erin Brockovich* to a $200,000 Ford Foundation grant—shift perceptions and ultimately action.

Repression

Integrating China studies and contentious politics also means comparing China to other authoritarian states. The next generation of research on Chinese protest may look more like Wright's essay: a side-by-side comparison of the dynamics of mobilization in two illiberal regimes. At the very least, China specialists need to read work from the Middle East, Latin America, and other places where limited opportunity and state surveillance shape collective action.

The good news is that China scholars are already accustomed to viewing collective action from the vantage point of the authorities. When studying China, all contention reflects political constraints, and negotiates and contests these constraints (Yang, chapter 6). Popular action in China is a call-and-response, in which complainants take cues from officialdom, even as institutions are evolving in response to bottom-up pressure. Chinese approaches to public security, for instance, have been altered both by increased exposure to contention and signals from the top.[61] Nowadays, police reports often describe protesters not as class enemies but as "exploited," "marginalized," and "socially disadvantaged."[62]

Yet for all the advantages of a state-centric approach, China specialists tend to focus on a thin slice of repression. Most research on Chinese contention touches on repression—how could the topic be avoided?—but repression is often distilled to crackdowns against protesters. There is room for a much more expansive notion of how collective action is suppressed. The most obvious starting point is to move beyond instances of ex post repression to examine ex ante suppression through socialization. In China, uncertainty and self-censorship play a key role in discouraging contention. The very arbitrariness of state control of the media, to take one example, cows most journalists into providing limited coverage of dissent.[63] A more nuanced understanding of repression would give China specialists another entry point into the contentious politics literature, where analysts now use the term "protest control," and recognize that repression varies according to the amount of coercion, the form it takes, the audience for it, and the identity of the repressor.[64]

Thinking about contention in today's China takes us beyond massive eruptions, like the Communist Revolution and the popular movement of 1989, into the quotidian world of resistance and response. Here, protest is rich and varied, encompassing camouflaged dissent, such as subversive doorway couplets, and boisterous demonstrations, such as traffic blockades by retirees who have lost their pensions.[65] In this volume alone, the disgruntled are found writing collective petitions, making claims on the internet, leafleting fellow workers, and taking to the streets, often quite disruptively. China offers a full palette of claims making. Episodes of contention that might go unremarked in an open, pluralist system illustrate much in a place where opportunities are limited, mobilizing structures must leave a faint footprint, and framing requires a deft touch.

The prominence of the words *opportunity, mobilizing structures,* and *framing* throughout this collection underscores the mainstreaming of

China studies. Although this trend has fragmented the China field to a degree (we no longer all meet in *China Quarterly* or *China Journal* to the extent we once did), it also provides an opportunity to make research on Chinese contention difficult for other social scientists to ignore. As China specialists contribute to wider conversations, there is much to be learned about how varieties of authoritarianism and domestic variation shape collective action. The essays that follow aim to bring research on China deeper into the study of contentious politics. We hope that some readers of this volume will take this venture a step further.

1 | Student Movements in China and Taiwan

Since the 1990s, the field of contentious politics has been enhanced by two related developments. First, scholars increasingly have turned their attention to closing the "gap between studies of movements in liberal democratic systems and those in the rest of the world."[1] Second, attempts have been made to refine the study of political opportunity structures by breaking down opportunities and movement characteristics into discrete elements and by specifying the linkages between particular structures and outcomes. This chapter builds on these developments by identifying and comparing the influence of specific illiberal political opportunity structures on student organization and mobilization in the mass protests of 1989 in China and 1990 in Taiwan. Rather than assuming that opportunities are automatically translated into activism, this study focuses on *how* activists translate opportunities into particular kinds of activism—both to their advantage and their detriment.

In these two cases, four elements of opportunity were particularly important: (1) single party monopolization of state institutions; (2) official control and manipulation of the flow of information; (3) official control and manipulation of social organizations; and (4) an official propensity to violently repress certain social groups. The importance of these factors varied not only from regime to regime but also over time, and during the course of each movement.

When these illiberal structures were more pronounced, student fear and distrust were magnified. As a result, the crucial collective action resources of organization and mobilization were impacted in ways that limited their expansion and effectiveness.

Illiberal opportunity structures hindered organization by heightening the need for pre-existing bonds of friendship to overcome student distrust and fear, and by exacerbating tendencies toward factionalism. When movement infiltration and repression were extremely likely, networks based on anything less than the most trustworthy connections tended to be characterized by suspicion, leading

---

Liberal	Illiberal

Single-party monopolization of state institutions
Official control and manipulation of information flows
Official control and manipulation of social organizations
Official propensity to violently repress specific groups

Lesser   ⬅   **Fear**   ➡   **Greater**
                          Distrust

Organizational instability
- Need for pre-existing bonds of friendship
- Tendency toward factionalism
- Tendency toward radicalization

Obstacles to broad-based mobilization
- Perceived need to demonstrate "purity" of ranks
- Perceived need to avoid connections with groups having uncertain membership and/or proclivities
- Perceived need to avoid connections with groups historically subject to official repression

Figure 1.1   The Impact of Illiberal Political Opportunity Structures on Mobilization and Organization

to organizational instability and ineffectiveness. In such a risky atmosphere, successful organization was possible only when it was based on personal friendship networks.

The fear-laden and distrustful environment created by illiberal opportunity structures also stimulated radicalism and factionalism. When the ruling regime remained intransigent in the face of conciliatory protest behavior, disagreement arose as to whether or not more radical measures were needed to force a response. In a high-stakes atmosphere, those calling for more radical activities were unwilling to abide by democratic decisions; indeed, in the cases studied here, such individuals chose to exit existing organizations rather than abide by a decision that they felt was too timid. For these individuals, more confrontational behavior was seen as proof of one's loyalty to the cause, and moderation was viewed with suspicion. Consequently, organizations tended to become less unified over time, and exhibited little ability to reach binding decisions. Illiberal political opportunity structures also lent legitimacy to this "radical flank," giving it power over more moderate groups.

At the same time, the risk, fear, and distrust engendered by illiberal political structures stymied cross-sector mobilization. To protect themselves from the real threat of official slander and repression, protestors felt pressed to demonstrate the "purity" of their ranks from outside infiltrators. Owing to a need for absolute certainty regarding the motivations and behavior of those within their ranks, protestors were unwilling to unite with groups whose proclivities or membership was uncertain. To further guard against repression, protestors avoided overt connections with groups that had been the target of official repression in the past. These necessities placed great constraints on each movement's ability and willingness to mobilize different social groups, and may have detracted from their ability to provoke meaningful change.

Political Opportunity in Nondemocratic Regimes

This chapter draws from and elaborates on two developments in the study of contentious politics. First, it builds on recent refinements of "political opportunity" theory. Initially formulated in the 1970s, this approach has come to dominate the field of contentious politics.[2] Its main assumption is that "activists' choices—their *agency*—can only be understood and evaluated by looking at the political context ... in which those choices are made—that is, *structure*."[3] Yet, despite its popularity, many have expressed concern that this theory often has been applied in a sloppy, incoherent, and mechanical fashion.[4] As a corrective, McAdam calls on analysts to be more explicit in identifying "*which* dependent variable we are seeking to explain and *which* dimensions of *political* opportunity are germane to that explanation."[5] And he emphasizes that analysts need to be more systematic in their examination of "the differential effects of particular elements of political opportunity."[6] The notion of regime "openness" must be disaggregated, such that the specific—and often differential—effect of regime characteristics on different groups can be clarified.[7] Similarly, the specific, and again often differential, effect of regime characteristics on movement resources, such as organization and mobilization, must be illuminated. Meyer also calls on scholars to pay more attention to "how distinct political opportunity variables might affect the relative prominence of particular forms of claims-making differently, as elites or authorities can channel dissent into particularly unthreatening, and perhaps less effective, forms of activism."[8] Finally, it is not the simple existence of "opportunity structures" that matters, but rather the *perception* of those structures by potential activists.[9]

These refinements in the political opportunity approach have dovetailed with the emergence of new studies of protest in non-Western and nondemocratic systems. Through the 1980s, theories of contentious politics largely were based on studies of protest in western Europe and the United States. Since then, scholars have begun to investigate the effect of more repressive and illiberal opportunity structures on collective action resources and outcomes.[10] Though the foci and conclusions of these studies differ, they generally find that the variables and assumptions of the political opportunity approach can be usefully applied to illiberal regimes. At the same time, these studies suggest that opportunity structures in democratic and nondemocratic regimes do exhibit some fundamental differences.

Perhaps the most noteworthy and consistent finding is the relative importance of media access and information flows in nondemocracies.[11] As Schock argues, these contextual factors do not vary greatly in democracies; consequently, they have been given less emphasis in earlier studies of protest. In authoritarian societies, however, press freedom and access to information vary substantially, both between regimes and over time.[12] Moreover, a free flow of information can facilitate mobilization even in repressive and unified regimes where mass opposition otherwise seems unlikely.[13]

Studies of protest in nondemocratic contexts have also explored how repression affects contentious politics. Of course, repression and violence are always possible when a popular movement pressures a government that controls the means of coercion.[14] Still, some forms of contention are inherently less likely to spur violent repression than others, and some regimes are less likely to use violent repression than others. Indeed, one of the clearest differences between democratic and authoritarian regimes lies in the latter's greater proclivity to use coercion to stifle public protest. Given this, scholars have explored how an increased likelihood of repression under illiberal regimes influences protest characteristics. The major conundrum here is the "repression-dissent" paradox: the finding that in some cases, repression has a radicalizing or mobilizing affect on the populace whereas in others, repression extinguishes popular dissent. Brockett explains this paradox by arguing that repression stimulates mobilization only during the ascendant phase of protest, when political opportunities are widening.[15] Others have found that the effect of repression is similarly dependent on the larger configuration of political opportunity structures within which repression occurs. These scholars argue that repression may spur greater protest when strong social networks exist, repression is considered illegitimate, a free flow of information is available, or influential allies are present.[16] Although these conditions are more prevalent in democratic societies, they can appear in nondemocratic settings as well.[17]

Although these findings are important, in general, the literature on protest under nondemocratic regimes focuses only on the question of *when* social mobilization is likely to occur, rather than *what form* it is likely to take. A notable exception is the work of O'Brien and Li, who show how a particular form of social mobilization—what they call "rightful resistance"—arises from specific political opportunity structures in post-Mao China.[18] In so doing, O'Brien and Li explain not just the presence of social mobilization, but its character. Similarly, my study of student protest in China and Taiwan shows how specific mobilizational features arose from particular illiberal political opportunity structures.

At the same time, this study adds to an emerging literature that looks at the impact of illiberal opportunity structures on protest *organization*. Looking at El Salvador from the 1960s–1980s, for example, Almeida documents how shifting levels of openness (specifically, the degree of institutional access and extent of competitive elections) first created civic organizations, and later spurred their transformation into more radicalized revolutionary groups.[19] In the same manner, my focus is not simply on the presence or absence of organization but also on the specific organizational features that arose from particular illiberal political opportunity structures, as well as their changes over time.

Political Opportunity Structures in China in 1989 and Taiwan in 1990

Following the counsel of students of contentious politics, rather than simply assessing the "openness" of the overall structure, I examine particular contextual features that impacted the daily lives of university students in each case: (1) the nature and extent of single-party controls over state institutions; (2) the nature and extent of official controls of information; (3) the nature and extent of regime manipulation and control of social organizations; and (4) the regime's propensity to violently repress specific social groups. Although both cases exhibit illiberal characteristics with regard to these four measures, these features were more extreme in mainland China in 1989. As a result, the student protesters' fear and distrust in China were also more pronounced.

In both China and Taiwan, a single party had dominated the governmental for over 40 years. Yet in each case, beginning in the late 1970s, ruling elites had initiated substantial economic and political reform. At the same time, by the late 1980s, Taiwan had moved much further in the direction of political liberalization and democratization than China.

In China, with the passing of Mao Zedong and rise of Deng Xiaoping in the late 1970s, the CCP trumpeted the goal of economic modernization. State controls over the economy were dismantled, and the CCP was repopulated with younger and more technically trained leaders. In the late 1980s, open and competitive village-level elections were legalized. Yet at the same time, the CCP evidenced no intention to diminish its monopoly on political power. Indeed, party elites viewed village elections as a way to strengthen party power by defusing rural unrest and ensuring compliance with unpopular policies.[20] Further, when confronted with political activism, such as the "Democracy Wall" movement of 1978–1979 and the student protests of 1986–1987, Deng made it clear that public calls for systemic political reform would be swiftly suppressed.

Even so, some top leaders within the party supported moderate political loosening. Most prominent among these were (1) former CCP general secretary Hu Yaobang, who had been removed from this post in 1987 owing to his support of the student protests, and (2) Zhao Ziyang, who had been chosen to replace Hu in the top party post. It was Hu's death in April 1989 that spurred the massive outpouring of mourning that soon mushroomed into the student movement of 1989.

In Taiwan, in contrast, by 1990, democratic activism had been legitimated by the ruling elites, and systemic political reform was well under way. In the late 1940s, the Guomindang (KMT) had invaded the island of Taiwan, bringing with it a government that had been elected on the mainland, as well as roughly two million KMT-affiliated "mainlanders." Local "Taiwanese" opposition to KMT rule was brutally repressed, and justified by martial law. In addition, the KMT-dominated National Assembly that had been elected on the mainland in the late 1940s was frozen in place by a series of "Temporary Provisions" that postponed the Assembly's reelection until the mainland was retaken. Following the death of KMT leader Chiang Kai-shek in 1975, his son, Chiang Ching-kuo, assumed control. Almost immediately, the younger Chiang initiated a series of political reforms, including amnesty to many political prisoners, the recruitment of local Taiwanese into party and government posts, and new checks on military intervention in politics. Encouraged, members of Taiwan's newly emergent middle class began to press for greater political liberalization. Along with publishing new independent periodicals, many Taiwanese activists ran for local office as "non-party" *(dangwai)* candidates. By the early 1980s these non-KMT candidates were winning roughly 30 percent of locally contested seats. In 1984, Chiang Ching-kuo selected a Taiwanese, Lee Teng-hui, to serve as vice-president. In 1986, Chiang announced that martial law soon would end, and that civil liberties would be protected. Shortly thereafter, *dangwai* activists announced the establishment of Taiwan's first true political opposition party, the Democratic Progressive Party. Instead of repressing it, the KMT legalized the formation of alternative parties. In December 1986, Taiwan held its first election involving competition between two independent parties. In 1988, Chiang Ching-kuo died, leaving Lee Teng-hui as acting president. When Chiang's term as president ended in 1990, Lee faced reelection.[21]

It was in this context that the student protests of 1990 emerged. Although Taiwan had undergone substantial political liberalization, the president was not to be directly elected by the citizenry of Taiwan. Instead, in accordance with the "Temporary Provisions" that had been enacted in the late 1940s, the aging KMT-dominated National Assembly would choose the president. Thus, the presidential election stood as a stark example of continued KMT control of the political system, and a lack of democracy at the highest levels.

Similar features characterized the nature and extent of official controls over information in both China and Taiwan. The ruling party dominated virtually all media outlets. As the vast majority of citizens under each regime received nearly all of their information through party-controlled news media, official reports had a large impact on popular perceptions. Moreover, the official media in both cases had long attempted to discredit protests with accusations that the demonstrators were puppets of outside forces bent on creating social turmoil. By the late 1980s, these controls had been somewhat relaxed in both regimes, especially in Taiwan. In post-Mao China, unsanctioned journals and newspapers were sometimes tolerated, and even official media occasionally expressed views that deviated from the party line. At the same time, all official and unofficial media outlets remained under the watchful eye of the party, and quickly met with repression if they were perceived as a threat. In Taiwan, by 1990 the media had been liberalized to a much greater degree, such that nonparty newspapers and journals enjoyed legal circulation and a small but substantial readership. Still, virtually all major newspapers, as well as radio and television stations, remained under KMT control.[22]

A similar pattern is apparent with regard to social organization: although the regimes in both Taiwan and China sought to penetrate and dominate social groups, in Taiwan these controls were more relaxed. In university life, in both cases the designation of key administrative figures, for example university presidents, was by the party-controlled ministry of education, and for the most prestigious institutions it often required consultation with top party leaders.[23] Curricular content and admissions quotas also were centrally dictated.[24] And in both cases, students were tested on party ideology on college entrance exams, and required to continue this study in their undergraduate years.[25] Student organizations were similarly penetrated. In both China in 1989 and Taiwan in 1990, students were allowed to form organizations only under the sponsorship and oversight of the party. The student campus government was to act under the guidance of the party, and student officers typically were selected by party-controlled student groups. Finally, official campus newspapers were controlled by the ruling party, and student-produced publications had to be submitted to a party-dominated committee for screening.

In China in the post-Mao period, these controls over education had been relaxed to the degree that unsanctioned student groups occasionally appeared, particularly at the ultraelite Beijing University. Yet these groups were never tolerated for long. In Taiwan, by the end of the 1980s, autonomous student organization was far less regulated. Many independent students had openly flouted campus regulations, not only running for campus office, but often winning. Consequently, the authorities tolerated the appearance of reformist student governments at many universities. In addition, other students with a more leftist bent were allowed to organize autonomous groups focused on social and economic justice. Nonetheless, at most campuses the KMT maintained a party branch, and each student was assigned a KMT-sponsored "counselor" (*jiaoguan*); these lived with students in the dormitory and kept close tabs on their behavior.

Finally, in both Taiwan and China, the ruling party displayed a high propensity for harsh repression of students who disobeyed official regulations. At the same time, cooperation with and loyalty to the party was often were rewarded with desirable employment and, in the case of Taiwan, scholarships. Typically, punishment involved expulsion or the entry of unfavorable remarks in a student's permanent record; in both Taiwan and China, such sanctions could severely impact a student's future.

In both cases, entrance to university was available to only a tiny percentage of the population.[26] A student who was expelled could not simply enter another university. Should a student not be expelled but still accrue unfavorable notes in his or her official record, the consequences could be equally traumatic—especially in the case of China. In 1989, the vast majority of university graduates in China still were assigned jobs by the state. Thus, a blackened record was almost certain to have a devastating effect on a student's future livelihood; not only would it guarantee denial to coveted posts but also it might bring exile to a position in a remote, undesirable region. In Taiwan, a sanctioned student had more freedom in job choice, but his or her alternatives were still limited by a tainted record. In addition, in Taiwan all males were required to serve two years in the military; here, a marred political record typically would lead to an undesirable posting and rank.

Even more ominously, in both cases the threat of imprisonment and physical violence was quite real. In China, persons designated "traitors" to the socialist cause often faced years of imprisonment, forced labor, and even torture, despite the party's halfhearted attempts to emphasize the rule of law after Mao's death. Although China's 1982 judicial code stipulated that detainees had to be tried and sentenced within 60 days, in reality public security staff widely ignored this regulation. Indeed, individuals regularly remained in detention for many months, or years. During this time, prisoners typically would have no contact with the outside world. Those who eventually were tried faced slapdash and arbitrary proceedings, leading to almost certain conviction and lengthy prison terms. Throughout this process, prisoners commonly suffered physical and mental torture, as well as forced labor. For most, even the completion of one's sentence did not result in freedom. Though one's formal status changed, many were required to remain in "Reeducation Through Labor" camps or other forms of forced job placement. Those fortunate enough to avoid this continued to experience surveillance and occasional harassment once they rejoined society. Under this cloud, few were able to eke out more than the most basic existence.[27] In Taiwan, such harsh treatment of opposition activists had become far more rare by the late 1980s, yet students and citizens vividly remembered similar violence directed against dissidents in the recent past.

Students in both cases were aware that the regime was particularly harsh on specific social sectors. In China, perhaps due to the party's waning claim to represent the working class, dissenting workers generally were treated more stringently than dissenting intellectuals. In Taiwan, activists associated with the opposition Democratic Progressive Party tended to receive especially harsh punishment.[28]

At the same time, it is important to note that in both cases, the state's ability and propensity to engage in repression was influenced by the larger geopolitical context within which it was enmeshed. Although most work on political opportunity ignores international factors, Meyer—drawing on Skocpol and Gourevitch—reminds scholars of contentious politics that the larger international environment "constrains or promotes particular opportunities for dissidents within the state."[29] In China in 1989, the most salient feature of the international environment was the dramatic change underway in the Soviet Union under Gorbachev. In particular, Gorbachev's policy of glasnost simultaneously emboldened Chinese students and hardened the resolve of Chinese ruling elites to avoid similar reforms. The increasing power of Solidarity in Poland had a similar effect. Thus, in many ways, the world-historical and geopolitical context in 1989 set the stage for the dramatic, yet ultimately tragic, clash between activists and political authorities in China. In Taiwan in 1990, citizens and officials acted within a very different temporal and geopolitical context. Most important, Taiwan's ruling KMT was in a precarious and dependent international position: it claimed to be the legitimate ruler of "China," yet was denied such status by virtually all world powers and international organizations. In addition, it was almost entirely dependent on the United States for military protection. The KMT had also publicly and enthusiastically supported the mainland Chinese protesters of 1989, and had vocally joined the international outcry in response to the CCP's repression of the demonstrators. Together, these factors limited the KMT's ability to forcefully crush popular protest, and thus also lessened citizen fears of repression.

In sum, students in both China in 1989 and Taiwan in 1990 labored under regimes that had become less repressive and suffocating yet still retained elements of their more oppressive pasts. Even so, the political opportunity structure in Taiwan was much more open than in China. As will be shown, varying degrees of illiberal social and political controls stimulated fear and distrust among protesting students in both China and Taiwan, leading to organizational ineffectiveness and factionalization, as well as concerns about cross-sector mobilization. But these features were less pronounced in Taiwan than in China.

At the same time, it is important to emphasize that the opportunity structures were not static. In each case, regime responses fluctuated between repression and concession, and regime controls over the media waxed and waned.[30] As this transpired, student perceptions of opportunity shifted as well. As a result, in both cases, the major features of student organization and mobilization fluctuated in tandem with changes in relevant political opportunity structures. Repressive responses heightened student fear and distrust, and diminished the leverage of those calling for compromise and moderation. This, in turn, led to an increase in factionalism and an inability to agree on binding decisions. Conversely, more conciliatory regime responses strengthened the hand of moderates and made students more willing to compromise with one another, thus facilitating organizational effectiveness. Similarly, the regime's use of the media to discredit protests and justify repression spurred organizational incapacitation and exclusive mobilization strategies. When official media controls were relaxed, the fear and distrust that tended to stymie organization and mobilization was diminished.

Constraints on Organization: China

During the 1989 movement in China, problems with distrust and fear led to organizational instability.[31] These difficulties were especially prominent at Beijing University, where the movement organization did not arise through the efforts of students who knew one another well. Members of the group thus were extremely suspicious of one another.

The new student movement organization that arose at Beijing University had its start in an anonymous poster calling for an on-campus public meeting. Hundreds gathered on April 21, at the appointed time and place, but knowledge of the CCP's presence on campus and the resultant risk involved in action rendered most students afraid to speak. Finally, a student named Ding asked for volunteers to lead a new autonomous campus organization. Those in attendance were profoundly aware that any persons willing to volunteer likely would face severe punishment, as it was almost certain that official spies were in their midst at that very moment. Consequently, although the students exuberantly voiced their collective support for such an organization, Ding's request met with silence.[32] Finally, Ding suggested that the few who had spoken earlier be the leaders. As a result, those students had no choice but to back up their words and step forward.

With this, the Beijing University Autonomous Union (BAU) was established. However, because most of the students who had "volunteered" to lead the group were not well acquainted with one another, the group was plagued by divisions and discontent. Although some of the new members had been involved in previous autonomous organizations, few had been involved in the *same* organizations. As a result, they lacked trust in the others' competence and dedication, and each feared that some of the others might be infiltrators.

At the group's first meeting, this lack of trust caused turmoil. Opening the meeting, Ding Xiaoping expressed suspicion that the group already had been penetrated by individuals sent by the Public Security Bureau, warning the group's members that they "must be extremely careful."[33] According to another member, the students present were highly concerned that "opportunists" might "enter the movement for their own political benefit."[34] This member also said, "Because we didn't recognize each other, every new student that came [to a meeting] had to be sponsored by another student."[35] Despite these precautions, the next morning a student CCP member informed the group that school authorities already knew of the group's plans.[36] A few days later, one group member charged another who had since quit with being a spy for the official graduate student union. On another occasion, a "very suspicious person" attended a BAU meeting; as one attendee relates, "everyone thought he was a party plant."[37] When asked to present his student ID, this student did not, explaining that he was "a very unique student at Beijing University, studying some confusing trade . . . living off campus, and having no classmates."[38] Owing to these suspicions, each leader had doubts about other members, and the group experienced almost continuous infighting and paralysis.

At the same time, a second autonomous student group formed at neighboring Beijing Normal University. The group there was the work of three close friends. The deep trust that existed among them and the absence of unknown students enabled this group to enjoy much greater stability and effectiveness than the BAU.

To establish a new student group at Beijing Normal, the three friends simply put up a poster announcing the formation of the Normal University Autonomous Union (NAU), asking interested students to join. By the end of the day, students from virtually every department on campus had registered. From the start, the NAU was effective and stable. The friendship-based trust of the initial leaders also gave these students the confidence to initiate the formation of the All-Beijing Student Federation. Meanwhile, the mutual suspicion among members of the BAU left it mired in its organizational conflicts and uninvolved in the formation of the larger organization.

Having found success in their establishment of the NAU, the student leaders at Beijing Normal pasted up an announcement of the formation of the All-Beijing Students' Autonomous Federation, calling on interested students to meet at the university's soccer fields.[39] On the day of the planned meeting, school authorities called NAU president Wu'er Kaixi's father to campus and warned him that his son's actions could have serious repercussions. Concerned yet undaunted, Wu'er announced the establishment of the new federation to the assembled crowd. A few days later, representatives from virtually all Beijing universities held the federation's first meeting. Not only was the BA Union uninvolved in the founding of the federation, it never even became a formal part of it. Aware of its flawed and weak organization, the BAU informed the federation that it would be unable to join until it could work out its campus-level organizational problems.[40] Before the federation's next meeting, a threatening report in the official media heightened the atmosphere of risk. As the federation representatives gathered, Central People's Radio broadcast the text of a *People's Daily* editorial that was to be published the next day. Entitled "It Is Necessary to Take a Clear-Cut Stand against Turmoil," the article read: "During the past few days, a small handful have engaged in creating turmoil . . . some shouting, 'Down with the Party' . . . beating, looting, and smashing . . . [and] calling for opposition to the leadership of the party and the socialist system. In some universities, illegal organizations have formed to seize power from student unions . . . If we tolerate this disturbance, a seriously chaotic state will appear . . . Under no circumstances should the establishment of any illegal organizations be allowed."[41]

At the federation meeting that followed, students worried that the group's next move could have dire consequences. Yet after heated and emotional debate, the students agreed to go forward with a demonstration they were planning that would call for freedom of association and the press, as well as greater government transparency. At the same time, to counter the editorial's charges, the students agreed to chant "Long live the Chinese Communist Party." They also agreed to hold hands to show that their ranks did not include the alleged "small handful" of people whom the party claimed had engaged in disruptive and unlawful behavior.

The following day, new actions by campus authorities caused nearly every major student leader to have second thoughts about holding the demonstration. At Beijing University, school administrators called in two members of the BAU, telling them that if the demonstration was called off, there would be a good chance for a dialogue. Meanwhile, at Bejing Normal, an NAU leader was informed that the primary school across the street contained 1,000 soldiers, waiting to meet any protesters. Feeling a "very heavy responsibility," this student met with the other NAU leaders to express his confusion and fear. Almost simultaneously, federation president Zhou Yongjun suddenly announced that due to extreme danger, the federation had decided to cancel the demonstration. In actuality, Zhou had consulted no one before announcing this change of plan. Apparently, he, too, had been under immense pressure from school and government authorities, and felt that he could not be responsible for placing students' lives in danger.[42]

Despite this confusion and fear, the demonstration was held, on April 27. Miraculously, it seemed to be an overwhelming success: over 100,000 students, representing every school in Beijing, marched for hours, passing through numerous police blockades, to Tiananmen Square. Hundreds of thousands of city folk lined the streets to watch and express their support.

When the federation met on the following day, the mood was triumphant; perhaps the regime's tolerance of the march signified a loosening of the political opportunity structure. At the same time, many were angered by Zhou's attempt to cancel the demonstration. Federation members understood that fear drove Zhou's actions, but they felt that they could no longer trust him in such a powerful position. Thus, as the first order of business, they forced Zhou to resign from the presidency. Further, showing the students' distrust of *anyone* in a position of power within the federation, they degraded the power of the president. Nevertheless, in the more hopeful atmosphere engendered by their successful march, the group decided to hold another mass demonstration a few days later.

The day before this action, the federation held a special meeting to discuss tactics. To guard against infiltration by party spies and to discourage official claims that the movement was being directed by a "small handful" of nonstudents, participants were checked strictly for their qualifications. The fear and distrust engendered by the illiberal features of the ruling regime made such caution indispensable. To further ensure and demonstrate that the student ranks would contain only persons with "pure" motives and peaceful intentions, the students reconfirmed that while marching to the square, they would hold hands to demarcate the student protest body. Although the students desired wider connections with other social groups, they felt that the greater imperative was to avoid CCP slander and repression.

This next demonstration succeeded in bringing over 100,000 students to the square. Nonetheless, government representatives refused to negotiate with student leaders. Frustrated, six student leaders met at a small restaurant to discuss the idea of a hunger strike. Some were members of the BAU, the NAU, and the federation, yet no effort was made to contact the entire leadership of any of these groups. These six students felt that the risk-laden environment made it more important for them to proceed quickly with what they perceived to be the "correct" approach.[43]

When the leadership of the BAU gathered the next morning, three of the students who had met at the restaurant suggested that the BAU join them in a hunger strike the following day. The hunger strike proponents noted that this would be two days before the visit of Soviet president Mikhail Gorbachev, and thus would press the government to respond.[44] The assembled BAU leadership was divided. Many feared that such an action would raise the risk level unbearably; others felt that a hunger strike was the students' only means of influencing the government. With no opposition parties, impartial government bodies, or independent media to which to appeal, the strategies available to them were extremely limited. Street demonstrations had been met with official indifference; now, a hunger strike seemed their only option. Those favoring the hunger strike did not feel compelled to reach a compromise with the BAU, and ultimately declared that they would begin a hunger strike regardless of its decision.[45] Faced with an ultimatum, the BAU decided that although it would not officially sanction the strike, its members could support the hunger strikers as individuals.

The determination of the hunger strike advocates also caused conflict with the federation. After the BAU had been contacted, students favoring the strike entered a federation meeting, announced the initiation of the hunger strike, and demanded that the federation lend its support.[46] Some federation members erupted in anger, declaring that these students had no right to use the federation's resources to engage in an unsanctioned action.[47] The hunger strike proponents defiantly responded, "No matter what you say . . . we will do it."[48] Again, those students who believed that a hunger strike was the "correct" action feared that compromise would destroy the movement. Consequently, they chose to exit the existing organizational structure. Meanwhile, those favoring a more moderate course of action were sidelined.

The hunger strikers gathered at Tiananmen Square the following day. But Gorbachev's visit passed without a compromise. As the number of hunger-striking students grew, participants began to realize the need for some sort of organization. Yet because the hunger strikers feared that compromise with others might result in devastating consequences, they agreed only to establish a coordinating body to protect the lives of hunger-striking students; the organization would have no authority to force decisions on its members.[49]

With no strong organization at work, the square soon was in crisis. Daily, thousands of students from outside Beijing poured in, and hundreds of new students joined the hunger strike. By May 17, close to 1,000 students had collapsed. Exacerbating the dangerous atmosphere, the authorities announced the imposition of martial law. Student fears rose exponentially; as one leader relates, "this seemed to be the final battle. Everyone seemed to be making a final fight against death."[50] In this environment, students became even more leery of compromise.

In late May, an important meeting was held to ameliorate this dangerous situation. Representatives of all of the major factions and groups that had formed during the movement attended, and after intense debate all agreed to withdraw from the square on May 30. In the interim, however, some prominent hunger strike participants reconsidered this decision. Concerned that a May 30 withdrawal would end the movement with no concrete success, the hunger strike group held a separate meeting.[51] Voting down the May 30 proposal, the hunger strikers announced that they would remain at the square until June 20.

The authorities had no intention of allowing the students' action to continue that long. By June 4 the square had been cleared, and hundreds, if not thousands, lay dead. Certainly, the government must be viewed as the main culprit in these events. However, had students been able to maintain organizational unity and abide by decisions with which they disagreed, they would have left the square days before the bloodshed began. Ironically, though, the extremely dangerous atmosphere engendered by the oppressive opportunity structure made students hesitant to compromise with those holding views different from their own. In this environment, alternative views were seen as not simply different but dangerous. Furthermore, the illiberal atmosphere lent legitimacy to those calling for more radical tactics, enabling them to outflank more moderate voices.

Constraints on Organization: Taiwan

As in the movement of 1989 in China, students in Taiwan in the spring of 1990 experienced organizational difficulties deriving from distrust and fear. In Taiwan, too, student protesters did not trust those they did not know well, and student behavior became increasingly radical and factionalized as the government remained unreceptive. As in China, students in Taiwan had undertaken organizing prior to the movement. Indeed, by the beginning of 1990, numerous campus underground press and reform-oriented student groups had formed, and the official student government at many universities was controlled by activists. Nonetheless, these previously existing groups often complicated the organizational process during the movement, creating conflict and divisions as students unacquainted with each other were forced to work together. In addition, as in China, more radical students initiated an unsanctioned hunger strike. At the same time, since the political environment was not as dangerous in Taiwan as in China, students' organizational difficulties were not as extreme. Consequently, as the regime turned to more conciliatory behavior, a more moderate solution was reached.

The immediate cause of the student movement of 1990 was the impending choice of a new president, scheduled for March 21, 1990. As noted, the president was to be selected by the National Assembly, a body that had not faced wholesale reelection since 1947. Many Taiwanese were dissatisfied with this method of presidential selection. Interestingly, however, unlike some who later joined in, the three students who initiated the "Month of March" student movement had no previous protest experience.

On March 15, at National Taiwan University, one of these students, Zhou Keren, informed the student union president, who was a reformist and a seasoned student activist, that he and two others planned to begin an open-ended sit-in at the Chiang Kai-shek Memorial in Taipei the following day. The student union president then convened a meeting of various dissident groups to discuss this development. Feeling that it would be rash to initiate such an action without more planning, those present decided not to immediately join or formally sanction Zhou's planned sit-in but to plan a united school action a few days later.[52]

Undaunted by this lack of support, the following day Zhou and two friends sat down in front of the main gate of the Chiang Kai-shek Memorial, raising banners listing their demands for political reform. As the afternoon passed, many more students joined them. That evening, the three initiators asked students to send a representative from each campus present at the square, to form an "Inter-Campus Association" to help organize the movement. To expedite decision making, a five-person "Policy Group" was also formed.[53]

The next day, however, divisions became apparent as more experienced student activists joined the protest. The student union officers who entered the movement at this time felt that their prior experience of organizing and subverting KMT control made them the most competent leaders. At the same time, the movement leaders who had never been involved in student government leadership were suspicious of the student officers. For example, at the start of one meeting, when the chair announced that formal rules of conduct would be used, the student representatives who were unfamiliar with these rules suspected that the chair's intimate knowledge of and preference for these rules demonstrated that she was a KMT plant.[54]

By the third day of the movement, student representatives in the Inter-Campus Association had begun to demand a larger role in policy making, expressing dissatisfaction with the decision-making powers that had been accorded the small Policy Group. Finally, it was agreed that the Inter-Campus Association would act as the highest policy-making body, and the Policy Group would act only as an executive body. Thus, as in China, students were unwilling to cede decision-making power to others.

Students further displayed this attitude with the initiation of a hunger strike. At an Inter-Campus Association meeting, a delegate proposed that students begin a hunger strike. When the motion failed, a handful of students independently began a hunger strike.[55] As in China in 1989, these more radical students felt that the future of the movement was so important that majority decisions must not be allowed to block the implementation of "correct" strategies. In addition, as on the mainland, this action undermined the legitimacy of the pre-existing organization. Just as the BAU, the NAU, and the All-Beijing Students' Federation were forced belatedly to announce their support of the hunger strike in 1989, the Inter-Campus Association soon announced that despite its decision not to sanction the action formally, it would support the hunger strikers.

Unlike the movement of 1989 in China, however, the relatively favorable government response to student demands defused the tense situation and allowed the students to agree to withdraw. On March 21, the reform-oriented Lee Teng-hui was elected president. That evening, he consented to meet with representatives of all student groups at the square. At the meeting, he promised that the students' demands would be addressed within the next few months.[56]

When the student representatives returned to the square, the Inter-Campus Association and hunger strike group held separate meetings to discuss withdrawal. Late that night, the hunger strike group voted to withdraw the following morning, and shortly thereafter the Inter-Campus Association was almost unanimous on this point. Thus, as dawn broke, the students began their formal retreat. The partial government concession to the students' demands had relaxed the tense atmosphere; consequently, students no longer felt compelled to engage in extreme actions. In fact, in these relaxed circumstances, such behavior would have appeared ridiculous rather than courageous. In this way, those calling for more radical action were marginalized, while proponents of moderation and compromise were strengthened.

What do these findings tell us about the relationship between trust and organization in illiberal environments? To be sure, protest movements even in the most liberal of settings operate in an uncertain and dangerous atmosphere. For this reason, trust is always crucial to any movement organization, and virtually all movements have experienced organizational stress due to a lack of trust among members. In addition, tendencies toward radicalization and factionalism appear in almost every movement. Yet in these two cases, these problems were more intense than is typically the case in less oppressive circumstances. The risk and fear involved in political protest in places such as China and Taiwan were much greater than in more free and open systems. Thus, in both cases organizational instability was enhanced, and more radical activists enjoyed legitimacy. As the political environment in China was relatively more threatening than that in Taiwan, these features were more pronounced in the Chinese case.

Constraints on Mobilization

Along with organizational difficulties, in both movements the illiberal political environment also made student protesters extremely hesitant to welcome nonstudents into their ranks. The students' past experiences had taught them that the appearance of disorder, or an alliance with groups the regime found particularly threatening, would likely provoke negative media coverage and/or a severe response by the authorities. Official actions during the course of each movement only reinforced these fears. As a result, students felt that an exclusive mobilization strategy was their only sensible choice.

China

Student leaders of the movement of 1989 in China relate that past incidents of official slander and repression made them exceedingly fearful of allowing nonstudents into their ranks. These fears were reinforced by government actions during the course of the movement, for example the imposition of martial law. One influential participant in China explained to me: "The security line [separating students and nonstudents] was employed mainly because the students feared government repression. During every democratic movement, the government said it was 'chaotic,' that the demonstrators were 'used' by others. The students had to be very careful, so the government couldn't say they were inducing violence or chaos, or that freedom leads to bad things."

Similarly, another student leader related in an interview: "In order to control the movement and keep it nonviolent, we needed a security line. From the April 5th Movement [of 1976, when people gathered in Tiananmen Square to demonstrate in memory of the late premier Zhou Enlai], we learned that the party may have plainclothed agents who can burn a car or something else and later accuse the people in the demonstration. This happened many times in PRC history, and happened again in 1989." A third interviewee told me: "The security line was especially important after martial law. We had to be well-organized in order to protect ourselves. Any small violence could have had huge repercussions." In brief, student leaders were well aware that the party had found pretexts to suppress popular movements in the past. The students had also witnessed similar official behavior in the present. To guard against official slander and repression, the students adopted measures to enforce order and student "purity."

The students were particularly concerned that until workers were more organized, broad-based actions would only bring disorder to the movement. As interviewees and scholars noted, even the most organized worker group (the Beijing Workers' Autonomous Federation) was small, with a core of only some 150 activists, whereas tens of thousands of students formed hundreds of autonomous organizations.[57] Moreover, the Beijing Workers' Autonomous Federation did not publicly declare its existence until mid-May, by which time students had already been organizing and engaging in large-scale marches and demonstrations for a month.[58] Even more important, the authorities had made it clear that whereas students would be allowed to engage in sustained protest activities, even the slightest worker activism would be severely punished. No students were arrested from the beginning of the movement on April 15 through its end on June 4, despite the fact that students had engaged in a great many illegal and embarrassing activities. Prior to June 4, the only persons arrested were workers.[59] The government seemed willing to tolerate sustained, large-scale activities on the part of students yet crushed even small-scale worker activism. Thus, the students felt their safety could be ensured only through clear separation from workers.

Taiwan

Student leaders in Taiwan cite similar reasons when explaining their decision to maintain a separation between students and nonstudents. Most important, students in Taiwan wished to remain separate from protesters demonstrating under the banner of the Democratic Progressive Party, the major opposition party in Taiwan. Indeed, many students reported that although they themselves belonged to it, they knew that explicit association with it would only bring the movement trouble, and possibly repression.

Like student leaders in China, those in Taiwan feared that the KMT would use the appearance of disorder as a pretext to crack down on the movement. In the words of one interviewee: "We feared that if the masses mixed in with the students, the KMT might use more forceful measures to control the movement . . . We wanted support from [the masses], but also didn't want to act with them because we feared KMT suppression. It was a contradiction . . . we did not really want the security line, but we needed it to ensure our safety."

Student leaders in Taiwan also emphasized that KMT domination of the media made the students fearful that their actions would be criticized in newspaper, radio, and television reports. One leader told me: "Our biggest question was how to avoid being slandered, being accused of being used . . . or being infiltrated by bad people. With the security line, everyone could see that we were all students."

Thus, students in both Taiwan and China feared that a more inclusive mobilization strategy would result in official denunciation and repression. At the same time, especially in the case of China, it is likely that this narrow mobilization strategy hindered the students' ability to pressure the government successfully. In the end, students were stuck between a rock and a hard place—official repression or official indifference.

Wider Comparisons

These findings apply only to the illiberal political contexts of China in 1989 and Taiwan in 1990. However, to the extent that sustained single-party domination of state institutions, monopolization of the media, penetration of social organization, and a high propensity for repression are present in other countries, one might expect to find similarly constrained forms of protest. Indeed, a look at political protest in other nondemocratic states indicates that many of the limitations and concerns that appeared in China and Taiwan also characterize dissent in other illiberal contexts.

Many scholars of Latin American, eastern European, and African politics have observed that a "culture of fear" characterizes social relations in the illiberal regimes of these regions.[60] Corradi, Weiss Fagen, and Garreton note: "Free societies . . . do not know fear as the permanent and muffled under-tone of public life."[61] Most likely, they add, this is because in democratic societies, "the decentralization of power, the exercise of self-governance in local communities, the existence of myriad voluntary associations, the separation of state and religion, the plurality of sects and creeds within religions, the possibility of rapid social and geographical mobility, and, above all, the functioning of representative institutions . . . have relegated fear to being either an intimate or a transcendent experience of life."[62] In authoritarian societies, in contrast, "fear is a paramount feature of social action."[63]

Even more interesting, these scholars find that fear resulting from illiberal features is accompanied by the same lack of trust that undercut the student protest movements in China and Taiwan. For example, Lechner explains that the repressive atmosphere of authoritarian societies "is manifested in the mistrust that pervades social relations."[64] Similarly, Weiss Fagen finds that "restrictions on social gatherings, on elections in social and sports clubs, and censorship of the press, television, and popular songs all conspire to draw people away from public life and into private spheres. Fears about talking freely in front of neighbors and colleagues, suspicions about people in unaccustomed places, and a reluctance to pursue friendships with new acquaintances follow."[65] In addition, Moreira Alves finds that in Brazil, the aim of the authoritarian regime was "to make individual citizens feel uninformed, separate, fragmented, and powerless . . . uncertainty was also encouraged."[66] Consequently, political organization in nondemocratic regimes is exceedingly difficult.

Indeed, the hallmark of an illiberal polity is the lack of the kind of independent associational networks that form the basic building blocks of social movement organization in democratic societies.[67] In more liberal contexts, these associational networks often arise from common interests or goals. When the possibility of repression is relatively low and institutional access is easy, a shared purpose alone can foster the trust that is essential for effective organization.[68] Of course, bonds of friendship are useful in democracies as well.[69] Yet even so, in liberal societies, such bonds do not appear to be essential for movement organization.

In more closed and repressive political environments, in contrast, networks based on friendship may be virtually the *only* sound basis of organization building. As with BAU in 1989, shared goals may not be sufficient to engender the trust that is needed for effective organization and decision making. When involvement in movement leadership entails a real risk of lifelong unemployment or imprisonment, individuals must have absolute trust in the competence and loyalty of their fellow leaders. Because the risks involved in protest in nondemocratic societies are inherently higher than in democracies, personal ties are vastly more important. As Dieter-Opp and Gern conclude in their study of the East Germany protests of 1989, "in authoritarian regimes trust is mainly placed on friends."[70]

At the same time, it is important to remember that political opportunity structures should not be viewed as dichotomous—simply "open" or "closed." Rather, as illustrated in the two cases studied here, opportunity structures exist along a spectrum from the most liberal to the least. Similarly, as emphasized by Almeida and Boudreau, the features of an illiberal regime vary over time, and should not be treated as static.[71]

It must also be recognized that even under a single political regime at a single moment in time, different social groups will be differentially affected by existing opportunity structures. In both China and Taiwan, some groups were more subject to official repression than others. Here, too, it is worthwhile to stress the role of individual or group *perceptions* of the opportunity structure they face. For example, Vala and O'Brien (chapter 5) show that unregistered Protestants in contemporary China have quite successfully recruited strangers to join what are technically illegal groups. Yet my study suggests that the key reason for this is that the recruits do not (at least initially) perceive their participation as being laden with risk, and thus are not fearful of the consequences of their action. Student protesters in 1989 in China and 1990 in Taiwan, in contrast, were quite aware of the political nature of their actions and thus the danger involved. And they were painfully aware that their contention was on display in perhaps the least "safe" space imaginable—the central square of the capital city.[72]

Studies of other nondemocratic regimes have also found that a fear-laden political environment encourages radicalized behavior among political activists, thus leading to organizational factionalism and an inability to agree on binding decisions. It is also true that some protest movements in democratic settings have tended toward escalation and radicalization.[73] Nonetheless, it appears that illiberal environments exacerbate these tendencies. As Corradi notes, "the sacrifice an individual has to make to serve the common purpose of the group is much higher in a despotic than in an open regime."[74] In a study of political protest in Chile, Martinez adds that as a result, expressions of protest in authoritarian contexts "follow the unequal distribution of courage among individuals."[75] In Iran, Kurzman notes, repressive acts by the illiberal ruling regime "frequently . . . led to increased militancy."[76] Student protest in predemocratic South Korea also evidenced this tendency. As Dong relates, many have noted a "tendency among the Korean student activists . . . 'the more radical and extreme, the greater the moral superiority of the activist leaders.'"[77] Echoing these findings, in a comparative study of student protest in Thailand, Burma, Malaysia, and Singapore, Silverstein found that in each case, "when the battle [was] joined and compromises [were] offered . . . those who accept[ed] appear[ed] to be 'selling out.'"[78] This phenomenon is perhaps best encapsulated in the words of a prominent Uruguayan dissident: "I rather think that all the radicalization of the youth was . . . generated by the authoritarian framework itself."[79]

In more open (and thus less risk-laden) environments, radical actions often appear irrational and unconstructive; as a result, such behavior is more easily marginalized from the mainstream of a movement. In more illiberal settings, in contrast, great danger lends legitimacy to the "radical flank," such that it may successfully overpower moderate actors and tactics. In such circumstances, compromise—both among movement participants and with the regime—becomes next to impossible.

The comparative literature also underscores this study's findings on limitations on mobilization. As seen in China in 1989 and Taiwan in 1990, the need for trust based on bonds of friendship may negatively impact a movement's prospects for greater mobilization by constraining activists' willingness to form wider connections. Dieter-Opp and Gern, as well as Kamenitsa, reach a similar conclusion, noting that in East Germany, the opposition's ability to create alliances was undermined by the suspicion that arose among members who did not know each other.[80]

Studies of protest in other nondemocratic contexts likewise support the finding that narrow mobilization strategies may be seen as necessary to counter official charges of movement infiltration by undesirable elements. As Brockett argues in his study of peasant mobilization in Central America, "challengers not only respond to current regime actions, but also must anticipate future actions, calculations that in turn are based on memories and stories of past elite behavior."[81] Bratton and van de Walle, studying Africa, concur.[82] Pointing in the same direction, Kamenitsa argues that "in political terms, experiences in the previous opportunity structure may affect activists' willingness to cooperate with particular groups."[83]

Similar strategies appear in other nondemocratic contexts. For example, Prizzia and Sinsawasdi find that in the Thai student protests of the early 1970s, the students' "strategy for the organized protest allowed for each university and school having students in the demonstration to assemble in a particular area so that leaders could detect any 'third hands.'"[84] Moreover, this exclusive behavior appears to have been justified.[85] Similarly, Silverstein notes that during student protests in Malaysia in the fall of 1974, the "government took the line that the students had been manipulated by sinister forces."[86] In the wake of student demonstrations in Singapore the same year, "the Foreign Minister and others spoke about outside forces seeking to weaken the nation and bring it down through the use of students. He was quoted as saying, 'By themselves, the students are manageable . . . It is a different matter when outside forces intervene.'"[87]

What lessons do these findings hold for political opportunity theory? To begin, this study supports earlier findings that open information flows are particularly important in nondemocratic settings. However, rather than focusing broadly on how media controls generally enable or prohibit mobilization, my findings show how particular forms of official media manipulation affect the *character* of mobilization in illiberal contexts. Similarly, instead of focusing on the question of *when* repression spurs increased protest, this study shows how the fear of repression affects the *character* of mobilization and organization.

With regard to organization, in both China and Taiwan, the ruling party's penetration of social groups, manipulation and control of the media, and use of repression aroused student fears and suspicion, resulting in organizational ineffectiveness. At the same time, the relatively less severe atmosphere in Taiwan mitigated the intensity of these reactions among the protesters. Furthermore, fluctuations in specific features of the political context during the course of each movement led to fluctuations in these organizational traits.

With regard to mobilization, student fears that were aroused by illiberal opportunity structures frustrated the formation of strong links across social groups. This suggests that protesters in illiberal contexts face a conundrum: narrow mobilization that is the ultimate outcome of state repression may be insufficient to propel real change, yet mobilization that includes groups which the regime finds threatening is likely to provoke repression.

Of course, protest is risky in any setting, and social movements in even the most democratic countries have often met with government slander and selective repression. However, in situations where there are no independent political parties, social organizations, media sources, or autonomous judicial system and there is a high likelihood of repression, the risks of protest are heightened immensely. This is evident in an extreme form in countries such as mainland China, where even nonviolent and reform-oriented political activists are routinely detained, tried, and sentenced to years of imprisonment and often excruciating torture. In this kind of political context, organization and mobilization may be inhibited to such a degree that effective, reform-oriented political protest is close to impossible.

2 | Collective Petitioning and Institutional Conversion

When ordinary people challenge authorities or a political system, ironically, they often turn to their targets for resources. In the meantime, it is not rare for the agents of a repressive regime to facilitate or even encourage popular mobilization. State authorization and facilitation are especially important in high-capacity authoritarian regimes, where the state controls most resources for mobilization. In such circumstances, what matters most is not whether "free spaces" or a civil society free from state domination exist but whether ordinary people can locate resources and support from state actors.

Students of mass mobilization in China have noticed a strong role of the party-state, not only in political campaigns of the Maoist era but also in popular action since reforms began in 1978. Thus Elizabeth Perry remarks: "The close relationship between state authorization and social movements in China raises some questions concerning the applicability of general theories of contentious politics, developed for the most part on the basis of European and American cases. Although these theories have certainly not ignored the role of the state, they have generally been content to suggest a negative correlation between state strength and politically threatening social movements . . . but the Chinese experience argues for acknowledging a larger, more pro-active role for the state."[1]

Similarly, in his study of the 1989 student movement, Andrew Walder wrote:

> I am arguing not simply that elite divisions and the loss of discipline within the party-state apparatus combined to create an opening for protest; I am arguing that defecting members of the regime acted themselves to mobilize the general population into the streets, signaling to the populace that staged shows of support for hunger strikers were reasonable, even encouraged. Instead of an "additive" effect usually implied in studies inspired by resource mobilization theory or reasoning about historical conjunctures, I am arguing that the interaction of regime defectors with street protesters had a "multiplicative" effect that vastly expanded both the scale of the street protests and the paralysis of the government in a very short period of time.[2]

Since political institutions in an authoritarian regime are usually designed to inhibit collective action, a proactive role of the state implies *institutional conversion*. As Kathleen Thelen defines it, this is a process in which institutions with one set of goals in mind are redirected to other ends.[3] This is not a phenomenon unique to China. In their study of regime transition in southern Europe and Latin America, Guillermo O'Donnell and Philippe Schmitter identified "the conversion of older institutions, such as trade unions, professional associations, and universities, from agents of governmental control into instruments for the expression of interests, ideals, and rage against the regime."[4]

Although some studies have shed light on the role of institutional conversion in mobilization, there is much more to be learned. In particular, it is not clear under what conditions or through what mechanisms repressive institutions are converted into instruments of popular action. This study aims to address these questions through an examination of the Chinese petition system, known as the "letters and visits" system *(xinfang)*.

Popular action has dramatically increased in China since the early 1990s. Although this contention involves a variety of groups and claims and takes a range of forms, from contained behavior such as letter writing to disruptive action such as blocking highways and attacking government officials, much of it revolves around collective petitioning, for two reasons. First, almost all contention is primarily intended to deliver a written or verbal demand to the government. Second, and more important, popular action, even if it is disruptive, is generally an effort to make claims though channels established by the party-state. Even disruptive and sometimes illegal actions are an extension of legitimate forms of petitioning.[5]

The evolution of the *xinfang* system has enabled collective petitioning to surge. *Xinfang* are one of the primary institutions the regime uses to handle state-society relations.[6] As a mechanism for controlled participation, it largely worked as designed before the mid-1990s.[7] Although some petitioners resorted to "troublemaking tactics" to push state agents to satisfy their demands, overall popular participation was tightly managed. After the mid-1990s, however, this system began to create strong incentives for collective action, to exert tremendous pressure on local officials to promptly deal with protest, and to increase the costs of repression.

Why has an institution designed to inhibit collective action started to facilitate it? To explain this, I will draw on a term introduced by X. L. Ding: *institutional amphibiousness*. The *xinfang* system shares with some other institutions a paradoxical nature: designed to serve the party-state, it can come to be used for popular mobilization. This potential is realized through two mechanisms: (1) changes in institutional configuration, and (2) an appropriation-reaction process.

It bears noting that the conversion of the *xinfang* system helps explain not only the dynamics but also the forms and strategies employed by protesters in China. When petitioners successfully convert elements of the state apparatus, this commits claims makers to work within constraints built into existing channels and leads them to, for instance, refrain from direct action.

An examination of the conversion of the *xinfang* system also advances our understanding of "political opportunity structures" and how they evolve. As a core concept in the social movement field, these structures have hardly been ignored. Still, more attention to the processes and mechanisms through which opportunities open and close is needed. In particular, a study of institutional conversion can contribute to our understanding of the temporal dimension of a political opportunity structure: when do opportunities open up?[8] Theorists have long been aware of the importance of taking a dynamic approach to opportunities.[9] But most studies still tend to treat elements of an opportunity structure either as stable or fast-shifting, while failing to examine how stable institutions can evolve and how a short-term change can take place in a stable structure. Along these lines, David Meyer has observed that most opportunity theories fall into two groups. One emphasizes stable aspects of government, essentially holding opportunities constant for cross-sectional comparison. The other underscores volatile aspects of opportunity, such as public policies and political alignments.[10]

Institutional change is, however, usually a mixture of continuity and change, and of stable and fast-moving elements. To understand it, we also need to examine continuity. As Sidney Tarrow remarked, changing opportunities must be seen alongside more stable structural elements—like the strength or weakness of a state and the forms of repression it habitually employs.[11] Yet few analysts have dealt with the connections and tension between continuity and change.

Weak conceptualization of continuity and change is not unique to the field of contentious politics. Ira Katznelson notes that historical-institutional theorists tend to unwisely draw too sharp distinctions between "settled" and "unsettled" times.[12] One solution advocated by Thelen is to specify modes of change, such as institutional layering and institutional conversion.[13] By focusing on institutional conversion, this study seeks to explain how institutions evolve and how evolution creates or closes off opportunities.

Explaining Institutional Conversion

Before discussing preconditions and mechanisms of institutional conversion, three caveats are in order. First, institutional conversion is not sufficient or necessary for popular mobilization in authoritarian regimes. As common as it is, this process is absent at times. For instance, the mobilization that led to the demise of communist regimes in Poland and Hungary was basically bottom-up, and involved minimal conversion of state institutions. Second, institutional conversion not only facilitates mobilization but also may contribute to demobilization. Elizabeth Perry illustrates this point in her study of the evolution of Chinese worker militias.[14] Third, institutional conversion may take different forms and involve disparate sets and sequences of mechanisms. A single case study thus cannot possibly produce an exhaustive list of conditions and mechanisms.

Amphibiousness

One favorable condition for institutional conversion is institutional amphibiousness, a term coined by X. L. Ding.[15] According to Ding, the nature of individual institutions is indeterminate: "an institution can be used for purposes contrary to those it is supposed to fulfill, and the same institution can simultaneously serve conflicting purposes."[16] The examples he gives include trade unions, youth associations, and women's organizations. According to Ding, in China these organizations "bore a strong resemblance to voluntary associations in liberal democracies but were actually pre-emptive organizations." They were set up both to serve "the regime's mobilization goals and . . . [in particular, to inhibit] the formation of private loyalties."

While Ding applies this concept mainly to "mass organizations," institutional amphibiousness can be found in a wide range of government agencies, too. The official media, for instance, are notably amphibious. Although they are designed to be a mouthpiece of the party-state, they also report ordinary people's opinions and reveal misconduct by state agents. It is not surprising, therefore, that the mass media briefly adopted an openly oppositional and exhortative role during the 1989 student movement.[17]

For this reason, amphibiousness is best treated like a variable. Not every state institution is amphibious, and some institutions have this trait more than others. Institutions of interest articulation in state socialist regimes tend to be more amphibious; in contrast, the function of the army, the police, and the party propaganda apparatus is more clearly defined, so they have little or no amphibiousness.

Amphibiousness is an enduring, even permanent feature of some state institutions. The official trade union in socialist countries is a case in point. Under state socialism, an official trade union sometimes shifts between the roles of "transmission belt" and corporatist organization. Jonathan Unger and Anita Chan observe that even in Stalin and Mao's era, when the peak trade union was charged only with disseminating central directives, it still allowed for articulation of grassroots rights and interests, especially during periods of liberalization. This is an important reason why Mao finally decided to dissolve the labor union during the Cultural Revolution.[18] During the student movement of 1989, the All-China Federation of Trade Unions once again played a significant part in facilitating contention.[19]

Amphibiousness is particularly common in regimes such as China's. This is due to the inherently paradoxical quality of contentious politics under state socialism. Jeremy Straughn's study of East Germany underscores this point. He remarks, "On the one hand, the state's ideological claim to rule 'in the interests of the working class' supplies citizens with myriad opportunities to test and contest the sincerity of this commitment, simply by 'taking the state at its word'; on the other hand, the ruling party's rigid intolerance of political opposition substantially magnifies the risk that any citizen petition, no matter how patriotically formulated, will be construed as an act of defiance."[20]

Clearly, amphibiousness creates favorable conditions for institutional conversion. Of course, it only facilitates rather than guarantees. Whereas an institution with a high level of amphibiousness is more likely to be converted, institutions that have limited amphibiousness can still, on occasion, be converted. For example, police may defect from a regime and support popular mobilization.

Two Mechanisms

Studies of contentious politics have recently isolated an important mechanism: institutional appropriation. This is a mechanism through which social actors convert or incorporate existing organizations or institutions for their own purposes. Doug McAdam's study of black churches in the civil rights movement is a good example of just this. Black churches provided an organizational base for the civil rights movement. However, "until the rise of the mass movement, the black church was a generally conservative institution with a decided emphasis, not on the social gospel in action, but on the realization of rewards in the next life."[21] Conversion was accomplished mainly though appropriation. As McAdam and his collaborators describe it: "To turn even some black congregations into vehicles of collective protest, early movement leaders had to engage in creative cultural/ organizational work, by which the aims of the church and its animating collective identity were redefined to accord with the goals of the emerging struggle."[22]

Institutions can be appropriated not only from outside but also from within. X. L. Ding argues that this pattern was at work in the spring of 1989 in China. At this moment, "because of the political orientation or personal connections of those working within, institutional structures were manipulated, becoming means for protest and opposition."[23] Although he calls such a mechanism "manipulation," it is essentially a form of institutional appropriation.

Indeed, institutional appropriation is a sensible choice for people who are unable or unwilling to create resources on their own. Other resources, too, such as ideological statements, the legal system, and state rituals, can be appropriated. For instance, O'Brien and Li identify appropriation of state rhetoric—whether framed in terms of Confucianism or class struggle—as a common pattern throughout Chinese history.[24] Similarly, Steven Pfaff and Guobin Yang find a propensity to appropriate social rituals for mass mobilization in socialist regimes. In their words: "Nascent protest movements in authoritarian regimes have few opportunities for effective action and are generally resource poor, operating chiefly within the sheltered niches provided by free social spaces. Dissidents attempt to counter this weakness by exploiting the doubled-edged character of official political rituals."[25]

However, social appropriation by itself is seldom sufficient to account for the dynamics or trajectory of mobilization, for at least two reasons. First, it does not explain success at some times and not at others. Institutional amphibiousness creates favorable conditions for appropriation, but at most times this potential will not be realized. Second, appropriation is usually only one element of state-society interactions. State agents will usually respond to such attempts, often quite forcefully. O'Brien describes how, in rural China, local cadres tried to overcome peasants' efforts to use law and state policies to press claims: "Many cadres use these conflicting norms and expectations to make rightful resisters appear unreasonable and to justify not implementing a popular measure or institutional protection ... [therefore] a strong legal case and the use of compelling normative language is merely the ante for rightful resistance."[26]

Therefore, I suggest two mechanisms that can account for the timing of institutional conversion: (1) changes in institutional configuration, and (2) an appropriation-reaction process. The first mechanism operates because an institution functions differently when it is located in a different institutional configuration. Take the example of black churches. Conversion was not accomplished by social appropriation alone. As noted by McAdam, some changes in social, economic, and political institutions came together to make appropriation possible. For instance, the rapid urbanization of blacks during this period (1930–1954) contributed to an increase in the strength of black churches and also made them more assertive on civil rights issues.[27] The first mechanism helps answer the "when" question of conversion. The second mechanism recognizes the importance of appropriating existing political space but also underscores the importance of state reaction to mobilization.

The Case of the *Xinfang* System

The dramatic rise of social protest in China since the 1990s has drawn attention from both the media and academia. In international media outlets, it is not hard to find such passages as "Chinese Protests Grow More Frequent, Violent."[28] Many academics have also highlighted the growing frequency of collective action and "increasingly open disgruntlement."[29] Protest has not only increased but also has begun to be routinized.[30]

To explain the rise and routinization of collective petitioning, many scholars have invoked shifts in political opportunities. As summarized by Kevin O'Brien:

> Post-Mao reforms have shifted resources toward non-state, local actors and have offered villagers unparalleled opportunities to press new claims. As de-collectivization and marketization have made villagers wealthier and less dependent on village cadres, the end of class labeling and mass political campaigns have made them less fearful. As increased mobility and media penetration have made them more knowledgeable about their exploitation and about resistance routines devised elsewhere, so too administrative, electoral, and legal reforms have given them more protection against retaliation and more violations to protest.[31]

Most of these changes can be considered aspects of the "unraveling of state controls," and they are certainly relevant.[32] They cannot, however, fully account for the dramatic surge of collective petitioning of late. After all, popular action in China still faces many obstacles. The party-state has worked hard to curb mobilization, and it still has the ability to do so, as seen in the suppression of Falun Gong.

What is missing so far is the role of state institutions in facilitating mobilization. A set of institutions, including the *xinfang* system, have spurred popular action. Indeed, even the fact that so many of the aggrieved resort to petitioning suggests the importance of the *xinfang* system.

How the Xinfang *System Facilitates Collective Action*

A group of 36 disgruntled fishermen came to the municipal government of City Y in Hunan province on the morning of October 25, 2001. They demanded to see the mayor to report excessive fees imposed by a local fishery management station. When some fishermen refused to pay, the station officials had seized their boats. At the offices of the municipal government, the petitioners were met by officials from the *xinfang* bureau. For *xinfang* cadres, fishermen were just one of many groups who "visited" the government regularly. In 2001, this bureau had handled 408 groups of collective petitioners, 12,735 petitioners in all. So the *xinfang* officials were not particularly surprised to see indignant fishermen in their office. They just followed standard procedures. First, they asked the petitioners to come into the government compound and to sit in the bureau's reception room, since it was important to avoid commotion around the compound gate. Then they called the agencies that were responsible for handling this case: the city and county bureaus of livestock and fishery. They also requested that the fishery station send a leader to the bureau immediately. Usually lower-level officials respond to such requests promptly. However, in this case, the officials from the county bureau and fishery station did not come until 4 p.m., and their tardiness was noted. Indeed a notice of criticism was circulated throughout the municipal bureaucracy reminding other agencies to handle collective petitioning promptly. In the end, the municipal authorities decided that the fees were inappropriate and should be revoked. Consequently, the fishery station was instructed to release the boats and return the fees it had collected.

Among hundreds of collective petitioning events every year, not every group in City Y was so successful. For example, in 2001 thousands of pensioners there directed 152 collective petitioning events at the municipal government, but their demands were only partly met. The government agreed to pay their current pensions fully and on time, but not to pay overdue amounts, or to reimburse medical expenses. Another petition wave protested the city's ban on using tricycles for passenger transport. The city government was concerned about transport safety, city image, and clean air, and despite fierce protests, held to its policy. Yet to pacify the petitioners, the government offered them 400,000 yuan (about $50,000) compensation. For some less lucky groups, the government refused to make any concessions at all.

Whether successful or not, such protests usually trigger a bargaining process. The petitioners acquire their leverage through contentious collective action. In order to demobilize them, government and party leaders often need to meet the petitioners in person, convene special meetings, and attach priority to their concerns.

Of course, petitioners do not acquire bargaining power easily. They need to mount collective action and employ "troublemaking tactics." Disruption is one of the most common of such tactics. Petitioners sometimes also engage in performative acts, such as kneeling down or even self-immolation. Besides directly exerting pressure on their targets, petitioners also often turn to third parties.[33] If they can engage higher-level officials or the public, they can enhance their bargaining power. For example, whereas ordinary petitioners seldom get a chance to talk to top city leaders if they petition the municipality directly, they often can if they "skip levels" (yueji). When a group of petitioners march on a provincial capital, for example, a city leader is likely to rush in to try to stop them. So there is saying: "If you want to meet the county head, go to the municipal government; if you want to see the mayor, go to the provincial capital."

Since most of such "troublemaking tactics" violate laws or official rules to some extent, repression is of course an option. However, the xinfang system tends to limit the use of force. Under this system, if repression causes a conflict to escalate, local officials often pay a high price.

Although the xinfang system provides a venue for petitioning groups to bargain with local authorities through collective action, at the same time it tends to frustrate moderate forms of complaint, such as individual visits and letter writing. Petitioners using these methods suffer from the "problem of the powerless."[34] Under no pressure, governmental officials are much less likely to offer them redress. A vast majority of these petitions never reach power holders. Among the few that do, many bureaucratic barriers still prevent their grievances from being attended to. When leaders handle such petitions, their instructions to underlings tend to be general and vague, and typically only have a limited impact. Even for the few cases that are investigated, the bureaucracy has a strong tendency to engage in cover-ups. Whereas investigations initiated by these authorities are more likely to yield the facts of a case, these authorities usually refrain from getting involved too deeply or directly. Therefore, the likelihood that individual petitions will be addressed is extremely small.

It is hard to imagine that authoritarian leaders in China intentionally created a system that encourages contentious collective action. In fact, the designers of the system were mainly concerned with facilitating information flow about popular preferences and misdeeds of public officials. So it is a striking institutional conversion that the *xinfang* system has started to encourage collective petitioning so strongly.

How has it been converted? Before discussing this further, it should be noted that to some extent the *xinfang* system was amphibious from its earliest days. In other words, it has always had the potential to serve conflicting purposes.

Amphibiousness of the Xinfang *System*

Chinese petitioners tend to appropriate the *xinfang* system to stage collective action with "troublemaking tactics" mainly because of (1) the low efficacy of normal petitioning, (2) the government's ambiguous attitude toward "troublemaking," and (3) officials' pressure on subordinates to maintain social stability. These three factors are built-in features of the *xinfang* system. In this sense, this system is amphibious by design.

To understand the design of the *xinfang* system, one must first understand the *mass line,* an ideological tenet that underpinned the *xinfang* system at its creation. As Phyllis Frakt has observed, mass line politics "combin[ed] a vanguard system with meaningful participation of the masses."[35] Richard Pfeffer also pointed out that such a system instituted "in a vanguard system the appropriate degree of accountability and responsiveness to the masses of people."[36] Based on the mass line, the *xinfang* system was set up to facilitate political consultation. Yet such consultation was to be carried out under party leadership. Thus while ordinary people could articulate interests and opinions, they were not to pressure the leadership through collective action.

In other words, the mass line emphasizes both centralized control and political consultation. Consequently, it produced an inherently inefficient channel for interest articulation, in which the amount of information in popular claims far exceeds the capacity to process it, most claims are about local issues, and leadership intervention from above is difficult. This low efficiency is manifested in *xinfang* procedures.

Generally, *xinfang* case handling involves four steps: information processing, written instruction, investigation, and solution and/or persuasion. First, *xinfang* officials must decide how to handle individual cases. Valuable information must be differentiated from less valuable information, and one basic principle has always been "to treat petitions differently."[37]

After evaluating the significance of a given case, a *xinfang* agency transfers it. In principle, higher-level agencies relay most petitions to lower-level agencies, and only county-level agencies handle cases by themselves.[38] However, agencies at every level are highly selective. The provincial bureau in Hunan Province, for example, received 17,975 letters from January to June 1996.[39] Among them, only 50 were sent to provincial leaders for review, and 70 were sent to leaders of relevant departments or lower-level bureaus; 255 other letters were filed and later sent to a relevant department. Even at the county, only a small number of cases are reviewed by leaders themselves.

If a petition is deemed significant, a written instruction is typically issued from ranking officials. Even so, there are still no guarantees that careful investigation and handling will transpire. Why is this so? The primary reason is that most instructions are quite general and ambiguous. They seldom express unreserved support. They only signal interest in a possible problem, and usually refrain from making a final judgment until an investigation is complete. Thus, in a majority of cases, leaders only request that subordinates investigate a complaint, and nothing beyond that. Of course there are ways to express different levels of concern. For example, a central leader may refer a case to a provincial party secretary or governor personally, or he or she may add a comment such as "pay attention to it," or "treat it seriously." If the leader wishes to express stronger concern, he or she may add more detailed instructions. But this still offers no guarantee. Premier Zhu Rongji acknowledged that even his written instructions did not always stir his subordinates into action. At a National Conference on Xinfang Work in 1996, he admitted that many letters containing his personal instructions disappeared like "a stone dropped into the sea."[40]

While upper-level authorities need information to make a decision, they usually avoid conducting investigations themselves. Instead, they delegate this to local agencies. However, owing to close ties among local officials, cover-ups are common, as they have been from time immemorial.[41] Given this, why do higher-level authorities usually fail to conduct investigations themselves? Limited resources, unfamiliarity with local circumstances, and fear of alienating their underlings all conspire to subvert the search for the truth.

In the end, "troublemaking tactics" are often a sensible choice for the aggrieved. It is virtually impossible for the government to outlaw all such activities, for three reasons. First, a highly selective sorting system needs such activities to distinguish significant petitions and valid claims from unimportant petitions and unfounded claims. Second, although the petitioning system is inefficient, it is one of only a few channels for interest articulation. Third, it gives party leaders a controlled way (and some levers) to hold local officials accountable.

For these reasons, the *xinfang* system has the potential to encourage popular mobilization, though this potential was seldom realized prior to the 1990s.

Changes in Institutional Configurations

The *xinfang* system was created immediately after the Revolution and developed during its first 40 years within the context of a planned economy. It worked with other institutions such as the work unit system reasonably well. However, many institutions that go back to that time have now declined or even completely disappeared. Work units no longer structure life to the extent they once did, rationing disappeared in the 1980s, and the custody and repatriation system was abolished in 2003. This wave of transformation has created considerable challenges for state control of petitioning.

The decline of the work unit, for one, has had a significant impact on the operation of the *xinfang* system. In earlier years, most interactions between ordinary people and state authorities occurred in work units, and were particularistic and featured a high level of dependency. State agents enjoyed more arbitrary power, and petitioners were in a weak position to turn the vagueness of petitioning norms to their advantage. That has now changed.

A second institutional change that has benefited petitioners recently derives from increased bureaucratic differentiation. Differing interests between upper and lower authorities have always existed in China. However, bureaucratic differentiation has increased recently.[42] In this situation, the *xinfang* system's function of holding local officials accountable has often led to coalitions between petitioners and upper authorities, thereby encouraging collective action directed against rogue officials at the grassroots.[43]

In the broadest terms, the *xinfang* system has operated under two quite different institutional configurations: (1) the *xinfang* system plus work unit system plus low bureaucratic differentiation, and (2) the *xinfang* system plus the decline of the work unit system plus high bureaucratic differentiation. Under the second configuration, the potential for the *xinfang* system to facilitate collective action has been enhanced.

Appropriation-Reaction Processes

Chinese petitioners are savvy. The amphibiousness of the *xinfang* system and new institutional configurations provide favorable conditions to appropriate an old channel to press new claims. Efforts to appropriate not only realize the latent potential of the *xinfang* system and secure a "safe-enough" space (see Vala and O'Brien, chapter 5) for collective action but also trigger a set of government responses. Although most of these aim to deter popular mobilization, paradoxically, some create even more opportunities for mobilization.

This arises first because of the traditional mass line approach of seeking both consultation and centralized control. In this regard, the Chinese political system has displayed impressive continuity. When collective petitioning became more frequent and more disruptive, party leaders adjusted the system to cope with popular mobilization.

This involved two measures: (1) enhancing *xinfang* bureaus' authority and clarifying their role, and (2) improving procedures for information processing, conflict resolution, and social control.

As *xinfang* agencies assumed heavier responsibilities in the 1990s, the regime began to upgrade their status and authority. Officials, especially those from *xinfang* agencies, often attributed their ineffectiveness to lack of power. The rationale for empowering *xinfang* agencies was that with more authority over conflict resolution, problem solving, and social control, they could handle more work independently, without disturbing leaders of other organizations.

Procedural reforms have also taken place. Requirements that local officials promptly report important cases to higher authorities have been strengthened. For example, a document issued by the Hunan provincial government in 2002 called for reporting of (1) collective petitioning by over 50 participants directed at county or higher governments; (2) potential collective petitions of over 100 people; (3) collective petitioning to the provincial government or Beijing; and (4) events that evolved from ordinary petitioning to "sudden mass incidents" *(tufaxing qunti shijian)* that disrupted normal work, production, business, or social order. The first three of these are to be reported within a day, the fourth instantly. Reports should include the time, location, number of participants, forms of action, claims, governmental responses, and the "overall trend" *(dongtai)*. When necessary, follow-up reports should be sent.

Though such measures may have made the system somewhat more responsive, they can also spur further collective action. First, petitions accompanied by disruptive or other "troublemaking" activities draw more attention than more moderate forms of petitioning. Second, lower-level governments are now supervised by their superiors even more closely. Both of these reforms encourage popular mobilization and offer more leverage to collective petitioners when they negotiate with local officials.

Party leaders have also implemented measures designed to enhance social control, including defining what types of petitioning are legal and instituting local responsibility systems. Again, these measures have been either largely ineffective in deterring popular mobilization or counterproductive.

Efforts to "bring *xinfang* activities onto the legal track" have entailed new rules that outlaw many varieties of petitioning. For example, the Regulations on Letters and Visits (1995, revised 2005) specify the agencies to which petitioners should deliver their claims. "Skipping levels" is prohibited. Collective action has also been restricted, insofar as petitions must be delivered by no more than five representatives. Similarly, many "troublemaking tactics" have been declared illegal.

Most of these rules, however, have been routinely violated. For example, thousands of petitions are delivered every day by more than five petitioners. Local officials do not dare reject these "illegal" petitions. Punishment is problematic, since the offense is so common. Refusing to meet petitioners is inappropriate, since it is the officials' duty to dissolve collective petitions. Common ways to deal with this conundrum are to pretend that there is no violation of the rules or to request that the petitioners elect five or fewer representatives on the spot. The second strategy is generally preferred, since it allows petitioners to demonstrate their numbers but at the same time fulfills the requirements of the law. In the end, such restrictions have done little to restrict "undesirable" types of petitioning.

The regime has also tried to use local responsibility systems to slow the rise of popular action. A basic principle has been to "confine disorders in localities rather than [being open to them] at the center." They have used two main strategies: (1) evaluating local government's performance by including petitioning as a measure of it, and (2) sanctioning local officials for failure to fulfill their duties to preserve social order.

The occurrence of collective petitioning is now often a component of local performance evaluation.[44] Local officials are under great pressure to head off mass complaints, if they do not, they can be punished. At the same time, however, repressive capabilities have diminished, and soft and preventive measures are preferred. With the decline of work units, cadre monitoring has become much more costly and less effective. A common practice nowadays is so-called five-to-one or four-to-one surveillance, which entails four or five state agents taking responsibility for one possible wrongdoer.

When petitioners reach higher levels, or are on their way to them, local governments are expected to intercept them and bring them back. Unlike the old system of custody and repatriation, the *xinfang* system relies more on persuasion than coercion. Although police occasionally participate, retrieval is usually carried out by *xinfang* officials and others from agencies directly relevant to a petition. This means less force is typically used, but also that the task is more difficult to complete. Local leaders even personally take a hand in important cases. Clarified and strengthened local responsibility for petitioning creates more bargaining chips for petitioners to deploy against local authorities.

In China's strong authoritarian regime, we can expect institutional conversion to play a continuing role in contention. Since civil society is severely underdeveloped, "bottom-up" mobilization remains difficult and less effective than "inside-out" mobilization.

Amphibiousness is present in many public institutions in China, and offers opportunities for existing channels of control and participation to become resources for mobilization. Recent efforts by activists to win a seat in a local people's congress are evidence of just this.[45] Of course, the conversion of other institutions will not necessarily proceed like that of the *xinfang* system. The mechanisms discussed here are only some of many possibilities. It remains for future researchers to specify which mechanisms apply where, and how they work together.

Institutional conversion is a process that illustrates how continuity and change can be integrated, and therefore is particularly useful to explain why modest (and often unintentional) institutional changes can provide a boost to collective action. Even efforts designed to sidetrack popular contention have further strengthened the *xinfang* system's proclivity to facilitate mobilization.

Methodologically, this study highlights the usefulness of Ira Katznelson's suggestion to "focus less on the causal importance of this or that variable contrasted with others but more on how variables are joined together in specific historical instances."[46] The configuration before the 1990s led to controlled participation; the configuration today, which features a market economy and a high degree of bureaucratic differentiation, has led to contentious bargaining. At the same time, unlike research that solely highlights elements of a political opportunity structure, a focus on processes and mechanisms can enhance the specificity and precision of one of the key concepts in the study of popular contention.

WILLIAM HURST

3 | Mass Frames and Worker Protest

The trade-off between structure and agency is as old as social science itself. The study of collective action frames has traditionally tried to bring a bit of agency and cultural contingency into a structure-dominated field. By emphasizing the agency of individuals and organizations in crafting and deploying cognitive scaffolds, the framing literature has largely limited its applicability to contexts in which relatively autonomous actors use mass media or public meetings to promulgate "liberal" or "elite" frames. But perceptions are far from meaningless in other settings. In some authoritarian contexts, like contemporary urban China, something that could be called "mass frames"—coherent worldviews shaped in large part by the *structurally rooted* collective life experience of social groups—can meaningfully take hold. My broader purpose here, therefore, is to bring some structure back into a field that has become too agency-dominated.

Frames: The Career of a Concept

Frames and framing have long been contested and variously construed concepts. William James famously argued in his essay *The Perception of Reality* that humans are capable of sustaining multiple realities, or "subuniverses," each real in turn as an individual's attention comes to be focused on it.[1] Erving Goffman later characterized James's argument as a "cop-out," substituting instead a series of "frameworks" to explain how individuals make sense of events and answer for themselves the question "What is going on here?"[2]

Goffman's work—the first on frames to have broad influence on contemporary social science—focused largely on so-called primary frameworks that are applied whenever an individual recognizes any event and are "seen by those who apply [them] as not depending on or harking back to some prior or 'original' interpretation . . . [and as] rendering what would otherwise be a meaningless aspect of the scene into something that is meaningful."[3] Beyond primary frameworks, a number of other sorts of frames can be employed, either consciously or inadvertently, across a range of situations. Neither James nor Goffman conceived of frames as overly conditioned or constrained by structural realities, though neither offered a clear picture of just how actors' agency shapes them either. One can muster support for a structuralist reading of Goffman's work.[4] But the use of frames in the social movement literature has been mostly taken up by those seeking to assert a greater role for some form of agency—usually focusing on "conscious strategic efforts of groups of people to fashion shared understandings of the world and of themselves that legitimate and motivate collective action."[5]

In the study of contentious politics, frames were introduced in the 1980s by scholars seeking to explain what structuralist analyses of political process or resource mobilization had left out. Early proponents of a framing perspective, including David Snow, Robert Benford, and William Gamson, emphasized the role of ideological and psychological factors in mobilization, as well as the tools and tactics used by "movement entrepreneurs" to construe social circumstances in ways conducive to collective action.[6] Until recently, however, frames and framing processes played at most a supporting role in most theories of social movements and contentious politics. Factors like the tone set by a judicial decision, the oratorical skills of a movement leader, or the savvy handling of the mass media by an organization were considered interesting but still largely epiphenomenal; at most serving as intervening variables rather than key causal factors or outcomes in their own right.

A smaller number of scholars have eschewed an elite focus, concentrating instead on the more bottom-up agency of participants choosing to view social movements in particular ways. In this vein, James Jasper has argued for greater attention to the broader culture within and beyond social movement organizations: "both explicitly and implicitly, in both ideas and actions, culture helps us define or construct the world around us. . . . Culture involves meaning and interpretation. We can't ignore these mental constructions, even when we deal with apparently 'objective' phenomena."[7] Though termed "culture" rather than frames, the basic idea is strikingly similar to Goffman's frameworks, which are often shared across populations or subgroups. The important difference between this culturalist perspective and the classic social movement framing approach is that the process of frame construction occurs in the broader social arena (with a less clearly defined and more communitarian understanding of agency) instead of within the leadership of an organization or inside the mind of an individual leader.

Most recently, Doug McAdam, Sidney Tarrow, and Charles Tilly have deliberately distanced themselves from their allegedly "structuralist" and "static" previous stance on all aspects of contentious politics, substituting the still somewhat ambiguous concept of "mechanisms of social construction" for frames.[8] Unfortunately, their book gets us only part of the way toward where they want us to go.[9] Worse, the new concept of "mechanism" is slippery and inchoate, with the same mechanisms sometimes appearing to facilitate divergent, even mutually exclusive, outcomes.[10] Though I am generally supportive of their call to move beyond the classic social movement agenda, it is not worth killing off frames yet—not when a return to a more inclusive understanding of framing can provide most of the benefits, without the associated costs, that adopting the new concept of mechanisms might bring.

Even when scholars refrain from using the formal language of frames and mechanisms, many still feel the need to "leave the world of structure to explore perceptions."[11] I contend that frames and framing, to be analytically useful across the widest possible range of contexts, ought to be viewed as at least partly structural phenomena. Frames are not infinitely malleable, and framing processes are not completely dependent on the wishes or actions of movement leaders. Nor can we get much explanatory mileage out of simply retreating to looking at the broader culture without being able to pin down where this culture comes from or how it affects individuals. Rather, what in-

dividual participants come to believe collectively about their grievances and any real or potential action to be taken in response to them
is powerfully conditioned by the structural setting in which they live.

Mass Frames and Chinese Laid-Off Workers' Contention

For Chinese laid-off workers, conditions on the ground—neither social construction mechanisms nor the machinations of movement organizations or leaders—clearly help decide which frames promote
their mobilization, which frames convince them to stay off the streets,
and which frames are simply ignored by the vast majority. In a repressive context in which the mass media and the political arena offer
very little space for the promulgation of collective action frames,
frames are not constructed and disseminated only by movement leaders or organizations.

What Feng Chen (chapter 4) views as frames, I would classify as
rhetoric or metaphors of claim articulation. These are different from
what I study because they are part of the protest outcome and are
conscientiously deployed; the frames I look at act as independent or
background variables shaped by relatively impersonal structural
forces. My notion of frames also differs from Ching Kwan Lee's recent analysis of protest "subjects" or "subjectivities," in that for Lee, as
for Chen, Chinese workers deliberately and instrumentally adopt
particular rhetorical idioms or narratives in order to elicit particular
responses from their targets[12]—such subjects are thus more important in the process of claim articulation than how workers analyze
and initiate action in response to grievances.

In the restrictive setting of contemporary urban China, subna-
tional regional political economies and the position of workers within
these shape the frames through which laid-off workers perceive their
grievances and the potential gains or costs of seeking redress through
collective action. Three main regional political economies are important: China's heavy industrial heartland in the Northeast (Liaoning,
Jilin, and Heilongjiang provinces); the largely resource-extractive
and light industrial political economies of north central China (Henan, Shanxi, and Shaanxi provinces) and along the middle to upper
reaches of the Changjiang (or Yangzi) River (Hunan, Hubei, and
Sichuan provinces, plus the Chongqing municipality); and the boom-

ing new market economy in China's traditional centers of international commerce and investment on the central coast (Tianjin and Shanghai municipalities, in addition to Shandong and Jiangsu provinces).[13]

A frame that emphasizes that workers could be worse off than they are, that blames individual mismanagement and petty corruption for problems in particular firms, that sees finding a job to be the responsibility of each individual, and that recognizes the benefits of reform has clearly been accepted by many workers in the booming market cities of the central coast. This frame, which could be called "market hegemony," is very much along the lines of what Marc Blecher uncovered among workers in Tianjin.[14] It serves as the primary cognitive template promoted by the official media and many academics and officials throughout China, though it seems to find a much more accepting audience along the central coast than elsewhere.

One laid-off fish warehouse worker in Shanghai stressed that even though things had been more stable in the past, her family has acquired a television, refrigerator, and air conditioner between 1992 and 2002—unthinkable luxuries in the 1970s. She criticized the manager of her old state-owned enterprise harshly and complained about local officials (while admitting that most things are still better in Shanghai than elsewhere) but also said protesting would not be worth it and that her troubles were probably unique to her enterprise. A laid-off sanitation worker and a laid-off chemical worker in Shanghai expressed similar views.[15]

There are a few exceptions, however, even in Shanghai—especially in truly failing sectors like textiles. One laid-off textile worker compared life today to life before 1949: "Corrupt Chinese officials and rich foreign businessmen relax together in beautiful places, while the rest of the people are not allowed near them. . . . It is just like before liberation. Only the rich people have money to go to school or see a doctor. The rich keep getting richer and the rest of us keep getting poorer. This process continues from generation to generation. Where has socialism gone? We have returned to a class-defined society."[16]

In contrast to trends on the central coast, a frame that resonates particularly well in northeastern China could be called "Maoist moral economy" and is similar to what Ching Kwan Lee described in her earlier work on Liaoning Province.[17] This frame blames China's entire post-1978 reform project for ruining a basically healthy socialist order. The Maoist golden age was certainly dominated by hierarchical relationships, but a general promise of equity was honored, living standards were relatively stable, rights were respected, and patrons fulfilled obligations to their clients. What has replaced this in recent decades is social chaos and political breakdown in the context of suddenly imposed scarcity. Responsibility for this, according to this frame, rests squarely with the central leadership and the reform agenda it has advanced over the past 20 years.

One retiree in Benxi (an industrial city of just under one million people in northeast China's Liaoning Province) said, "Reform has brought nothing but problems. Political reforms have taken away rights from the people and undermined the revolution's victories. Economic reforms have brought lay-offs and poverty and have made Benxi's economy collapse. I have been 'on vacation' since 1988 and have protested many times because I often do not have enough to eat."[18] A miner on "long vacation" since 1993 said, "Reform and opening started around 1985. Since that time, everything has consistently gotten worse and worse. Wages don't get paid, people lose their jobs, inequality has become worse than it was before liberation [1949]. Even the Japanese managed things in the Northeast better than today's government. . . . The Northeast is dying and the Communist Party does not care about socialism anymore. During the planned economy we were all poor. But we were poor together. We were all proletarians. We all ate the food from the common pot. Now, the rich people get richer while we all get poorer. The special characteristic of Chinese socialism is that it is especially unfair!"[19] Finally, a laid-off chemical worker in Benxi said, "Workers have the right to protest and riot if local officials are not able to act, are incompetent, or refuse to listen to workers' legitimate demands. Chairman Mao said so himself; I remember studying this when I was young."[20]

Some elements of this frame have turned up elsewhere. Similar to the example from Shanghai noted above, one laid-off chemical worker in Beijing, who had found new work as a taxi driver, said, "When I was young, I was a Red Guard, one of the vanguard of the proletariat. Now, I am the modern Xiangzi.[21] I go here and there around Beijing and can never earn enough to live in peace. The taxi company boss is just like the boss in the story as well; by day he drinks my sweat, at night he sucks my blood. . . . No one cares about us workers anymore. Things were much better when Chairman Mao was alive and I was in the factory."[22] Though sentiments like these are shared by many, particularly older workers, in other regions, the whole frame appears to fully come together and spark widespread collective action only in the Northeast.

Both of these frames also appeal to certain audiences in the upper Changjiang and north central regions. There, workers belonging to large firms in still-viable sectors—mines, some defense plants, and certain other heavy industrial firms—often tend toward the market hegemony frame; whereas those from small firms or certain hard-hit sectors, like textiles, often tend toward the Maoist moral economy worldview.

Still more widespread, though, among workers from the largest firms and best sectors and from the smallest firms and worst sectors alike, in the upper Changjiang and north central regions is a third point of view. This could be called the "keep your head down and muddle through" frame, and is similar to what Dorothy Solinger uncovered among her interviewees in Wuhan.[23] This way of viewing recent events and changes in Chinese society holds that reform has brought about many problems, including widespread job losses and corruption, but also affords the dislocated a number of new opportunities. Adherents of this frame maintain that to make ends meet one must work exceedingly hard to find new opportunities that exist in the market, though there is little doubt that such opportunities *do* exist. These opportunities are thought to be sufficiently fragile that political or social upheaval on any scale could result in them being snatched away.

One laid-off textile worker in Chongqing said, "protest is of no use for us laid-off workers. No one ever gets anything from stirring up trouble, and people like me can't stop working [in odd jobs] and go protest. We have to feed our children."[24] A laid-off coal miner in Datong (a major coal mining center and railway hub with roughly two million inhabitants in northern Shanxi Province) observed, "I am afraid of what would happen if I were caught protesting. Some of my coworkers from the mine have protested violently and have been arrested. I am able to find enough work around town to feed my family, but I have no health insurance or pension. If I get in trouble, I don't know what would happen."[25] The party secretary of a large state-owned enterprise in Luoyang (an industrial city of two million people in Henan Province) also claimed that workers in his factory generally remained off the streets so long as they were able to find temporary work (as supposedly most of them could); the benefits of working combined with the threat of repression or lost income kept them off the streets.[26]

But why do these particular frames seem to hold sway in these regions? If workers cannot form social movement organizations or be recruited to action via the rhetoric or deeds of movement entrepreneurs, and if the media maintain silence regarding their situation, how do many of them come to see their grievances through common filters? Xueguang Zhou offers one possible explanation: China's state socialist institutions aggregate individual interests and motivations, giving them a collective character they might otherwise lack.[27] If it were this simple, however, we might expect workers across regions, living within similar institutions in state work units, to respond in similar ways. At the very least, we would expect characteristics such as sector, firm size, or overseeing bureaucracy to be the main forces shaping workers' frames. These factors (along with age and cohort effects) clearly play a role, as already discussed, but the role played by regional political economy appears to be stronger.

Mario Luis Small has described structural influences on framing among residents of a Boston public housing project. Specifically, residents who moved into the project at different times "framed the neighborhood differently. . . . because of the historical experiences through which they came to live in Villa Victoria. . . . These experiences are affected by the politicoeconomic environmental conditions each cohort faced as it developed its view of the neighborhood."[28] Similarly, laid-off Chinese workers frame their grievances in ways tied closely to their material, ideational, and political life experiences under socialism and postsocialism. These shared life experiences have given rise to broadly popular attitudes, ideas and narratives of workers' grievances in a way not unlike the way workers everywhere are said to develop shared dispositions that "map the terrain of lived experience . . . [and] . . . are plausible and meaningful responses to the circumstances workers find themselves in."[29] If shared dispositions can help build social classes, surely they can help class members frame collective grievances in the absence of active framing by social movement organizations.

The key point for Chinese laid-off workers' shared dispositions is that they are bounded by regional political economy rather than being class-wide. Northeastern workers experienced socialism as an economic boom. Their region continued the rapid state-led industrialization it began under Japanese occupation. Large firms making steel, railway or defense equipment, automobiles, and machine tools or extracting coal, oil, or metal ores were doted on by central planners who lavished resources on the Northeast. Workers' living standards improved markedly—particularly for the majority who were just a generation (at most) away from abject poverty and famine in rural northern China in the first decades of the twentieth century. Politically, northeastern workers were the heroes of the nation, lionized in campaigns to "study Daqing" and other successful northeastern firms.

Postsocialism has been a dystopian nightmare in which northeastern workers have seen their gains stripped away. Some have descended back into hunger and dire poverty. A few of my interviewees had been reduced to living without heat in Benxi's often subzero (Fahrenheit) winter temperatures and eating little more than scavenged scraps of rancid vegetables and insect larvae. The region has experienced the largest number of layoffs as a percentage of the pre-reform workforce and among the lowest reemployment rates of any area in China. Worse still, the very qualities for which northeastern workers were praised under socialism have come to be seen as liabilities in a nation where what had once been criminal activities are now smiled on. All of this makes a Maoist moral economy frame resonate well, as it does for some older workers elsewhere who also experienced the heady gains of high socialism and the messy consequences of its aftermath.

The central coast became industrialized mostly through foreign direct investment in the 75 years or so before 1949. Workers there were recruited from the countryside through village networks not unlike the contemporary ones that ease the flow of young villagers from Sichuan, Jiangxi, Henan, and Anhui to the sweatshops of Dongguan and Shekou.[30] Employment in the city was always precarious, in marked contrast to the "golden rice bowl" Japanese employers offered northeastern workers at the time.[31] Socialism on the central coast brought wage restraint and the cooptation or repression of a nascent labor movement.[32] It also spelled relative stagnation for what remains one of China's richest regions, as the rest of the country at least partially caught up.

Market reform has opened up countless new opportunities for many in central coastal cities (including laid-off workers), and even those left out by the boom are generally well taken care of through generous welfare programs. Incredible new development has transformed cities like Shanghai, raising living standards nearly across the board. No longer constrained by onerous duties to support the backward hinterlands or toe the socialist line, workers and others on the central coast are free to return to the old ways of globalized capitalist development. In such an environment, it is not hard to see how even the most disadvantaged laid-off worker could be at least somewhat susceptible to the market hegemony frame.

Similarly, in upper Changjiang and north central cities, workers experienced rapid industrialization after 1949 (with the exception of a few cities, like Wuhan and Chongqing, that were partially industrialized earlier), mostly in resource-extractive sectors like mining and in consumer goods light industries such as textiles. Many of the existing cities in these regions expanded greatly, absorbing workers from the surrounding countryside or other regions, particularly during industrialization campaigns like the "Third Front" (c. 1967–1973). Socialism thus brought a certain degree of growth and prosperity to relatively large inland cities that, despite the party's best efforts, remain backwaters to this day.

Postsocialism for north central and upper Changjiang workers has been a mixed bag—new opportunities along with new risks and insecurities. As markets have opened up and new capital has poured in, new jobs have indeed been created, and many enterprising entrepreneurs have done well. At the same time, these regions remain poor and isolated. Most workers are forced to look very hard for minimal opportunities to eke out a living. But, unlike the Northeast, these regions have not experienced a great degree of downward mobility or complete collapse of the job market. Most workers here are at least not drastically worse off in material terms than before reform and there do seem to be at least some employment opportunities to go around.

Chinese state-owned enterprises, then, are akin to American public housing projects, in that the circumstances under which workers came into them and lived in them, as well as how they left them, condition the ways they perceive their departure from the state's embrace. When pressed about why they do not like the reform project and its effects, northeastern workers often recount earlier life experiences. For instance, the Benxi miner who thought the current state of affairs was so unjust said, "Overall, life was better before the reforms started. When Chairman Mao was still alive, to be a worker was to be a hero. Today no one cares about the working class."[33] Even a shop-floor foreman, laid off from a midsized Benxi firm, explained, "It would be far better to return to the planned economy. Things then were much better all around. An iron rice bowl is far better than an empty rice bowl."[34] Underscoring the degree of frustration and despair among laid-off workers in the Northeast, a team of government researchers in Liaoning Province found that of 1,739,000 laid-off workers there who had not been able to find any form of gainful reemployment by the end of 2004, nearly 25% (421,000) had given up searching for work altogether, even in the absence of regular welfare subsidies.[35]

Things could hardly be more different for Shanghai workers. A laid-off worker from a state-owned wholesale and warehousing company there complained bitterly about a lack of management accountability and blamed his plight squarely on managers' corruption and incompetence. Still, though, he was confident that he could find a new job soon and did not seem worried when pressed about what he would do if he could not; "I can stand to live a simple lifestyle," he said.[36] A laid-off forklift operator who found a new job as a truck driver was even more optimistic, stressing that being laid off from the state sector is really a kind of opportunity for those willing to work. "Under today's conditions, if you have a relatively scarce skill, some patience, and go through formal and informal organizations diligently, you can definitely find a good job after being laid off in Shanghai," he explained.[37] A laid-off dock worker and auto worker also made it clear that they blamed corrupt managers, and not the reforms, for their being laid off. They also explained that things were much better now than they ever had been before reform; the auto worker added, "All it really took to find new work was time and perseverance and an understanding of the way things really work."[38] All these interviewees were committed to the reform project and believed they had benefited personally from it and could overcome temporary difficulties, even though none of those just quoted had received all the benefits they were entitled to.

Mass Frames and Framing: The Big Picture

The basic dynamics that give rise to Chinese workers' mass frames are not unique, though the precise contours of the framing process and the interaction of mass frames with other factors may vary widely elsewhere. Mass frames are likely important in many contexts. Others have found evidence for a similar influence of regional political economy in shaping frames far from the dreary grey housing blocks in Benxi or Datong or the glittering skyscrapers of Shanghai. Cathy Schneider demonstrated in her study of mobilization by Puerto Rican radical activists, known often as the Young Lords, in three boroughs of New York City that regional political economy at the neighborhood level can play a powerful role in shaping frames.[39] The ideas and attitudes popular on Delancy Street or East Broadway did not always go down well or spark the same feelings on Melrose Avenue or Bushwick Avenue, even though the main audience (working-class Puerto Rican New Yorkers) and grievances (lack of social services) were the same. Similarly, Chinese laid-off workers in Chongqing or Datong do not typically perceive their main grievances (being laid off and a lack of effective welfare and reemployment assistance) the same way as their counterparts in Benxi or Shanghai. It might be tempting to attribute these differences to divergent "cultural stocks" (or "repertoires of subjectivities") across regions or to the different "tool kits" movement entrepreneurs have to draw from in different places.[40] Though it might be fair to characterize the Young Lords as skillfully selecting the right tools from the appropriate kits for their mobilization efforts in each neighborhood, such a view would place too much emphasis on the agency of protest organizers in shaping Chinese workers' perceptions, or would shift the focus away from perceptions and onto instrumentally phrased claims designed to evoke a particular response from workers' interlocutors.

Without organizations to do the heavy lifting, Chinese workers' frames are shaped as much by historical legacy as anything else. The experiences of being poor and marginal, at the center but milked for resources, or placed in the spotlight and glorified under socialism, help workers decode the meaning of contemporary threats to their material survival and political and social status in ways that encourage either protest or quiescence. Paul Almeida recently observed that in El Salvador under military authoritarianism, "organizational infrastructures surviving past a period of political opportunity in which they were founded perform a key task in determining if threats will deter or escalate collective dissent."[41] I suggest that "ideational infrastructures" that coalesce during periods of formative political, social, and economic regional development can play a role that is at least somewhat like Almeida's "organizational infrastructures," particularly where organizations are dismantled or are blocked from forming by even more effective authoritarian governments than El Salvador's.

Proponents of a more culturalist approach to the analysis of contentious politics have criticized earlier theories for their alleged assumption that group interests were determined simply by their structural position.[42] Although there is merit to this criticism, in authoritarian settings, where organizations are unable to engage in strategic framing activities, structure does help shape which frames resonate with individuals' lived experience in ways that give collective action broad appeal despite its high risks and uncertain rewards. In fact, the very question of frame resonance in the broader literature is really a nod to the role of structure. Recent analysts of strategic framing have emphasized that the resonance of frames can contribute to the breadth of support and depth of influence a movement wields.[43] As McVeigh, Meyers, and Sikkink point out in discussing the way the Ku Klux Klan based its framings on local structural conditions of Indiana counties, "the most effective frames are those that resonate with the life experiences of those targeted for recruitment. . . . The diagnosis of the problem must be consistent with what the targets of recruitment perceive in their immediate surroundings."[44]

But can we really speak of frames when what we are referring to are little more than worldviews conditioned by and held widely within particular structural contexts? Might it not be better to retreat to a broader and vaguer concept like "mechanisms of social construction"? Keeping the focus on frames, as opposed to other new concepts, does indeed make sense, provided we are willing to return to a more inclusive definition of frames. We can begin with the basic insight that grievances are "subject to differential interpretation, and . . . variations in their interpretation . . . can affect whether and how they are acted upon."[45] Frames could then be basically defined as patterns of interpretation through which individuals or organizations perceive their circumstances that influence their behavior with regard to collective action. Frames deliberately shaped by leaders and formal organizations can be seen as but one possible subtype of frame, which could be called a "liberal frame," or more accurately, "elite frames." These tend to play important roles where social movement organizations are relatively free to form and operate, even only sometimes, as in praetorian El Salvador.

Mass frames are a different but equally common subtype. They are not shaped or deployed by leaders or organizations but rather are widely held by people in similar social, political, and economic contexts. Their specific contours are also shaped through historically contingent lived experience of individuals and groups. They can affect behavior just as strongly as elite frames, and in many authoritarian contexts, it is only loosely organized individuals, usually without access to resources needed to deploy elite frames, who are capable of independent (i.e., not state-initiated) collective action. Mass frames can also be active in democratic and pluralist contexts, though in such cases their influence can frequently be superseded by elite frames. Mass frames also buy us more leverage than the broader concept of mechanisms of social construction. If mass frames are coherent collections of perceptions or worldviews that are widely shared among identifiable groups of people in particular situations, they should be easier to discern and measure (particularly in contexts where the work of framing remains hidden for fear of repression) than "collective efforts at interpretation and social construction" or "the reimagining of the legitimate purposes attached to established social sites and/or identities."[46] We can see mass frames not as deliberate efforts to interpret but as readily available fallback interpretations for people who are not inclined or permitted to engage in open collective efforts.

Mass frames can also exert a powerful influence in instances where deliberate efforts at reinterpretation or elite framing fail, because of a lack of resonance or coherence, strategic mistakes, or other blunders that harm leaders' credibility, or in the many settings when countermovements crowd the discursive arena with dissonant rhetoric and contradictory frames.[47] It would be unreasonable to assume that individuals or groups are capable of mobilization only in contexts where successful promulgation of elite frames or deliberate collective efforts at reinterpretation have occurred. Conversely, it would not be valid to assume that such collective efforts or elite framing was successfully completed in every context where the outcome of contentious mobilization is observed. Systematically addressing mass frames and their role in promoting mobilization can help scholars understand how perceptions shape contention, even when they are not themselves shaped through deliberate efforts of leaders or collectivities.

Some might object to mass frames on the grounds that they represent little more than a return to the older concept of cognitive liberation. That concept, at least in McAdam's formulation, is geared toward measuring when and how potential movement participants recognize political opportunities and develop "injustice frames," rather than toward understanding broader schemata of interpretation.[48] Cognitive liberation also appears to be essentially an all-or-nothing proposition closely linked with the presence of "indigenous organizations." He argues: "shifting political conditions supply the necessary 'cognitive cues' capable of triggering the process of cognitive liberation while existent organizations afford insurgents the stable group-settings within which that process is most likely to occur."[49] Thus, cognitive liberation remains conceptually distinct from mass frames in its focus on the role of organizations and injustice frames, as well as in its being a basically dichotomous variable (either present or not).

If organizations are not a factor, the media are off limits, and we are looking for something more verifiable than broad ideas of identity or culture, just where do mass frames come from and how can we measure them? It is easy—too easy—to retreat to structural conditions as the root of mass frames. More specificity is needed. One approach would be to look for the roots of mass frames in the institutions that control authoritarian societies, arguing along Xueguang Zhou's lines that the "similarity in structural dependency and vulnerability to the rhythms of state policies implies that social groups in China not only live in a similar political and economic environment but also tend to share similar life experiences . . . [that] have produced similar behavior patterns among individuals across workplaces and localities."[50] Such an approach, though clearly suited to China's structural environment, fails to explain the regional variation observed in the mass frames of laid-off workers and would likely preclude the analysis of mass frames in pluralist settings.

I propose a modified version of Zhou's rubric for uncovering the roots of Chinese workers' mass frames. Institutional structures obviously play a role, but the more subtle variation across regions and sectors must be emphasized. It is not possible, in other words, to root workers' frames entirely in the basic structures of Chinese work unit socialism, but the specific forms these structures take on in particular contexts do matter. An important element of these structures that Zhou mostly leaves aside, moreover, is the housing and other living arrangements that structure workers' lived experiences.[51] Also important is the "ideational infrastructure" put in place during earlier periods of class-based mobilization. In the Chinese case, such mobilization was nearly always led by the state or the CCP. Such structural elements help Chinese workers develop mass frames or shared dispositions.

Thus, we can arrive at a picture of structure that is multidimensional and takes into account key aspects of cultural and historical contingency. There are at least four major factors that influence the development of mass frames. First, the general social, political, and economic environment in a particular area helps shape perceptions and worldviews. Second, cultural, social, and other norms held across members of a society or group are reinforced through daily material life and interactions with institutions, and influence perceptions and interpretations of the world. Third, shared lived experience during particular historical periods, particularly experiences of collective action during times of great social or political change, strongly affect the sorts of frames adopted. Fourth and finally, the specific lived experience of otherwise unconnected individuals shapes worldviews in important ways (as occurs, for example, among sufferers of particular diseases, victims of crime, lottery winners, and so on). Sorting out more precisely how each of these factors, from the most purely structural to the more idiosyncratic, interacts with the others and the role each plays in molding mass frames remains a task for future research.

One further question that arises is whether frames and framing processes—in either elite or mass form—can be properly analyzed in isolation from other aspects of contentious mobilization. I agree with McAdam, Tarrow, and Tilly that to understand and explain contentious outcomes, analysis of cognitive processes and templates must be integrated with studies of relational and environmental mechanisms or opportunities, grievances, and mobilizing structures. But I believe that nailing down how key variables or mechanisms are shaped and the specific ways they influence actors in particular settings is a useful preliminary enterprise. Once the contours of the various pieces are better understood, we can begin to fit the larger puzzle together, revealing a clearer picture of the process of mobilization in China and beyond.

The most obvious and important question about mass frames is just how far they can travel as a concept. Is there any point in searching for or thinking about them when studying contention on American university campuses or in the streets of Paris? I believe there is. Clearly, powerful organizations and individual leaders can create facts on the ground through their strategic actions. Clearly also, skillful use of the mass media and virtuoso performances on the political stage can change the way people interpret their grievances. Where these markers of strategic elite framing are found, they often play the leading role.

What is less obvious in many cases is the part played by mass frames, even in pluralistic societies with active social movement organizations. As suggested earlier, the idea of frame resonance is an implicit admission of the importance of this role, but as currently construed this concept does not get us all that far. Some recent scholarship has suggested that resonance is more important than is often recognized, largely determining the degree of support even the most strategic framers can muster, because only those frames that "resonate with structural conditions" will appeal to targets of recruitment.[52] Replacing the general concept of structural conditions with the more specific, contingent, and historically and culturally embedded concept of mass frames would add greater subtlety and clarity to such arguments.

Though mass frames may sometimes fall into a supporting role when strategic or elite frames are in the limelight, they step to the lead in contexts where organizations and movement leaders are forced into the wings or are received poorly by audiences. In pluralist settings, mass frames may only be supplementary; in authoritarian settings, they are often central.

4 | Worker Leaders and Framing Factory-Based Resistance

Market reform in China has led to widespread protests by workers from state-owned enterprises (SOEs). Some of these incidents are best considered "primitive rebellions" or "crowd" phenomena.[1] They are often precipitated by accumulated frustration or "suddenly imposed grievances" related to reform policies that damage workers' interests.[2] Taking place on the streets or in front of government buildings, these gatherings last for a few hours or a few days, and have minimal organization. However, an increasing number of worker protests are well organized, strategic, and consciously planned, raise clear demands, and continue for a relatively long time. For such challenges to emerge, a variety of factors must be present. An indispensable one is leadership, insofar as it is crucial for defining goals, formulating strategies, mobilizing followers, and galvanizing organization.[3]

Leadership remains one of the more understudied issues in the social movement field. As Erickson and Bob point out, this lack of attention is due to four beliefs that some social scientists hold about emphasizing leadership—that it would (1) reduce complex episodes of popular action to the whims of a disgruntled agitator; (2) ignore deeper, long-term processes and mass behavior; (3) discount consensus-based decision making and the critical role of rank-and-file activists; and (4) downplay the role of structure and culture in shaping collective action.[4] When we turn to labor contention in China, two more reasons can be added. First, since the CCP has long suppressed the emergence of "civic leaders" *(minjian lingxiu),* attention has not been paid to people who perform leadership roles in collective action. Second, most labor protests in China are factory based and do not have wide societal impact. Their organizers are often obscure figures who are not readily accessible, not least because of security considerations. However, with collective protests growing of late, questions about leaders of popular action inevitably arise. Who stands up to lead? What inspired them? How did they organize resistance in an environment unsympathetic to extrainstitutional action? What role do they play in shaping contention? Without answers to these questions, our understanding of China's labor protests remains incomplete, as it leaves out the agents who turn mass discontent into action.

This chapter examines the role of worker leaders in framing contention and in choosing tactics from the repertoire of contention. As the literature has established, framing and repertoires are two key constituents of contention. Framing provides beliefs and meanings that inspire and legitimate movements,[5] Repertoires of contention enable the disgruntled to make claims.[6] Both are shaped by various factors, but they often reflect the orientation of protest leaders, which are in turn shaped by leaders' values and lived experience.[7]

This essay stems from a striking finding that emerged in my fieldwork: almost all instances of factory-based resistance were led by people who strongly believed in Maoist socialism, and most of the leaders were former Cultural Revolution activists whose thinking and actions showed a strong imprint of that time. I cannot claim that this is typical, as the number of people I interviewed was not great. With limited data, I cannot generalize but only provide a partial answer to the questions "Who are worker leaders?" and "What motivates them?" I also examine how these worker leaders' backward-looking orientation affected the ways they constructed frames and staged contention, and how it reflected the context in which they operate.

My focus on the role of leaders in framing is not necessarily at odds with William Hurst's (chapter 3) emphasis on the structural roots of frames. Indeed, despite being a "subjective" phenomenon, frames and framing processes are conditioned by "objective" circumstances, tied to both history and reality. Thus movement leaders cannot freely construct frames out of whole cloth. In fact, as Hurst argues, workers' injustice frames are rooted in their material, ideational, and political experiences under socialism and shaped by current economic conditions. However, Hurst's concept of a "mass frame" does not pin down how this perception translates into action. Framing is a stirring-up process that must be accomplished by certain agents. Worker leaders are one of these agents.

Framing, Repertoires, and Biographical Experiences

The worker leaders I interviewed played a critical role in framing contention and choosing tactics from the repertoire of contention. A collective action frame is indispensable for any movement, as it provides a "set of action-oriented beliefs and meanings that inspire and legitimate social movement activities and campaigns."[8] Its construction is a process through which social actors, media, and members of society jointly interpret, define, and redefine states of affairs.[9] But this description, derived from experiences in the West, cannot be readily applied to framing in a society like China's where public debates are controlled, the media is censored, and freedom of speech is limited, especially for politically sensitive issues. In short, framing as defined above is always difficult in places where the public sphere is under tight control. Indeed, this control is one of the major obstacles to the emergence of social movements in China. However, this does not mean that factory-based contention takes place without the mobilization of symbols or the construction of an injustice frame. Instead, framing largely results from leaders defining, interpreting, and articulating perceived problems, rather than through media and consensus mobilization.

A repertoire of contention, as Tilly defines it, is "the ways that people act together in pursuit of shared interests."[10] As a structural and cultural concept, a repertoire spells out not only what people can do in a given clash but also what they know how to do and what others expect them to do.[11] While some "contentious gatherings" are largely spontaneous and leaderless, organized contention is characterized by movement leaders' deliberate choices.[12] As this study will also show, the repertoire of labor contention in Chinese factories is often a direct product of worker leaders' decisions.

How worker leaders frame their contention and choose tactics is profoundly shaped by, among other things, their personal orientations, which in turn have a great deal to do with their "biographies."[13] Biography refers to lived experiences but is more than a simple aggregation of occurrences. A biography is entrenched within the culture, ideas, values, and social practices of a time. Biography shapes personal cognition and involves the "interplay between individual meaning and more structured public system."[14] It provides heuristics for a person to make sense of his or her current environment and to act on that perception. Biographical factors not only define who workers are but also account for what ideational resources they have and what ways they can deploy them during contention.

The worker leaders I interviewed were involved in contention in three state-owned enterprises that underwent privatization.[15] Their biographies typically reflected an era when personal experiences were deeply permeated by ideology. These worker leaders generally remained enthusiastic about Maoist socialism and nostalgic for the Cultural Revolution. They all strongly criticized market reforms, using prereform rhetoric to express grievances and demands. Their common perspective, which was shaped in the Maoist era, generated for all of them a similar discourse on and reactions to a situation they now perceive as renewed "class struggle." Of course, this orientation has a popular basis. Mao, despite being blamed for the disastrous policies of his later years and despised by many for his political fanaticism and persecution, remains an iconic figure among workers in SOEs as well as other disadvantaged social groups.[16] To many workers who have lost jobs or are facing a decline in economic status, Mao has come to symbolize a system that embodied socioeconomic equality and protection for working people. This common longing for the Maoist past implies the existence of a "collective definition" of a situation, but it does not automatically produce a "collective action frame" that stimulates mobilization.[17] A frame is dependent on protest leaders articulating workers' discursive nostalgia in a relatively coherent way; connecting it to abstract cognitions of unfairness and injustice; translating it into perceptions, evaluations, and claims; and thereby creating legitimacy and solidarity.

Cultural Revolution experiences also account for how these worker leaders organized contention, as well as their leadership ability, style, and mobilization skills. The Cultural Revolution was a time when people learned to rebel, argue, criticize, mobilize rhetoric, and organize group activities. These experiences conditioned how they react to disputes, particularly those they perceived as "class struggle." The symbolic and the organizational methods that they currently use, including leaflet distribution, group meetings, mass rallies, placards, slogans, red armbands, and factory takeovers, reveal the imprint of "rebellion" during the Cultural Revolution. As was evident in the leaflets, petitions, and commentaries they drafted, as well as in the interviews, most worker leaders were articulate and adept at analysis and had a strong propensity to connect concrete issues to ideological tenets, all tendencies that may have been shaped by Cultural Revolution experiences. Another notable trait they displayed, perhaps traceable to the same source, was their militancy, expressed in both discourse and action. Their critique of SOE reform was often packed with Cultural Revolution rhetoric, and they were eager to turn to confrontational and disruptive action when official channels failed.

Their orientation toward labor struggles also was related to two more recent considerations. First, the regime often justifies market reform in socialist language. This encourages worker leaders to seek moral justification in the ideology of days past and to frame their claims in the rhetoric that deeply permeated their lived experience during the Cultural Revolution. Second, institutions constrain choices of how to protest. Here, although worker leaders view suffering from marketization as class-shared, they must confine their defiance to a single workplace, avoiding crossfactory action and other forms of prohibited escalation.

Maoist Rhetoric and the Action Frame

The Cultural Revolution ended a generation ago, and fundamental socioeconomic changes since then have undercut the ideology of Maoism and left few detectable vestiges of the "ten years of turmoil." While the turbulence of that time may be hard to forget, it seems to have little contemporary relevance for most Chinese. However, the Cultural Revolution has not been swept away. For the labor activists I interviewed, experiences from the Cultural Revolution remained a source of ideas and inspiration, as well as a reminder of the pride proletarians felt at a time when they enjoyed immeasurably higher political status.[18]

Some worker leaders retain a strongly positive view of their participation in the Cultural Revolution. During interviews, Mr. L and Mr. D proudly mentioned their experiences in the 1960s and 1970s. Mr. D joined the 2/7 Commune, the most famous rebel organization in his province, when he was still in middle school. Mr. L was a propagandist for a university Red Guard group. They both still believed that Mao had been correct in launching the Cultural Revolution and preventing the country from turning capitalist. For Mr. Z, who was Mr. D's comrade in factory A and a member of a worker rebel group, the Cultural Revolution represented a time of social equality and clean government: "[At that time] cadres did their jobs in accordance with Chairman Mao's instructions. They were not corrupt and did not have many privileges. . . . Worker rebels followed Chairman Mao's revolutionary line and some outstanding representatives of the working class, like Tang Qishan, became the members of the Central Committee, and provincial Party Secretary and Deputy Secretary.[19] They never made use of power and position for the pursuit of individual interests. They grasped revolution and promoted production, enjoying a very high reputation. Compared with current cadres, it is like the difference between heaven and earth."[20]

These leaders' positive view of the Cultural Revolution was accompanied by a strong belief in Maoism and nostalgia for industrial relations that prevailed during Mao's time.[21] They viewed China prior to reform as a society where working people were protected and enjoyed social equality, something they said was denied under capitalism. This perception was the benchmark against which they made sense of market reforms. Mr. D, one of the principal leaders from factory B, did not conceal his affection for Mao and Mao's era:

The epoch of Mao Zedong was the greatest one in Chinese history, which nobody can deny. This was an era when Chinese people felt proud and elated, and when workers and peasants were the masters. . . . People lived a happy life without worry and anxiety and got paid for their work. Everybody worked hard for the country without trouble back home, as the state provided housing and medical insurance. . . . Mao established a worker-peasant regime, which wholeheartedly served the people and did not pursue self-interest. So I think that the epoch of Mao was great. The working class misses Chairman Mao very much. . . .

Many workers here paid homage to Mao by laying flowers at the foot of statues of him on his birthday, National Day, and Qingming Festival every year. . . . I still study Mao's works and recite his poems, which make me feel good and cheerful.[22]

Mr. D's feelings were shared by other labor activists. Mr. L, a central figure in contention at one factory, remarked that Mao's system was best for workers' interests. He fondly recalled an era in which there had been no need for a labor law because workers were masters of their enterprises, and he criticized the current labor law as mainly serving the interest of employers.[23] Mr. C, one of the activists leading resistance to the privatization of another SOE, said, "we were all crying and hoping that another Mao Zedong would emerge."[24] Mr. Z, who had been removed from his party post as one of "three kinds of people" *(sanzhongren)* at the end of the Cultural Revolution, and later led labor protests in several factories, upheld a staunch Maoist position in his comments, decrying reform during an interview in early 2004.[25] On September 9, 2004, the twenty-eighth anniversary of Mao's death, he was arrested while distributing flyers dedicated to the memory of Mao. Charged with libel, because his leaflet criticized Deng Xiaoping and Jiang Zemin, he was imprisoned for three years.

With a deep attachment to Mao and the old system, worker leaders severely criticized market reform, especially the restructuring of SOEs. Market reform was seen as deviating from socialism and a betrayal of the working class. In other words, lived experience under Maoism became an ideational resource deployed to define and assess current problems. A popular critique of SOE reform among worker leaders and workers held that it was extremely unfair because it violated their rights to factory property. In this view, since workers had contributed their youth, and indeed their entire working lives, to a factory, this justified a share of factory property. Privatization amounted to deprivation without compensation. For example, when the workers at one factory confronted a private entrepreneur who had "merged" their factory, the new owner asserted that the factory was now his, insofar as the government had sold it to him. "On what do you base your claim to the factory?" he said. "It is based on our work and struggle at the factory for several decades!" Mr. Z, one of the principal worker activists leading resistance in that factory, shot back.[26] As Mr. L insisted, workers opposed privatization down to the marrow of their bones.[27]

To these worker leaders, the plight proletarians were facing was directly due to market reform. In a leaflet distributed to workers, Mr. D stated: "The Chinese working class joined the revolution in order to control the means of production, factories, and equipment. The working class's control over the means of production has determined the nature of our country. . . . Now [those officials] want us to give up the factory and give the means of production to capitalists and they still call this socialist. It is a gross deception."

Mr. L questioned the direction that market reform was taking, arguing that privatization went against the CCP's own "purpose" (zhongzhi) and undermined the foundation of the regime by downgrading the vanguard of the revolution. Mr. Z, Mr. D's comrade, thought that market reform was wrong from the outset because it "aimed to negate the basic principles of socialism." For him, ongoing privatization was retaliation by the capitalist class against the working class.[28]

As former Cultural Revolution activists, labor leaders were not hesitant to call their contention "class struggle," a term officially shelved by the government after the reforms began. At one meeting, the new owner of a factory accused activists of "carrying out class struggle" (gao jieji douzheng) in an attempt to delegitimize their contention. However, Mr. Z struck back, saying, "What's wrong with class struggle? What you are doing is class revenge!" Mr. D, from the same factory, told me without hesitation: "Our struggle [against privatization] is a manifestation of class struggle. Oppression and polarization inevitably lead to class struggle."[29] In leaflets drafted by Mr. L and his comrades, privatization was described as "restoration" (fubi) and "replacement of proletarian dictatorship with boss dictatorship." They labeled their resistance a "proletarian movement" that had the aim of defending their "homeland" (jiayuan).

For these worker leaders, the core issue was ownership of the enterprise. They portrayed privatization as negating socialism as well as their basic interests. Differing from many subsistence-oriented "moral economy" protests by laid-off workers hurt by downsizing, closure, or bankruptcy, the resistance was framed as a means to stop privatization.[30] However, as an alternative strategy to save an ailing factory, only one group of activists that I studied devised a plan to transform a factory into a workers' collectively owned entity.

Nostalgia for the Maoist past can also be found in labor contention in other factories in Z city, as well as in other parts of the country, especially in places where workers could find few other jobs or did not receive much government assistance.[31] In addition to differences in regional political economy, the salience of Maoist norms can also be attributed to local history—Henan province, where the factories are located, is one of the areas most steeped in "memories of the Cultural Revolution" *(wenge zhongzaiqu).*[32]

Is the Repertoire of Contention Learned from the Past?

Many of the elements of a repertoire of contention are inherited.[33] In this section, I show that some tunes from the repertoire can be traced back to the years of "rebellion-is-justified" *(zaofan youli).*

In the history of the People's Republic, there have been two major episodes where the working class launched collective action. The first wave of protests took place in 1956–1957, as a result of tensions in the workplace precipitated by socialist transformation. The Hundred Flowers Campaign, despite being directed at intellectuals, also encouraged workers' open expression of their grievances at this time. In Shanghai alone, major labor disturbances erupted in 587 enterprises, and similar protests occurred in other parts of the country.[34] I would argue, however, that this strike wave has had little influence on the current working-class struggle, as it is not known widely by today's workers, because information of it was suppressed at the time and it occurred only in a limited number of locations.

Rebellion during the Cultural Revolution, the second major episode of workers' collective action since 1949, is, however, very much a part of the lived experiences of older workers experiencing market reform, and hence has had a bigger impact on current contention.[35] Although the contemporary working-class struggle is not a replica of contention during the Cultural Revolution, in the cases I examined, much of the repertoire of contention appears to have been "learned" from Cultural Revolution experiences.

Leafleting and Slogan Making

Leafleting and slogan making were widely used by rebel groups during the Cultural Revolution. As former Cultural Revolution activists, worker leaders in two of the factories I examined effectively made use of both methods of claims making and consensus mobilization. Like other ordinary citizens in China, workers have limited access to the media or other channels to express grievances and mobilize contention. Leafleting was an alternative through which worker leaders could present their views in written form to rank-and-file workers. Producing effective leaflets depended on a protest leader's ability to write well and provide convincing evidence. The two activists who wrote most of the leaflets in one factory said they acquired this skill during the Cultural Revolution.[36] Since their contention was factory based, leaflets focused on enterprise-specific issues and were disseminated within the confines of the enterprise. This explains why leafleting was not prohibited by the authorities.[37]

As both factories I studied show, a primary purpose of leafleting was to "expose the truth" (*jielu zhenxing*).[38] Whereas many workers strongly suspected that the transfer of factory property to private hands was unlawful and involved corruption, they did not know much about the details of the deals between private buyers and management. In leaflets, the labor activists provided a meticulous rundown of the transactions, gathered through their own investigation. For example, they revealed the tremendous difference between the real value of factory assets and the price they had fetched. One of the factories, whose assets were worth 240 million yuan, was sold to a private firm for 47 million yuan. An "empty-shell" private company was merged into the other factory, worth 88 million yuan, for 12 million yuan. The leaflets also illuminated the attitude of local authorities, who leaned toward private buyers in disputes over factory property.

Leafleting was also used to suggest alternatives to privatization. For example, protest leaders at one factory distributed a "propaganda outline" that proposed measures to restore and develop production if the planned merger was terminated. Its purpose was to convince workers as well as the local authorities that privatization was avoidable and that the factory could be run under a modified form of public ownership.

To mobilize workers, leaders in both factories formulated slogans and disseminated them through leaflets. Slogans were the most concise and pointed expression of opposition to restructuring, and set the tone for later protest actions. The slogans can be separated into several types, which reflect the aims and tactics of worker leaders, as well as their demands on behalf of other workers. The first type was used to embolden workers; for example, "We workers have strength! Unity means victory!" "We are the working class and the master, not slaves!" The second type put forth workers' claims and demands; for instance, "Seize back state property from private hands!" "Reform does not allow privatization!" "The working class must not follow the capitalist road!" "The factory is a public-owned enterprise!" "Defend workers' interests and pay back suspended wages!" The third type focused on self-defense. Worker leaders were fully aware that to sustain popular action and avoid suppression, they had to appear politically correct. Thus, slogans included "Closely united around the Central Committee of the Party with the core of comrade Jiang Zemin," "Only the CCP can rescue China!" and so on.

Organizing and Mobilizing

The experience of factional strife during the Cultural Revolution informed organizing and mobilizing strategies used in antiprivatization resistance. In one factory, an informal group successfully convened a Staff and Workers' Council meeting, which rejected a merger proposal and then quickly transformed itself into a formal organization called the 10/28 Committee (October 28 was the day the council was held).[39] Mr. L was elected "general representative" (*zongdaibiao*) of the committee. To mobilize workers, each building in the factory's residential area was assigned a liaison who was responsible for keeping workers informed of new developments, encouraging their participation, and distributing leaflets. The leadership group at another factory, including Mr. D and Mr. Z, emerged one day in 2000 from the security booth at the factory entrance, where disgruntled workers often gathered to discuss the factory's situation, and staged a rally that was attended by over 1,000 workers. At the rally, they declared that the Staff and Workers' Council sought to take over management of the factory, which had been under the control of a private firm. In yet another factory, some key leaders came from the leftist Zhongliu Study Group, which had existed for some time before the privatization started. *Zhongliu* (Midstream) was a Beijing-based magazine that often published articles supporting orthodox socialism and criticizing market reform; the study group, composed of workers as well as retired cadres, met once a month to discuss articles in the magazine. When the magazine was shut down in 2001, the group was renamed the Mao Zedong Thought Study Group. Although no formal organization was set up during the resistance to privatization at this factory, individual activists from the Zhongliu Study Group were instrumental in coordinating several actions.

Taking over a Factory

In organizing defiance, worker leaders tended to use more institutionalized means first. There were three such means. One was the operation of the Staff and Workers' Council within the factory. These councils had been largely ineffective and powerless organizations in most SOEs. However, because of their legally designated power to discuss and approve decisions concerning enterprise restructuring, councils often became critical arenas to seize in order to press a case within approved channels. To revoke a merger plan, worker leaders in one factory aggressively lobbied members of the council to vote against it, both before and during the meeting. At first, worker leaders also wanted to bring their dispute to the council for resolution. Only when the new employer declared the old council defunct did worker leaders decide to form their own committee.

The second officially sanctioned channel was lodging collective petitions to government authorities. Like many workers at SOEs nationwide, the disgruntled workers I studied lodged repeated complaints to various bodies, including municipal and provincial governments, provincial people's congresses, municipal courts, the All China Federation of Trade Unions, the *Workers' Daily*, and so on. The purpose of petitioning was not only to "reflect the situation" (*fanying qingkuang*) but also, as Mr. C, a leader from factory C, said, to demand that "the government take a clear stand on a dispute" (*xiang zhengfu yao ge shuofa*). Visits to government agencies were headed by worker leaders, who drafted petitions usually in the name of "all staff and workers of the factory." When trips to Beijing were made to appeal to higher authorities, worker leaders conducted fundraising in the factory to cover a petitioner's travel expenses.

Workers also sought legal redress for harm caused by industrial restructuring, even though existing laws were seldom helpful. A dispute over privatization in one factory reached the district court, which ruled in favor of the workers. However, municipal authorities overrode the court's ruling. Court officials told the litigants that they could do nothing about a "government action" *(zhengfu xingwei)*. As Mr. D, who was involved in the lawsuit, explained, the government had to intervene because it realized that the court ruling in favor of workers could lead to a chain reaction across the city, where about 150 enterprises had undergone similar privatization schemes.[40]

Workers from a second factory also sought to bring a dispute over privatization to the district court, but it refused to accept their case. According to Mr. C, "all courts [in the city] have been ordered by the government authorities not to take such cases."[41] Indeed, China's labor laws were largely ineffective in resolving, and were even irrelevant to, disputes caused by industrial restructuring. According to state policy, many consequences of industrial restructuring are not open to legal challenge.

The failure of officially sanctioned channels often induced workers to deploy extrainstitutional means to press their claims. In one factory, nearly 600 workers joined a two-day strike called by activists, most of whom were members of the Zhongliu Study Group. Protest leaders in another enterprise called a mass rally that led to the formation of a workers' committee. When workers became truly desperate, they took to the streets and blocked traffic. This occurred in many SOEs.

The most radical action taken by workers, however, was taking over a factory. This had both symbolic and substantive meaning. It was symbolically significant because it demonstrated workers' belief that they had a legitimate right to the factory. Substantively, it was intended to increase pressure on opponents to concede. At one factory, when workers had exhausted all institutional avenues and more moderate means of exerting pressure, activists decided to take the factory forcibly. Mr. L said, "Since the state does not take care of the factory, we will take care of it by ourselves."[42] In five ways, this dramatic action was reminiscent of the "seize power" *(duoquan)* campaigns of the Cultural Revolution. (1) All workers joining the action wore red armbands in "defending the factory team." They stormed the factory and tore down its name plate. All managerial personnel of the private company were expelled from the grounds, and all offices were sealed. (2) Placards were erected on the factory gate; the biggest one read "Reform Does Not Allow Privatization!" (3) A few days after the seizure, activists issued three "announcements" proclaiming their takeover. All physical assets, as well as accounts, cash, contracts, and legal documents, were declared to be under the control of the workers' committee. (4) Leaflets were widely distributed and posted in the factory to promote, as one leader said, "our ideas." (5) Finally, arrangements were made to sustain the action. The leadership was broken into two groups to prevent interruption if arrests occurred. Participating workers were divided into three teams that guarded the factory in shifts: retired and female workers were on duty in the daytime, and male workers took over at night.

During the two months of occupation, the local government dispatched a work team to the factory to demand that workers end their action. Under mounting pressure from the authorities, the leadership split. One younger leader, Ms. Liu, suggested backing down and negotiating with the government, but Mr. L refused and insisted on "carrying out the revolution to the end." Ms. Liu explained their disagreement:

> He was somewhat a Cultural Revolution-type person, a *zaofanpai* [rebel] type person. He was indeed a *zaofanpai* in the Cultural Revolution—this was what he said to us. . . . I revised much of what he wrote. I told him that if I had not revised it, we would have given a handle to the authorities against ourselves. . . . I said to him that what we were doing [i.e., continuing the occupation of the factory] was not proper. It was no use saying "let's carry out the revolution to the end"; we had to face reality.[43] I did not mean that we must end the occupation immediately. But we should sit down and talk with the government. He [Mr. L] did not let us contact the work team and had no intention of breaking the stalemate. . . . I stopped attending the meetings he called, though I continued to join the action of protecting the factory.[44]

Mr. L's Cultural Revolution experience, as another observer also pointed out, accounted for his radical and uncompromising tactics, as well as the language he used to describe his contention.[45] His arrest after the crackdown and Ms. Liu then becoming the central figure in the leadership brought about a shift in tactics. The dispute was now framed more in legal terms than in class language. The Staff and Workers' Council was reestablished as an arena for dispute settlement, and more petitions were written to request government intervention. Consistent pressure from workers finally forced the private buyer to terminate the merger scheme.

Protest repertoires are drawn from a dense thicket of experiences.[46] As a turbulent episode that engulfed the whole population, the Cultural Revolution offers a reservoir of choices, especially for people who were activists in that period. Here local history is relevant again. Henan is a province that witnessed a particularly strong "worker rebellion movement" during the Cultural Revolution that produced a large number of ideologically oriented workers familiar with a variety of approaches to protest.[47] It is thus not surprising that these people played a key role in activating idioms, symbols, and tactics of the past to frame resistance against privatization.

Facilitating and Constraining Factors

Although we do not know how widespread the role of Maoist-oriented activism is in factory-based labor contention nationwide, there is strong evidence that Maoist norms are still attractive to many workers and laid-off workers.[48] Maoist framing clearly has a deep emotional and socioeconomic basis (Hurst, chapter 3). This is of course far from unprecedented—the history of labor movements elsewhere shows that workers' defiance is often influenced by the values, norms, and experiences of the past.[49] Chinese workers were immersed within socialist ideology, as well as Maoist practices, for decades. They were thus ready targets for worker leaders who used familiar ideas and language to interpret a situation and frame claims.

Yet historical memory is not the whole story. The government's ideological strategy, that is, maintaining an official legitimation of socialism during China's transition, has also had an impact. Socialist rhetoric still matters to the Chinese government. It matters not because it is effective for generating "diffuse support" for the regime or for guiding policies and social life but because ideology remains a critical symbolic constituent of the state, and its open abandonment would invite political challenge.[50] Thus, despite his unwavering position on market reform, Deng Xiaoping never intended to shed communist ideology. Nor have his successors. Even though market reforms have already remolded China's economy along capitalist lines, the top leadership has still insisted that what is happening by no means amounts to a departure from socialism. In industrial reform, for example, the transfer of SOEs to private hands is never called "privatization" (siyouhua). Instead, it is often described in official discourse as minyinghua (ownership by the people), gaizhi (restructuring the system), or guoyou zichan zhuanrang (the transfer of state assets). On several occasions, state leaders have openly denied that privatization is occurring. For example, in 1995, Jiang Zemin, then party secretary, stated: "We . . . are absolutely not going to practice privatization. This is a big principle from which we should never waver in the slightest degree."[51] Likewise, as workers have been driven out of factories and thrown into poverty more recently, the official discourse on the political primacy of the working class has remained largely unchanged. This class is still deemed the master of the country or the "main force of the reform" (gaige de zhuliujun).[52]

This maintenance of socialist pretensions has created a disjuncture between official ideology and social reality, and has been a major source of workers' confusion, frustration, and resentment. However, it has also provided legitimate grounds for workers to challenge SOE restructuring and make claims. In their verbal as well as written critiques, worker leaders I interviewed kept asking why privatization should be permitted in a socialist country or, to put it another way, under "the reign of the Communist Party" (gongchandang de tianxia). Whereas market reform has indeed created deep disillusionment with official rhetoric, the government's ideological strategy seems to have delayed changes in cognition and reinforced a notion that reforms have deviated from the "right" track. As long as socialism is still an official commitment, many workers feel it is proper and justified to criticize restructuring schemes that "betray" the interests of the working class.

Of course, the use of Maoist rhetoric to frame claims and actions should not be viewed only in terms of belief and nostalgia. It might also reflect tactical considerations—an effort to make resistance politically unimpeachable. The strategy for criticizing market reforms amounts to what O'Brien and Li call "rightful resistance" by a subaltern class—poaching rulers' ideology and their theater of legitimation to reduce vulnerability and make actions more palatable to officialdom and especially potential elite allies.[53] The worker leaders I studied consistently employed rhetoric and language that they recognized the government could not question unless it sought an open rupture with communism. Worker leaders were not hesitant in their interviews to call the state a "bureaucratic capitalist state," but during open protests, no antigovernment slogans were raised. On the contrary, and in a more dramatic way, they employed slogans such as "Support the Chinese Communist Party!" "Only the Communist Party Can Save China," and "Long Live the Chinese Working Class," as well as Deng Xiaoping and Jiang Zemin's earlier promises to uphold public ownership. By shouting these slogans, protest organizers indicated that their actions were not politically deviant—that they were not targeting either the party or the government.

Such behavior seems to support James Scott's argument that "it is not at all necessary for subordinate classes to set foot outside the confine of the ruling ideals to formulate a critique of power."[54] However, I would argue that to view worker leaders' resort to this rhetoric purely in terms of tactical consideration might ignore a key constraint that faces the working class: the lack of alternative ideational resources.[55] Whereas the past decade has witnessed a surge of new ideas and ideologies among China's intellectuals, few of them have reached the working-class struggle. For Chinese workers, the old socialist rhetoric is not only a ready-made "raw material" to be used in contention but also the only ideational resource that is available to them for articulating grievances and framing claims. The state has cut off workers' access to alternative ideologies by restricting their contact with intellectuals and forbidding them to link up with dissident labor groups outside of China.[56] The lack of an alternative cognitive framework has contributed to the predominant role of Maoist-oriented activists as well as the popularity of socialist rhetoric among SOE workers.

At the same time, if worker leaders could actively play on socialist rhetoric to frame their claims and actions, their role in framing and organizing was also informed by the broader context. Privatization has already affected a wide spectrum of the workforce and produced a disgruntled proletariat and no shortage of workers waiting to be mobilized. Cognitively, the worker leaders I studied, as well as some of their followers, comprehended and interpreted their firm-specific grievances as class-wide and openly interpreted privatization in terms of class conflict. My fieldwork also made clear that some worker activists from different factories in one city maintained personal contacts with each other and even had occasional meetings to exchange information and discuss tactics. Labor activists were obviously clear about, and interested in, contention in nearby factories. One protest leader also indicated that he once offered tactical advice to activists from another factory.

However, all these favorable conditions did not lead to concerted action or broader claims. In the end, protests against privatization all remained factory based and focused on firm-specific concerns.[57] This outcome pointed to an overriding constraint on workers' contention: no crossenterprise, sector, or regional coalescing would be tolerated by the authorities. To avoid repression and sustain their momentum, worker leaders had to avoid wading into class-wide claims making. For example, when the workers at one factory were fighting privatization, their counterparts in a dozen SOEs located along the same boulevard were also protesting similar schemes, but no crossenterprise coalescing took place. Mr. L related that the worker leaders insisted to all participants that their action must remain within the factory gate. During days when a factory was occupied, one of the important tasks of the "factory defense team" was to prevent workers from going onto the streets or contacting protesting workers in neighboring factories. Worker leaders were all in agreement that the authorities would suppress such attempts immediately. Indeed, the government's intolerance of crossfactory action was most evident in its crackdown after a protest in Liaoyang in 2002 that attracted thousands of workers from six enterprises. Following this incident, three protest leaders received long prison sentences.[58]

China's transition to the market economy, while striking a heavy blow to the working class, has not been accompanied by a broad labor movement based on class solidarity at the sectoral or societal level. Nevertheless, in factories numerous protests have occurred, some of which have been organized and lengthy. Worker leaders have been instrumental in framing and organizing factory-based contention. That they confine framing and organizing efforts to single factories underscores a fundamental constraint on Chinese labor contention: framing and concerted action that go beyond the factory are currently impossible. While it is hard to make generalizations about the background, ideas, and behavior of labor activists due to a shortage of data, this chapter has attempted to show that at least some of these activists share beliefs and experiences rooted in the Maoist era, and that such beliefs and experiences have shaped their role in framing and organizing contention.

That Maoist-oriented activists led contention was not accidental. As members of a social group that once enjoyed higher socioeconomic status, SOE workers have been hit hardest by market reform. Having been excluded from a process of restructuring that has often devastated their lives and forced to watch helplessly as state property is transferred to private hands, many workers harbor a strong sense of unfairness and injustice. Their nostalgia for a Maoist economic system they perceive as egalitarian is a natural response to their plight. Maoist-oriented worker leaders, as this study has shown, echo the prevailing sentiment of nostalgia among many SOE workers. Their action frame, in this sense, embodies one of the "mass frames" (Hurst, chapter 3) shared among workers. Using familiar language to interpret the situation, define victims and perpetrators, and identify the root of grievances, the appeal of "mass frames" and their mobilizing power is considerable.

The emergence of worker leaders can often be attributed to prior experiences with collective contention. As former "rebels" in the Cultural Revolution, my interviewees tended to be more assertive, militant, and steadfast than most.[59] Furthermore, they possessed a variety of practical skills, honed during the Cultural Revolution, that helped them conduct mobilization and contention.

Still, the prominence of Maoist-oriented worker leaders highlights a profound dilemma facing the Chinese working class in the transition to a market economy. As a social group that more than any other has borne the cost of transformation, SOE workers can be expected to continue to express grievances and defend their interests. However, if market reform is irreversible, a resort to socialist rhetoric is anachronistic. It may even hinder workers from recognizing, defining, and articulating their interests and rights in new labor relations, and may slow their search for a long-term solution to their predicament. In fact, ideologically based "rights" are no longer truly enforceable; few protests by laid-off workers address their "rights" problem. Although marketization has caused inequality and corruption, a return to the Maoist system is not in the cards. A nostalgic critique of market reform and resort to slogans with Cultural Revolution flavor might also alienate other urbanites, especially the middle class and intellectuals, and diminish their sympathy for working-class problems. Furthermore, worker leaders with a Cultural Revolution background are often susceptible to the accusation of being the "three kinds of people" (i.e., leftovers from the Cultural Revolution). This makes it easier for the authorities to delegitimate and suppress them for "creating disturbances" *(zhizao dongluan)*.[60] The shortage of ideas that could inspire a new direction for the working class points to constraints that continue to exist. Cognitive liberation, as one social movement theorist points out, occurs most readily in stable group settings.[61] In other words, without independent unionism, there may be little chance for the development of alternative visions of the labor struggle in China.

CARSTEN T. VALA
KEVIN J. O'BRIEN

5 | Recruitment to Protestant House Churches

New members generally do not join a political or religious movement simply because they believe in its message. More often than not, they must be recruited. And recruitment, even of those so inclined, is far from automatic. Potential participants have many calls on their time and resources, and even for causes that speak to deeply felt needs (or grievances), grabbing a person's attention usually requires effort.

Springing largely from studies of American social movements of the 1960s and 1970s, researchers have homed in on one leading way to facilitate movement recruitment: social networks. Participants are typically drawn into political and religious movements by people they know, as "recruitment flows along lines of pre-existing, significant social relationships of positive-affect."[1] For political movements, friends, roommates, coworkers, or relatives bring a person to a march, a meeting, or a demonstration. For religious movements, a current member connects someone they know with a community of believers, places a text in their hands, or sits alongside them through a broadcast.[2]

In this way, social bonds with the already mobilized can create a context for new identities to emerge. Close personal ties enhance feelings of trust and offer newcomers reassurance, while also providing recruiters with opportunities to apply subtle forms of pressure ("If you go, I'll go, too"). Preexisting relations enable those who share values to influence each other and ease the circulation of information about a movement's message and its activities. Social networks, in short, are a crucial "pull factor" that connect recruits with a chance to participate. They activate feelings of solidarity and offer a variety of interpersonal rewards.[3] In a host of ways, networks (and the social bonds they are built on) allow recruiters to exploit the rapport that friends, relatives, colleagues, and neighbors have and help get newcomers on the streets (for political movements) or jump-start the process of conversion (for religious movements).

Prior ties are generally thought to matter even more in nondemocratic states. They have been found to be especially important, for example, in Leninist regimes, where they often substitute both for organizations and the media.[4] In communist-era Poland, Maryjane Osa observed, social networks helped overcome barriers to participation by opening channels for uncensored materials to circulate, diffusing the risks of association, and, most broadly, substituting for a public sphere and forming a context for micromobilization.[5] East German dissidents, like Chinese student protesters in 1989 (Wright, chapter 1), in an effort to reduce the likelihood of repression, also relied on a circle of intimates to decide who could be trusted and with whom heterodox ideas could be shared.[6]

Social bonds have likewise been found to be important in drawing new adherents to religious groups, not least because conversion may entail a wholesale reordering of beliefs that requires regular confirmation from others. Networks provide opportunities to discuss an unfamiliar faith and ease the decision to make a commitment. For newcomers, personal relations with church members often carry feelings of warmth and friendliness, opportunities to be socialized to new beliefs, occasions to be urged to participate, and contact with people they already trust who can help them resolve doubts about a religion's claims.[7]

Researchers for over a generation have highlighted the role social bonds play in religious recruitment, with some going so far as to argue that "faith constitutes conformity to the religious outlook of one's intimates."[8] In two landmark studies, Snow and his colleagues showed that social networks yielded 60–90 percent of the new members of several religious groups, and Stark and Bainbridge isolated personal ties to religious activists as the best predictor of recruitment to established faiths (Mormonism) and unconventional sects (doomsday groups).[9] Door-to-door proselytizing, on the other hand, seldom proved fruitful for Mormons or American Pentecostals, and early efforts to recruit members to the Unification Church through radio spots, public meetings, and press releases usually floundered, once recruiters went beyond members' extramovement networks.[10] To this day, one of the key findings of research on religious recruitment is that "the network channel is the richest source of movement recruits."[11] Even more unambiguously, "all faiths rest on network influences."[12]

Recruiting Strangers

But friends, acquaintances, roommates, coworkers, and relatives are not the only recruits to religious or political movements. Sometimes strangers are also drawn in. Animal rights activists in the United States have relied on shared values, "moral shocks," and skillful use of the media to activate already developed motivations and attract new recruits. Dutch peace activists have courted sympathizers with whom they have no links through appeals in local newspapers, peace stands, posters, billboards, and banners. In the 1960s and 1970s, Hare Krishna devotees in the United States adeptly exploited the biographical availability of alienated, isolated youth who had few other ties. Strangers also flocked to the American antiabortion movement in the immediate aftermath of the *Roe v. Wade* decision, largely owing to moral outrage.[13]

Each of these nonnetwork pathways to participation depended on unpatrolled spaces in which to act. Animal rights activists in the United States were able to set up booths where graphic, shocking images of laboratory animals could be displayed. In the Netherlands, peace activists conducted their recruitment drives partly through publicity stands that distributed pamphlets and sold buttons, stickers, and posters. Hare Krishnas flooded countercultural neighborhoods, such as Haight-Ashbury in San Francisco, where they had the run of city streets to play their drums and chant.[14] Even antiabortion activists in the United States enjoyed the right to advertise efforts to reverse *Roe v. Wade* and to picket clinics where abortions were performed.

What if public spaces are not readily available and if door-to-door recruitment and other types of direct, personal contact are discouraged or illegal? In China, for example, public religious recruiting is forbidden, and potential recruits hear little about religion in the official media and receive nothing concerning any faith in the mail. How do activists in such circumstances reach out to strangers? What, in particular, does stranger recruitment to unregistered Protestantism in China tell us about the mechanisms that draw people into activism and how networks can be done without, at least initially?[15]

Methods and Data

Studying religion in China is a "very sensitive" *(hen minggan)* matter, said a professor at a major Chinese university to one of us, and the best way to go about it would be to concentrate on published materials that could be found in libraries and bookstores. Having gained official approval to examine the development of Protestantism in China, however, and with introductions to potential interviewees already in hand, it was possible to press ahead with care.

In the end, more than 50 interviews were conducted with current and former pastors, provincial religious leaders, unregistered church leaders, foreign missionaries, and members of both registered and unregistered churches. Most of our informants were contacted through long-term foreign residents who had won the trust of local Protestants. Church leaders themselves opened the door to some interviewees locally, regionally, and even nationally. Interviews were conducted in Mandarin and took place wherever informants felt most comfortable—in apartments, in secluded coffeehouses, in private rooms of restaurants, and, once, on a busy public street. The varied locations meant that recording interviews was seldom possible, and with most informants, even taking notes created anxiety. Hence, in many cases, responses were reconstructed after the informant left the interview site.

Given these challenges, two points are worth emphasizing. First, the most telling information was derived from stories informants recounted. Second, the recruitment techniques described here are illustrative rather than representative, not least because it was impossible to gain approval to survey a population for which few records, public or private, exist.

In addition to interviews, the data derive from a variety of written sources. Materials consulted include central and provincial government descriptions of Protestant home meetings in the 1950s and 1960s, policy texts and document collections used to train religious affairs cadres at the Central Party school, a provincial official's account of more than 10 years of managing religious affairs, narratives of Chinese evangelism penned by Western missionaries and foreign church scholars, and studies of Chinese Protestantism by researchers in Taiwan, Hong Kong, and the United States.

Northeast China proved to be an apt site to study religious recruitment, partly because access to both registered and unregistered church leaders could be obtained and partly because the main research location, Heilongjiang Province, has experienced church growth since the mid-1980s that is "nothing short of breathtaking."[16] According to official figures, the Protestant population in Heilongjiang exploded from 35,000 in 1985 to 300,000 in 1995, before adding another 100,000 by the year 2000.[17] This meant that many Protestant activists could do more than recite a long list of attempted recruitment techniques; they could recount successful outreach strategies that had stood the test of time. Nonetheless, the extraordinary growth of Protestantism in Heilongjiang is further reason to view the techniques discussed here as indicative rather than representative.

The Growth of Unregistered House Churches

Shortly after the CCP took power in 1949, Protestant leaders established the Three Self Patriotic Movement (TSPM) to gather all Chinese believers into one party-approved organization. Pastors nationwide were pressured to join the TSPM association, while those who resisted were arrested or withdrew from public life, as their churches were shut down.[18] Throughout the latter half of the 1950s, many Protestants left TSPM churches, home meetings became more common, and lay leaders began to develop.[19] By the time Chairman Mao launched the Cultural Revolution and religion came under attack as a superstitious holdover from the "old" society, even Protestants meeting at home found it difficult to worship.[20]

After the most violent assaults on religious believers died down in the late 1960s, Protestants once again began meeting in secret, recruiting new members to house churches that sometimes grew to several hundred believers. These underground or unregistered churches attracted old Protestants as well as many new converts.[21]

In the late 1970s, the Party launched a full-scale reevaluation of the Cultural Revolution and made an abrupt reversal in its stance toward religion. First, in a 1979 *People's Daily* editorial, religions were distinguished from superstition by their scriptures, doctrines, and religious rites. Then, Document 19 appeared in 1982. The CCP's most complete and definitive statement on religious policy since the 1950s, it stated that religion would no longer "die out within a short period" and that cadres using "coercive measures" against religious practice were "entirely wrong." Instead, religion would only "disappear naturally" over an extended period of time.[22]

Accommodation of religion, not persecution, was the new policy, but only "normal" religious activities were granted protection.[23] In other words, religious practice was permitted only within authorized sites and under the auspices of approved religious organizations. Document 19 explicitly declared: "No religious organization or believer should propagate or preach religion outside places designated for religious services."[24] By 1980, the CCP had begun to reopen shuttered churches, into which rehabilitated TSPM staff sought to draw a growing population of old and new believers. This effort to corral all worship and recruitment into designated sites continues today, and means that all churches must register with the state, so that they can be monitored by the Religious Affairs Bureau and fall under control of the TSPM association. Registration also establishes where meetings can take place and who can attend, and requires that all religious leaders be approved by the authorities.[25]

Yet many Chinese Protestants object to these restrictions for three reasons: inadequacy, excessive control, and lack of intimacy. First, they say there are too few registered churches, especially in rural areas and small towns. In 1999, there were 16,000 TSPM churches and about twice as many approved meeting sites in the entire country. Many of these sites, moreover, were only large enough for a handful of believers. By 2005, Harbin, the capital of Heilongjiang Province, had only 25 registered churches for 160,000 Protestants, and worship services there were often packed to capacity.[26] In the countryside and small towns where most Protestants live, the situation is more serious;

as there are few registered sites, and they are often far from believers' homes.[27]

Even more important, some Chinese Protestants believe that registered churches are too dependent on the government, because party restrictions on religious preaching, worship and recruitment mean that whereas "the head of the house churches is Christ . . . the head of the Three Self churches is the government."[28] Whether because children are officially not allowed to participate, because public preaching is limited to registered sites, or because the government can close churches, as happened during the outbreak of severe acute respiratory syndrome in 2003, unregistered Protestant leaders typically reject registered churches as "false" (*jiade*) and feel driven to create their own autonomous communities of believers.[29]

Churchgoers also complain that party monitoring of TSPM churches can create an atmosphere of mistrust that makes congregants uneasy about developing close ties with each other. Instead of lingering after services and chatting, members stream right out of some larger TSPM churches once the last hymn ends.[30] In unregistered churches, by contrast, many participants discover a more trusting environment, in part because believers meet frequently in small groups.[31] During these intimate gatherings, members may confess their shortcomings and discuss problems as sensitive as spousal friction, and so develop a familiarity with one another that is more difficult to achieve in above ground churches. One unregistered leader in Beijing spoke of trust "like a family," such that when a member or even a member's relative falls ill, other Protestants hasten to deliver food and make bedside visits. Unregistered Protestants also commonly play an active part in services and other small gatherings by taking turns preaching, singing, or leading Bible studies.[32] And when the entire congregation meets as one, believers often feel free to relate their personal experiences to the whole church, thereby creating an open, informal atmosphere unlike that found in the more impersonal TSPM services.[33]

Drawing on these advantages, unregistered churches have grown to some 20–40 million worshipers, compared to the 17–20 million members of TSPM churches.[34] (Uncertainty surrounding all estimates continues, however, owing to persistent official underestimation of the number of Protestants, the failure of many TSPM pastors to keep membership rolls, believers who worship in both above- and below-ground churches, and the clandestine nature of many unregistered churches.)[35]

Religious Recruitment as Political Threat

The rapid increase in Protestant numbers has triggered fears because many officials see Christianity as an ideological and organizational threat to regime stability. Top CCP leaders interpreted the role of churches in the collapse of eastern European communist regimes as a "tragic lesson of [how] some Communist Party–led countries lost political power" and therefore attacked those in China who were "clothing themselves in religious garb" to "struggle with [the CCP] for the [loyalty of the] masses, especially the youth."[36] These fears have taken concrete form in a number of steps designed to stem the growth of unregistered Protestantism. First, a raft of new regulations has been issued from the national to local level to contain religious activities within registered sites and stop freelance preaching.[37] Second, Beijing has allocated new funds to train cadres to enforce these regulations.[38] Third, local governments have required registered church staffs to report any unregistered recruitment activity, helping to dramatically curtail Protestant growth in some areas.[39] Finally, unregistered Protestant sects that grow large enough to develop national networks are targeted for eradication as "cultic organizations" in periodic, countrywide campaigns of suppression.[40]

Networked Recruitment to Unregistered Churches

Though it is clear that unregistered churches are flourishing and provoke no small alarm among CCP cadres, we still need to know much more about how church membership has increased so dramatically over the past 25 years. A large part of this growth, of course, took place through social networks, as Protestants introduced their friends, classmates, and relatives to Christianity. In one northern China location, for example, members of an unregistered church invited friends to attend a program of Christmas music. At the performance, the newcomers heard their Protestant friends play songs about the prodigal son and other Bible figures on traditional Chinese instruments. Without prompting, most of the potential recruits would have had no occasion to go unaccompanied to a service, and certainly none of them would have found this unadvertised event. Throughout the evening, the congregants introduced their faith by drawing on trust fostered in previously existing relationships, using a familiar style of music to communicate new beliefs and demonstrating the pleasures of participation. These all made recruitment to Protestantism more attractive. By the night's end, 50 of the 150 newcomers had joined the church and, after one year, church membership had doubled to 1,400.[41]

Other unregistered churches use social networks to draw new recruits by tapping into widespread interest in contemporary Western culture. In northeastern China, for example, some Protestant students asked their university classmates to an American-style Thanksgiving dinner in a private restaurant.[42] This invitation-only evening featured a variety show in which the centerpiece was a rendition of Shakespeare's *Romeo and Juliet* with a new twist: a Christian wedding supported by the young lovers' families replaced the double suicide finale. In addition to engaging a fascination with all things Western, the event was both personal and participatory, as students recounted how conversion had changed their lives and wrapped up the night by initiating conversations with their classmates about their readiness to believe in God.

When networks connect activists to targets with whom they share an existing interest (e.g., the West), social bonds can facilitate recruitment greatly. As university classmates curious about Western culture discuss Christianity, their conversations fulfill a common desire to explore what makes the West distinct, and this can open the way to evangelism. Networks also offer opportunities for recruiters to interact with potential members in a variety of settings, as trusted friends, for instance, run into classmates in dorms, at the cafeteria, or outside classes, where they can bring them to the point of conviction and help confirm what commonly begins as a tenuous decision. Finally, when the political environment is laden with uncertainty, as in a corroding state socialist regime, networks reduce risks. By connecting activists with a ready supply of prospective recruits whom they trust not to turn them in, networked recruitment may proceed in a discreet, even covert, fashion.

Attracting Strangers to Unregistered Protestant Churches

Despite the advantages networks afford, in the recruitment of unregistered Protestants in China, a surprisingly large amount of contact is made with strangers: individuals who only become part of an evangelist's social network after conversion.[43] Lacking bonds of friendship or family to prepare the way, recruiters have learned how to reach new populations without the long-standing trust, easy channels of communication, and social pressure that networks provide. To attract people with whom they have no personal ties, proselytizers have had to address three key issues: *who* is best at making the initial contact; *how* nonnetworked people can be reached; and *where* to do so.

Making first contact with strangers is facilitated when recruiting agents and potential recruits share the same social location. As religious and social movement scholars have long known, "like attracts like": the individuals most available for recruitment are similar to existing participants, since people have the most contact with others whose attributes mirror their own.[44] This is true for networked recruitment; it also holds for those with whom proselytizers have no personal ties. Along these lines, university students from an unregistered church in northeastern China served as natural recruiters for other students. In the course of handing out pamphlets entitled *The Four Spiritual Laws* to passersby on campus, Protestant students struck up conversations about Christianity with students they did not know. Painters who established a Protestant enclave outside Beijing also sought to evangelize their fellow artists. Some rural women in Guangdong Province set up a food stall to spread Christianity to farmers coming to market.[45]

Homophily, however, implies more than just moving in the same circles. Individuals from a similar background are more likely to share attitudes, influence each other, and discuss common worries. Relying on this, Protestant evangelists in China fashion appeals using a vocabulary that is drawn from daily life and resonates with potential recruits. Two female recruiters from Henan Province, for example, made skillful use of agricultural metaphors from the Bible to attract rural strangers in the Northeast.[46] The Henan women had grown up laboring in the fields, so they shared a mutual language with the northeasterners about planting, tending, and harvesting crops. Drawing on this familiar vocabulary and knowledge of the rhythms of the planting season, the Protestants knew how and when to communicate biblical ideas via farming language. When the evangelists, for instance, spoke about "scattering seeds" *(san zhongzi)* on rocky or fertile ground, their targets could immediately grasp how this referred to spreading the faith among resistant or receptive people. "Harvesting the crops" *(shouge zhuangjia)* as a metaphor for recruiting new converts also made sense to rural listeners and tied their new beliefs to everyday concerns.

Attracting strangers to Protestantism requires that recruiters know more than just what to say. Students of religious movements in other parts of the world have observed that successful recruitment depends on developing flexible strategies that attract target audiences and have called for more study of "how movements solicit, coax, and secure participants, and more attention to the factors that account for variations in recruitment strategies and their efficacy."[47] Recruitment techniques are especially crucial for unregistered Protestants in China, given the many challenges they face eluding official scrutiny and avoiding repression. To gain access to prospective converts and draw them into their orbit of influence (much like Hare Krishnas in the United States in the 1970s), recruiters have tailored the ways they communicate to suit different environments.[48]

In the Chinese countryside, evangelists have at times employed a private form of communication to attract strangers: door-to-door proselytizing. By going to one farmhouse after another, recruiters approach families one at a time until they locate someone who is receptive to their message.[49] Unlike evangelists in the West, who face a solicitation-weary population and are rarely successful in door-to-door recruitment, strangers on one's doorstep are a novel sight in rural China, and may be ushered inside out of curiosity as much as spiritual interest.[50] Unregistered Protestants using this approach make direct contact with potential recruits, gauge their interest in private, and avoid any public display that might invite official punishment. Once the first strangers are drawn in, further recruitment typically extends outward through existing networks of personal ties. The Henan evangelists mentioned earlier started with private, door-to-door proselytizing and then turned to their recruits' social networks to spread Christianity throughout the Northeast for a decade.[51]

In Liaoning Province, a team of 10 rural proselytizers began by split-
ting into twos and threes to visit houses in search of new converts.[52] If
the farmers welcomed them and were willing to listen to their message, the recruiters sought to establish a base in their homes and offered to work alongside them in the fields while educating them
about Christianity. The farmers in turn suggested whom to seek out
next and whom to avoid, until dozens of villagers were drawn in
through personal ties. By limiting all their gatherings to 50 people or
fewer, the Liaoning recruiters also avoided unwanted attention from
the authorities and managed to establish six sites for worship with
300 members in three years.

At times, the effort to attract strangers has crystallized into immediate recruitment when sudden, providential healing has backed up
a recruiter's claim that divine power could cure physical ailments.
For example, the Henan evangelists encountered one family in the
northeastern countryside whose daughter had been stricken with
cancer.[53] Shrunken and yellowed by illness, the girl had seen doctors
who had diagnosed her case as too advanced for treatment. Desperate for a cure, the family promised to convert if their child was
healed. The Henan women fasted for two days, praying that God
might heal her. On her recovery, the whole family converted and offered their rural home as a permanent Christian meeting place. Similar reports from the countryside of "faith healings" are common.
According to one provincial director of a religious affairs bureau, the
majority of rural believers in some counties attribute their Protestant
faith to such events.[54]

Itinerant evangelists, in their work, tend to downplay doctrine to
emphasize pragmatic goals, and to emphasize signs "of the Spirit over
theological rigor."[55] Their displays of supernatural power act as
"demonstration events" that back up a recruiter's theological claims
and provide evidence of trustworthiness.[56] Moreover, because tales of
healing spread rapidly, a private mode of communication can be transformed overnight into a semipublic one as the curious are drawn to
hear more.[57]

Protestant recruiters have often relied on public or quasi-public
forms of communication as a second means to attract strangers, especially in China's cities. Students of political and religious movements
have discovered that skillful cultural work can open a person to re-

cruitment and build rapport faster than had previously seemed possible.[58] By embedding religious messages in popular cultural performances, Chinese evangelists heighten interest in Christianity among nonintimates and circumvent state restrictions on religious propagation. These public performances are ostensibly set up to appeal to cultural fascination with the West, but their real aim is to provide an occasion to bring Christianity to a new audience.

For example, recruiters put on Christmas celebrations in university auditoriums to exploit university students' interest in Western society and culture.[59] These performances are tolerated by school officials and prove immensely popular with students, who flock by the hundreds to see the birth of Christ reenacted. By "staging events for public consumption," student evangelists make contact with new populations of potential worshipers, note the names of interested students, and often form small Bible study groups that facilitate conversion.[60] An unregistered church in northeast China used this approach to attract newcomers at Christmas pageants that played to audiences of up to 900 students.[61] American Christians teaching English in China have also staged Christmas shows, inviting student onlookers to play Joseph or Mary and then helping them practice English and learn more about the Bible in small study groups.[62] In this way, student recruiters attract strangers to Protestantism through enticing "contact events" that give young urbanites a sense of "being in tune with modern culture." These Western-oriented youths see Christianity as "progressive, liberating . . . and universal" and are often recruited in places such as McDonald's restaurants, a favorite haunt that evokes cosmopolitanism and conveys the flavor of American culture.[63] Unlike converts in Greek cities of the Roman Empire, many of whom had lost their social ties and were drawn to Christianity owing to their isolation, Chinese university students are attracted to Christianity even while they remain connected to their families, friends, and classmates.[64]

A third mode of communication involves one-on-one, public conversation with possible recruits. Evangelists plant themselves in highly visible and densely trafficked areas and start up conversations about how belief in Christianity has changed them and will transform their listeners too. Unlike Hare Krishnas in the United States, who command attention with their distinctive dress and hairstyle, public recruiters in China drum up interest through the fervor with which they share their faith and the hardships they are willing to bear. One woman devoted much of her meager savings to renting a room in a busy hostel, solely to chat up travelers who were spending the night.[65] Fresh on the heels of her own conversion, the woman felt compelled to evangelize others, even if it caused her financial difficulty, and even before she, in her words, "really knew who God was." She seldom brought up church doctrine with the travelers she approached, but instead explained how her newfound faith had brought her "peace." Years later, she could proudly point to over 200 churches in her county and more throughout the Northeast, all set up as a result of her proselytizing. Such church growth is not unusual. The recruitment efforts of one Protestant leader in Heilongjiang Province resulted in three meetings in 1987 that grew to 20 the next year before finally generating 200 unregistered churches by 1991. A single church in rural Henan expanded from 10 to 190 participants in the space of a year, as four new offshoots were formed.[66]

Initial contact at other times is more happenstance, as evangelism amounts to being ready to discuss Christianity when the opportunity arises rather than setting out to disseminate one's faith. Consider a troubled, young woman who "pour[ed] out her heart" to a Protestant recruiter she came across in a public park.[67] The young woman had been doing morning exercises when she noticed the evangelist's "kind appearance." The woman initiated a conversation and confessed that her parents had upset her by insisting that she burn incense to Buddha—instructions that conflicted with everything she had been taught in school about eradicating religion. The evangelist patiently listened to the woman's story and then told her how believing in Jesus Christ would bring her calm. By simply being in the right place at the right time, and being attentive to a person who was searching for "inner peace," the proselytizer showed that recruitment can occur in nearly any space that is free from direct surveillance—so long as one is alert.[68] This particular chance encounter yielded a committed and energetic believer who promptly drew on her own ties to establish a new church. Within three months, she had evangelized 10 coworkers at her factory, and after a year and a half her meeting had grown to include 20 additional converts.

Regarding the third matter of where to find potential converts, evangelists recruiting strangers to social movements in Europe and the United States often make initial contacts through the mass media, mailings, door-to-door canvassing, sister organizations, or tables on streets.[69] In China, however, because the authorities frown on religious activism, Protestants typically must forgo direct solicitation through the media, the mail, or public displays.

Instead, evangelists create or appropriate "safe-enough" spaces that appear in the creases of a reforming authoritarian regime—spaces in which a religious message may be communicated without undue risk.[70] As noted, these spaces often emerge in the ordinary flow of life, be it in public parks, at hostels, on farms, or in open-air markets—anywhere evangelists can engage individuals below the radar of a distracted, increasingly porous state. Locations for proselytizing have multiplied, largely because government control over the ideological realm has diminished and recruiters deftly weave evangelism into their daily lives.[71] Protestants in China, like activists elsewhere, have become adept at exploiting spaces that are "at least temporarily shielded from social control."[72]

When the goal is to reach many strangers at once, recruiters typically adopt the aforementioned strategy of staging large events in public spaces (such as university auditoriums).[73] In these semiautonomous spaces, they are energized by bringing a faith nurtured in private into the open and to a large audience. For more timid members, a firsthand experience of impassioned performances drawing new recruits may encourage them to evangelize more.

The larger lesson in this is that "free spaces" perhaps do not have to be very free.[74] Surveillance can be frustrated when public events have mixed purposes or when private recruitment is integrated into everyday life. Even in regimes where most spaces are penetrated by state power, policing is subject to intrinsic limits, and "havens" can be found.[75] Safe-enough spaces, more broadly, may well be available wherever dominant and subordinate groups face off.[76] For only total institutions destroy all shelters and preclude all mobilization.[77]

What does Protestant evangelism in China tell us about stranger recruitment and about the role networks can play in building a political or religious movement? First, attracting strangers need not rely only on exposing potential members to "moral shocks" to jolt them into action or exploiting an unusual lack of countervailing ties. Strangers may also be opened to new beliefs through timely interactions and through "contact" or "demonstration" events that address prior interests and fulfill emotional needs.[78] In today's China, existing interests include a fascination with contemporary Western culture; emotional needs include overcoming a sense of powerlessness and achieving inner peace. "Contact events," like Christmas plays, broadcast the pleasures of religious participation, and "demonstration events" relieve feelings of powerlessness through "miraculous" healings. These events spark interest and open the door to further engagement, much as Fourth of July fireworks at American ballparks draw people to a baseball game they otherwise would never have attended. Shaping their outreach strategies to take into account the aspirations and longings of target audiences, Protestant evangelists have devised creative ways to draw in strangers.

A second payoff pertains to when networks promote movement participation.[79] Often researchers assume that social bonds are critical throughout the recruitment process: vital before individuals join up and then necessary to sustain mobilization and envelop new recruits. Student protesters in China in 1989, for example, mobilized successfully by limiting recruitment to members of friendship networks, because they feared infiltration by state agents (Wright, chapter 1). But the risks of repression for religious recruitment, high as they are, are much lower than for massive street protests, some of which have demanded regime change and all of which have targeted the state. Furthermore, as some have begun to note, personal ties actually come into play at different points during recruitment or conversion.[80] In China, the evidence suggests that social bonds at times play a smaller role and enter later in the recruitment process than is commonly thought. Of course, networks, when available, do facilitate recruitment to Protestantism. They offer evangelists channels for circulating information about outreach events; they enable proselytizers to build on feelings of trust that make conversion less a question of accepting unfamiliar beliefs and more an opportunity to join friends in fellowship; and they facilitate intimate conversations in which a reluctant relative, classmate, colleague, or friend can be urged to become a Protestant.

But social networks may sometimes matter less for drawing a person into a movement's orbit than for completing a conversion. Conversion (and its maintenance) may indeed require encapsulation in a network of believers, but that often occurs long after initial exposure, when newcomers to Bible study find their time quickly fills up with group worship and prayer activities, and countervailing influences weaken. Attraction is the first order of business for Chinese Protestants; and evangelists have become skilled at using spectacle and "miracles" to achieve it.

Does this mean that networks play only a small role in attracting new Protestants? Of course not. But focusing too much on the structural aspects of recruitment can obscure the cultural processes that networked and nonnetworked recruitment rest on. For Chinese Protestants, both types of recruitment build on an affinity and common identity shared by recruiter and target. It is, at least in part, the cultural meanings encoded in networks and the messages transmitted across them that constitute this identity and make networked recruitment effective.[81] For nonnetworked recruitment, the fact that evangelists can attract new believers beyond the reach of networks reminds us that there are other "workshops" in which mutual understandings and feelings of affinity can be tapped or discovered.[82] Recruitment, at root, may trace back to common identities rather than preexisting networks.[83]

Moreover, in circumstances where religious activism is discouraged, the advantages that networks offer—for example, credibility, trust, rapport, an uncensored flow of information—still foster participation, but these can sometimes be mustered even when networks are absent or have yet to be created. In an unwelcoming or even hostile environment like that of late Leninist China, attention to recruiting techniques such as locating targets who share a recruiter's social background, entering their daily routines, speaking in idioms they readily grasp, seizing opportune moments, and capitalizing on their cultural interests or sentiments can substitute for networks that do not extend as far as ambitious proselytizers might like. In private encounters between evangelists and potential recruits, Chinese Protestants endeavor to create an intimate, trust-filled setting by listening carefully and using familiar language that produces feelings of solidarity. Creative strategies, including the types of public events already described, help evangelists reach people where social networks do not extend.

These creative strategies have arisen out of ambitions to "Christianize" the nation by bringing in new believers, both opportunistically and through targeted engagement. One Protestant leader set a goal of recruiting 10 million believers by 2010; another decried the moral decay in society and claimed that "only if all of China Christianizes can things be much better."[84] To realize such lofty aims, leaders teach some Protestants to be ready to respond to the needs of those they meet in daily life. At the same time, other Protestants, such as itinerant evangelists and aspiring leaders, undergo months, even years, of training in underground Bible schools in both urban and rural areas. The goal of all such training is to develop resilient local communities and nationwide networks that can promote a cultural transformation of society.[85]

This research provides further proof that no single factor explains the onset of participation in a political or religious movement.[86] Although networks often facilitate recruitment, movements can still begin to grow without recourse to mobilizing friends, relatives, colleagues, or classmates. Chinese evangelists have, above all, discovered that there are many ways to contact nonnetworked persons, whether singly or en masse, and that even one-time events can get the effort underway. In the course of attracting strangers, Protestant recruiters have learned that new networks can be opportunistically stitched together when network intimates are not available. Social networks, in other words, are often a result of recruitment rather than a precondition for it.[87]

6 | Contention in Cyberspace

Popular protests have accompanied economic reform in China from the very beginning. With the development of the internet, however, contention has taken on some new forms. An important change is the rise of online activism. On the one hand, the internet is increasingly integrated with conventional forms of locality specific protest; it is, in this sense, used to mobilize offline protest events. I will refer to this type of online activism as internet-assisted contention. In many cases, however, popular contention takes place *in* cyberspace. It may spill offline, but its central stage of action is the internet. It is a type of radical, claims-making communicative action.[1] I will refer to this type of online activism as internet contention. This chapter focuses on this second type.

A Short History

Internet contention can be traced to the student movement in 1989. At that time, Chinese students and overseas scholars were already actively using email and newsgroups. As protests escalated in China, an intricate web of communication emerged that linked students inside China with the Chinese diaspora and the international community at large. Telephones, faxes, and the mass media played the most important role, but the internet had a presence as well. Chinese students overseas would call up their friends in Chinese universities to get updates about the movement and then report back to the popular newsgroup Social Culture China or email list Electronic Newsletter for Chinese Students. They also used the internet to help student protesters in China by raising funds, issuing statements of support, and organizing demonstrations in front of Chinese consulates. Of hundreds of Chinese usenet newsgroups at that time, Social Culture China became the one ranked highest in online traffic.[2]

Inside China, however, the internet was barely known. In 1989, only a select few Chinese scientists had email connections with the outside world.[3] China did not achieve full-function internet connection until 1994. Even then, access remained limited to a handful. Only after 1996 did the internet begin to become available to the average urban consumer, thanks both to state promotion of the information economy and efforts by private entrepreneurs to commercialize new information technologies.[4]

The first few years of internet diffusion in China saw only scattered reports of internet protests. One protest unfolded in 1996 on the electronic bulletin board systems (BBSs) of Peking University concerning territorial claims to the Diaoyu Islands by China and Japan.[5] In 1998, Chinese internet users joined the Chinese diaspora from New York to Amsterdam to protest against violence committed against ethnic Chinese in Indonesia.[6] Also in 1998, the release by Shenzhen Online of an investigative report about a murder case provoked protests and petitions that sought justice for the victim.[7] It is noteworthy that these first few internet protests were mainly about two issues—nationalism and harm inflicted on vulnerable individuals. These issues have come to dominate internet protests in China.

In the development of internet contention, 1999 was a year of significance. In May 1999, both in the streets and in cyberspace, large-scale protests occurred against the bombing by the North Atlantic Treaty Organization (NATO) of the Chinese embassy in the former Yugoslavia. The official *People's Daily Online* set up a BBS named Protest Forum for internet users to air discontent.[8] In the Maoist era, Chinese citizens had sometimes appropriated such a state-initiated campaign for their own purposes, in effect turning a party-led campaign into a popular protest.[9] The launching of Protest Forum produced a similarly ironic outcome. It unintentionally popularized on-line protest activities. It was perhaps the most important formative event in the short history of internet contention. Since then, internet protests have never stopped appearing.[10] The most recent cases include an environmental protest in the city of Xiamen in June 2007, in which the internet and text-messaging played an important role in mobilization. Some sample cases of internet contention from 1998 to 2007 follow.

October 1998: The publication by Shenzhen Online of a report about the murder of a female business manager in her hotel room led to online petitions for further police investigation of the case.

May 1999: Nationalist protests broke out in the streets and Chinese cyberspace against the NATO bombing of the Chinese embassy in Belgrade.

May 2000: The death of a student at Peking University led to online and offline protests against attempts by school authorities to cover up the news.

July 2001: Chinese internet users protested against the cover-up of a mine accident that killed 81 miners in Nandan, Guangxi.

November 2002: The detention of a popular internet writer was followed by online petitions for her release.

March 2003: An outraged online public protested the death Sun Zhigang, an apparently harmless vagrant, while in police custody in Guangzhou.

October 2003: The light sentencing of a wealthy woman who killed a poor farmer in Harbin drew internet protests.

November–December 2004: In the "Niu Niu Incident," a municipal party secretary in Shenzhen apologized after online protesters challenged his abuse of official position to promote his daughter's film.

April–May 2005: In several cities and on the internet, large-scale protests were mounted against Japanese school textbooks that whitewashed Japan's wartime actions and Japan's bid for a permanent seat on the United Nations Security Council.

March 2007: Citizen reporter Zola Zhou used his personal blog to cover the Chongqing "nail household" incident.

June 2007: In what has come to be known as the "Xiamen PX" incident, residents in the city of Xiamen used the internet and text-messaging to organize a demonstration against the proposed construction of an xylene (PX) chemical plant.

Characteristics of Internet Contention in China

The most obvious feature of internet contention is its symbolic and discursive form. Internet contention is radical communicative action conducted in words and images.[11] Language and symbols have always been an important part of popular revolt, but they have taken on new dimensions in the so-called information age. As Mark Poster argues, just as material resources are central to the Marxist mode of production in the industrial age, so linguistic resources have become central to the transmission of information.[12] For similar reasons, Alberto Melucci thinks of contemporary social movements as "symbolic challenges."[13]

Second, internet contention is usually reactive, episodic, and quick to diffuse. Although some online protests and petitions are organized, most happen spontaneously in reaction to critical events in the offline world. Social injustices trigger internet contention. In addition, its largely spontaneous nature means that it tends to be episodic and fluid. Its efficacy derives from its speed and unpredictability rather than from organization and planning.

Finally, in content, internet contention can potentially be about any issue, but in practice, three issues have been especially prominent. First is neonationalism. Examples include protests against the NATO bombing of the Chinese embassy in former Yugoslavia and several cases of anti-Japanese protest. Second is the rights of vulnerable individuals and disempowered social groups. Examples are the protests concerning the rights of children, women, migrants, and others. Third is social injustices committed by the powerful and the rich, reflecting new types of social conflict.

Internet contention thrives despite repression. Since 1996, more than a dozen regulations concerning internet use and services have been promulgated.[14] Besides using legal and policy instruments, Chinese government agencies intervene directly in internet use; for example, by exercising sophisticated filtering of internet traffic.[15]

Thus among countries with large numbers of internet users, China is unique in its combination of high levels of internet control and internet contention.

How does internet contention appear under conditions of control? To address this question, I will take an integrated cultural approach. It is integrated in the sense that I examine both macro conditions and micro dynamics. My approach emphasizes cultural factors, because culture and technology play a central role in internet contention. Specifically, I will argue that contention in Chinese cyberspace reflects conditions both external and internal to the internet.

Origins and Limits

One facet of contemporary Chinese life is a "polyphony of conflict and contention."[16] Many scholars have documented the proliferation of popular protests in China; internet contention is part of this larger mosaic. Online and offline contention share some common themes. The issues at the center of internet contention, especially those concerning the rights of disadvantaged groups, also feature prominently in street protests.

To the extent that these two forms of contention share similar concerns, they originate from the same structural conditions. The most important feature of China's current situation is economic reform, the ongoing transformation of a planned into a market economy, which has accelerated economic development. But this developmental path favors some social groups at the expense of others. Growth has been accompanied by social polarity, environmental degradation, the collapse of the socialist social security system, and so forth. As these problems worsen and dissatisfaction spreads, Chinese citizens are becoming more and more aware of their citizenship rights and increasingly active in their efforts to defend them.[17] This situation provides the structural conditions for popular protest.

Internet contention reflects the dark side of economic transformation. As the cases mentioned above show, internet contention is often a response to social injustice. The uproar after the death of Sun Zhigang is a case in point. Sun had been detained three days earlier merely for lack of a temporary residency permit. After the news broke of his death following a beating while in custody, an outraged public filled the internet with debates and protests, expressing sympathy for Sun and demanding criminal prosecution of the perpetrators. As often is the case, the protest went beyond Sun Zhigang's death. Discussion topics ranged from ways to curb police brutality to the protection of the rights of "disadvantaged social groups" *(ruoshi qunti)*. This episode of contention reflected widespread grievances about social inequalities.

Another way internet contention reflects dissatisfaction with the social costs of economic development is that street protests often spill over into cyberspace. In this respect, the internet has become an important channel for publicizing information about street protests. In one case, the popular website Yannan.cn, associated with Peking University, published such extensive and timely reports of peasant riots in the village of Taishi in 2005 that it was forced to close down.

The closure of Yannan.cn shows the political limits of internet contention. The reactive feature of internet contention suggests that, like many rural protests, it "is rarely directed at the national government; nor does it typically involve demands for wider political change."[18] In fact, the main issues in internet contention—nationalism, the rights of vulnerable individuals, and social injustices committed by the rich and the powerful—partly overlap with state agendas. For example, to the extent that neonationalism helps fill an ideological vacuum in contemporary China, the state supports its expression.[19] But state actors are careful not to give free rein to popular nationalism, which could spill over into other issues and affect China's international relations. This ambivalence provides space for nationalistic contention in cyberspace. More politically subversive issues such as the Falun Gong protests and discussions of the 1989 student movement enter Chinese cyberspace only in guerrilla forms, but censorship prevents these issues from coalescing into moments of internet contention.[20]

Cultural Belief in the Internet

Over the past decade, an expressive internet culture has emerged in China. The internet has become a prime space for self-expression and social interaction. Many scholars have described this new culture. Geremie Barme and Gloria Davies have studied online intellectual discourse.[21] Michel Hockx has examined online literary communities.[22] Yongming Zhou has analyzed *minjian* (popular) political writers who publish online and gain enormous influence.[23] Haiqing Yu finds abundant self-affirming AIDS talk online, as well as light-hearted but empowering wit and merriment.[24] These studies reveal a fascinating mix of intellectual and political discussion, personal expression, and humor and play. Internet contention is part of this internet culture.

One main reason people interact, express themselves, and, for that matter, protest online is that they believe in the power of the internet. The importance of beliefs in the making of reality is a familiar sociological axiom. Social interaction in general is based on the belief in the part one plays.[25] People are more likely to protest when they have a sense of efficacy. Studies of early Chinese newspapers show that the power of mass media "lies in the power of the imagination."[26] The media have power because people believe they do. Michael Schudson argues that "the power of the media resides in the perception of experts and decision makers that the general public is influenced by the mass media, not in the direct influence of the mass media on the general public."[27]

Chinese state authorities believe in the power of the internet; otherwise, they would not try to control it. There is abundant evidence that ordinary users also believe in the internet. According to a survey report published in January 2006, about 45 percent of respondents indicated a 75 percent trust in the internet, and 41 percent indicated 50 percent trust, while only 7.6 percent indicated 75 percent distrust.[28] Many people rely on the internet for news and are enthusiastic about new possibilities of personal expression online. The popular Strengthening the Nation Forum (QGLT) is a case in point. This BBS is affiliated with *People's Daily*, the leading official newspaper in China. It is censored more strictly than other bulletin boards and is thus a conservative case for analyzing public perceptions of the internet.[29] Even here the message is clear: users generally consider it a comparatively free and open space for public participation.[30] They speak of it as a place for ordinary people to discuss national affairs, communicate feelings, and express opinions, a place for self discovery and self-expression, a space for demanding democratic supervision and independent thinking, and a "coffee shop" that "cannot turn away customers, or dictate what they talk about."[31] They often compare the democratic potential of BBS forums with the lack of such potential in conventional media and are excited about new possibilities for freedom of speech. Thus, one posting said that QGLT is "a sacred temple where we had our first taste of the sacred rights of freedom of speech."[32] By and large, users consider the internet a space for public participation. This perception influences their proclivity to participate in online communication and interaction.

Network Structures

The network structure of the internet channels the diffusion of contention. The internet is not just another mass medium, but as Manuel Castells explains, a galaxy of networks.[33] Regulating internet activism entails regulating the internet galaxy. This does not mean the internet is impossible to control. Of course, insofar as the internet galaxy encompasses an entire society, complete control of the internet would entail totalitarian social control. But networks can reduce the chances of political repression, because although some nodes may be destroyed, others may survive.[34] Control is most effective when it penetrates entire networks. Resistance, however, can emerge at any entry point to the network.

Network linkages are essential for an effective network. To observers of Chinese politics, this is not new. From the Red Guard movement to the student movement in 1989, linking up has been an effective tactic of translocal mobilization and much feared by the state. The Chinese internet is linked up both internally and externally. Internally, a website can connect to another by setting up a hot link. Some scholars consider this kind of linkage an "online structure" for action meaning "electronic space composed of various HTML pages, features, links and texts within which an individual is given an opportunity to act."[35] Many websites and BBS forums in China are linked in this way and thus function as online structures. Websites with interactive functions are connected through the common practice of crossposting messages.[36] Often, an insightful or well-written message will be crossposted in many bulletin boards. In addition, internet users can use search engines to find linkages among different websites.

The internet has numerous external linkages. First, it is increasingly integrated into everyday life. According to a survey report released in July 2005 by the China Internet Network Information Center, regular internet users in China spend about 14 hours online weekly, almost equivalent to two full work days.[37] About 60 percent of them say that the internet is important or very important in their daily life, and more than three-quarters say it is important or very important for work purposes. This indicates that urban Chinese rely increasingly on the internet in all aspects of life. Second, it is increasingly integrated with other media. On the one hand, conventional mass media have gone online. On the other hand, large portal sites such as Sina.com and Sohu.com are acting like conventional media by providing news and news analysis. They compete among themselves and with mass media channels in providing timely coverage of current affairs.

Third, despite political control, the Chinese internet is linked with web sites and mass media outside China. International organizations and foreign media regularly monitor internet activities in China; their reports are sometimes posted back on Chinese websites by interested users, in English or Chinese translation. There are also connections between overseas and domestic Chinese-language web sites. For example, *New Threads,* a Chinese website based in California, is well known to internet users in China, so much so that in 2004 its editor, Fang Zhouzi, was selected as one of the 50 most influential public intellectuals by a Chinese newspaper.

The network structure of the internet means that critical information may be leaked to the internet at any time through any network node. At any given time, there are people using the internet, mostly for fun. As the occasion arises, however, these netizens can launch into action by filling the internet with queries, information exchanges, debates, and protest. The more outrageous the incident, the more likely it is to arouse the virtual crowd, always lurking and always on the alert. Though not always manifested, the possibility of contention is always there and hard to predict. Part of the power of the internet is that its technological structure harbors latent political potential. Such contingency is associated with moments of agency.

A Case Study

Macro factors are necessary but insufficient conditions for internet contention. Recent cultural theories of social movements suggest that the micro-level, internal dynamics of contention is equally important.[38] I will argue that at the micro level, internet contention is the result of what Charles Tilly calls "contentious conversation."[39]

To illuminate these micro dynamics, the following case study describes what has been called "the most serious student unrest there since 1989."[40] Widely reported in the Western media, this episode unfolded in May 2000 following the murder of Qiu Qingfeng, a first-year student at Peking University.[41] Although demonstrations and candle vigils took place on campus, it was in cyberspace that the protest first started; it then escalated into radical calls for 1989-style demonstrations, and was sustained for about 10 days amid fiery online exchanges.[42]

Like other first-year students, the victim lived on the Changping campus in rural Changping township, about 30 kilometers from the main campus in Beijing. On Friday, May 19, 2000, she went to the main campus for an exam. By the time the exam ended at 4 p.m., the last shuttle bus to Changping had left. She was last seen around 8 p.m. in a supermarket in downtown Changping, suggesting she was on her way back to the Changping campus, probably by long-distance bus and then on foot. She was found murdered the next morning. On learning of the murder, the university administrators covered it up and barred students from engaging in public mourning.[43]

At 11:19 p.m., May 22, 2000, a message appeared on Triangle, the university's BBS forum. This news shot across Chinese cyberspace. One of the first two messages that appeared on Triangle was forwarded to the news forum of Shantou University at 8:44 a.m., May 23; to the BBS of Xi'an Jiaotong University at 9:29 a.m.; to Netease's news forum at 3:46pm; and to Sohu's forum at 10:19 p.m. No post about the murder appeared on QGLT on May 23, but 56 did the next day. Figure 6.1 shows the distribution of posts in Peking University's Triangle forum from May 22 to May 31, 2000; Figure 6.2 shows the distribution in the other five bulletin boards.

While protest raged online, hundreds of students held demonstrations on the campus of Peking University on the night of May 23. The combined online and offline protest thwarted information control. On May 24, university authorities announced plans for memorial services and promised to compensate the victim's family and improve campus safety. A protest that started online ended with significant concessions by the authorities.

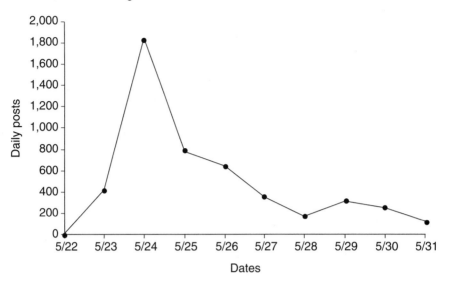

Figure 6.1 Daily posts on the Qiu Qingfeng murder case, Triangle forum, Beijing University, May 22–31, 2000

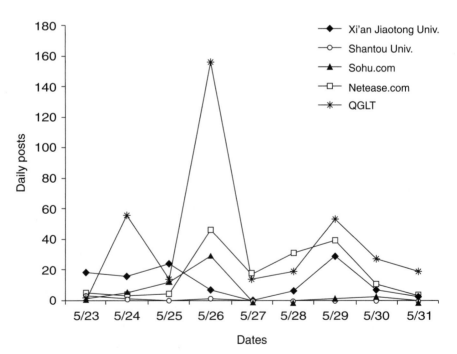

Figure 6.2 Daily posts on the Qiu Qingfeng murder case on six BBSs in China, May 22–31, 2000

Linkages, Control, and Protest Diffusion

Internet contention is a form of "contentious conversation." According to Tilly, "conversation is contentious to the extent that it embodies mutual and contradictory claims."[44] He proposes that contentious conversation cannot be explained away by referring either to individual psyches or to group interests. It happens "through historically situated, culturally constrained, negotiated, consequential interchanges among multiple parties."[45] In the case of the May 2000 protests, this logic of contentious conversation manifested itself mainly in three ways. First, diffusion was a function of various forms of linkages as well as political control. Second, despite the newness of the technology, conventions of protest still mattered. Third, dialogues and narratives were essential to the discursive dynamics of diffusion.

Successful mobilization everywhere involves some kind of organization, although the manner and means of organization may differ. The form of organizational effort in China most dreaded by the authorities is called "linking up" *(chuanlian)*. One important factor in the fast spread of the Cultural Revolution in the 1960s was that students traveled across the country to link up with students in other cities. Such linking up was a way of solidarity building and mobilization. It was possible in the 1960s partly because of state sponsorship. In the decades after the Cultural Revolution, especially at times of popular unrest, authorities became extremely wary of "linking up."

In May 2000, Chinese online protesters developed new ways of linking up through creative use of the internet. I call these spatial linkages. The most influential in this protest were the links between cyberspace and physical spaces, although there was also a notable new phenomenon—transnational links in cyberspace.

Links between cyberspace and physical space took three forms. First, some messages on BBSs were printed and posted on walls in campus areas. Wall-posters were traditionally a key repertoire of collective protest in China.[46] During the contention, the author of one post reported reading a campus wall poster that had first appeared on the internet.[47]

Second, online forums were used to announce campus protest events, thus turning the internet into a space for organizing offline activities. This happened both in Beijing and elsewhere. At Huazhong University of Science and Technology in Wuhan City, for example, small-scale memorial gatherings were organized by "net friends."[48] In Beijing, the march from Tsinghua University to Peking University on the night of May 23 was much publicized in a widely circulated posting.[49]

The third linkage between cyberspace and offline space was the almost instantaneous online broadcast of campus events. One posting described the evening vigil on May 23 in this way: "On the stairs near the Triangle area, a huge heart-shaped pattern was laid with flickering candles, with little white-paper flowers in the middle of the heart."[50] Online broadcasts helped to keep interested persons informed about what was happening on the ground. Sociologists have proposed that the "drama" of social movements needs to be sustained by keeping up the interest of the "cast" and the audience.[51] Online broadcast of the offline events served this purpose.

Besides links between cyberspace and physical space, there were connections between bulletin boards inside and outside China. Some postings were crossposted to Chinese-language forums in the United States. Some messages that appeared on BBSs in China were clearly posted by overseas users, who tended to identify themselves as Peking University alumni. The author of a message posted on May 29, 2000, argued that fighting for one's own interests, something common in the United States, was a sign of social progress. A message posted the same day on QGLT by "Wanderer," self-identified as a Chinese student in an American university. "Wanderer" praised the security measures on American campuses and suggested that Chinese universities learn from the American example. In these different ways, the linkages between online space and offline space shaped online and offline protest. The internet was used to organize and mobilize offline protest. Online broadcasts kept people in other places informed about events as they transpired.

As Figure 6.2 shows, however, the diffusion was uneven. The protest started in university-based BBSs and then spread to commercial and government-run websites. This pattern is consistent with diffusion theory, which would expect diffusion to follow communication channels and structures of social relations.[52] The initial diffusion of protest among university-based bulletin boards was due to the preexistence of a university internet culture. A high proportion of China's internet population was college students, with whom BBSs were especially popular.[53]

The uneven diffusion of protest also reflected different degrees of political control. Shantou University's BBS had the fewest posts. Xi'an Jiaotong University had the most—109. Furthermore, while posts appeared on May 23 in all three university bulletin boards and the two commercial bulletin boards, they began to appear on QGLT only on May 24. Although there are national regulations about internet services, enforcement varies. Some bulletin boards had more elaborate regulations than others, and some practiced censorship more strictly. Of all the university bulletin boards I visited before May 2000, those run by Shantou University had the most meticulous rules and regulations, indicating stricter control.[54] There is evidence that QGLT tried to restrict posts related to the murder case, which probably explains why the first message about it appeared there almost 40 hours after the news broke on Peking University's BBS.[55]

Why did QGLT begin to tolerate protests after May 24? Although initially the authorities attempted to cover up the case, they began to concede to student demands after protest started elsewhere. The university issued an official notice on May 23 acknowledging the murder and requesting students to use constraint in their memorial activities. But it no longer forbade such activities. It is unclear exactly why the authorities changed their approach, but the pressure of online protest and campus demonstrations was likely an important factor.

Conventions of Protest

Internet contention does not depart completely from other forms of protest long familiar in China, including sloganeering and the use of wall posters. During the Maoist era, shouting out and posting slogans were everyday elements of the repertoire of contention. Shouting typically happened in groups, but posters could appear in any public space and could be put up by individuals. Slogans are easy to write, do not require a great deal of analytical skill, express strong opinions and emotions, and are often memorable. "Down with so and so!" for example, was a favorite slogan during the Red Guard movement and even the student movement in 1989.

Protests in Chinese cyberspace are full of sloganeering. One message posted on May 25, 2000, on the "Current Affairs" forum of Sohu.com, entitled "Give back the safety and peace of the campus," consisted of the following slogans:

> Save our compatriots!
> Save ourselves!
> Stand up! Our determination!
> Our dignity!

The author of another message, posted on May 26, 2000, on the same forum, exclaimed: "I am angry not just about the murder of the female student in Peking University, but about what the university did before and after the student was murdered!!!!!"

Internet postings resemble big-character posters both in form and function. Like wall posters, online postings encompass various genres— essays, letters, poems, slogans, one-sentence statements, and single-word exclamations such as "Yes!" and "Nonsense!"[56] For example, during the protest over the murdered student, several poems were dedicated to the victim and circulated in online forums. One, entitled "Maple Flying: For the Soul of the Dead," laments the passing away of a beautiful young life.

Some users posted messages in the form of letters that conveyed a strong sense of solidarity. One letter begins thus:

> So glad to hear back from you in such a short time. Previously, I've read your postings about the Peking University incident in "Ji'an Forum" and the "China and the World Forum." I am not completely clear about the details of the incident (no time to follow everything), but based on what I know, I have developed my own views.[57]

The letter writer then went on to explain that the protest was important because it articulated the widespread problem that some segments of the population lacked protection.

In his study of English spinners' protests in the nineteenth century, sociologist Marc Steinberg finds that the challengers' discursive repertoire was limited. It was "dominated by a selective appropriation of political economy, political liberalism, nationalism, abolitionism, and other genres through which factory owners mapped out a hegemonic vision of a social order."[58] Chinese internet contention involves a great deal of appropriation of official discourse, as does "rightful resistance," but compared with "rightful resistance" it is distinctively plural in its speech genres.[59] This in itself challenges the authorities, who employ a more narrow range of speech types, such as public announcements and radio speeches by senior administrators.

The variety of genres is not an invention of internet contention but a common feature of protest in modern China. Poems, letters, essays, and proclamations abounded in earlier social movements. A collective memory of popular contention is carried in these genres, so that each time they appear, they give their authors and readers a sense of moral legitimacy and rhetorical power.[60]

Contentious Conversation

What *is* different now is the predominance of dialogues in internet contention. This reflects the unique features of interactivity and connectivity of the internet. Internet contention is par excellence a contentious conversation. In May 2000, such conversation was central to the dynamics of diffusion. The protest unfolded in cyberspace through dialogue and narratives.[61] It consisted of multiple individual voices and contentious interactions. From May 23 through May 31, more than 7,000 postings related to the murder case appeared on the six sampled bulletin boards. Countless others appeared on the hundreds of bulletin boards in China. Postings that resonated with public sentiments were circulated widely through crossposting. They served as narratives of mobilization and possessed emotional or rhetorical appeal. The following messages were among the most widely circulated:

> "The Murder of a Student of Peking University at Changping
>   Campus and the Responses of the University Administration"
> "Sad Thoughts upon the Murder of a Schoolmate in Peking
>   University"
> "The Conspicuous Absence: On the Silence of the Mass Media
>   over the 'Qiu Qingfeng Case'"

These were crossposted on all the six bulletin boards, often several times, until they took on great symbolic significance and, like the narratives studied by Gary Fine, became the moral expression of a group.

Besides the chorus of individual voices, dialogic interactions sustained protest. These interactions were peppered with questioning, dissent, arguments, and counterarguments. They spurred responses and carried the conversation forward in a dramatic fashion.[62] Because their basic feature was taking issue with one another, I will call this the issue-taking mechanism of internet contention. The following example illustrates how someone called "Obey the moderator" took issue with the students and how "Forum new user" talked back:

> Students should be more concerned about why there are still people in China who are forced to sell their own children, and why so many good women are forced into prostitution.
> "Forum new user": According to your logic, you should be more concerned with the problems of corruption or loss of jobs. Why are you talking about the students' concerns in this forum?

The next example from the same day illustrates a more elaborate exchange among four users, illustrating how taking issue carried contention forward:

> "Young face old heart": Please be reasonable. Don't go to extremes. The death is sorrowful, but don't indiscriminately blame the university.
> "Horse galloping in the air": You still don't understand what happened. This is not making senseless trouble. It is fighting for the right to mourn a victim who is our own sister.
> "Wild boar": This is not to blame the university, but to air grievances about its leaders.
> "Discussion and publicity": It's as simple as asking the police to solve the murder case.
> "Wild boar:" Solving the murder case will lead to punishment of the criminal, but the students' real purpose is to prevent such tragedies from happening again.

These are typical examples of contention in Chinese cyberspace. They show that internet contention takes place primarily through interaction. Taking issue—the questioning, clarification, and clashing of different views—sustains contention.

*   *   *

Contention in Chinese cyberspace reflects both external conditions and features specific to Chinese internet culture. Using an integrated approach, I have shown that three external conditions are conducive to it, namely, the network structures of the internet, people's belief in the internet, and the broader landscape of popular protest in a polarizing society. Furthermore, my in-depth case study demonstrates that internet contention has complex internal dynamics. It reflects sociological channels of diffusion and constraint, conversational mechanisms in online communication, and cultural conventions of protest.

Internet contention does not replace street protests, but it has influenced Chinese politics and society in at least three important ways. First, the best-known cases, such as those listed earlier, have shaped policy or the behavior of those who come under challenge.[63] An often-cited example is how online protests about the Sun Zhigang incident eventually led to the cancellation of China's vagrancy regulations. In May 2000, the Peking University protest likewise forced the university authorities to abandon their effort to cover up and led them to make a public commitment to improve campus safety.

Second, internet contention both responds to and shapes mass media behavior. Sometimes, it can open up domestic mass media channels; other times, it attracts the attention of the international media and produces a "boomerang" and "externalization of contention" via transnational activism[64] (see Thornton, chapter 9). For example, the internet protests about Sun Zhigang's death led to a wider public debate in the mass media. In May 2000, internet contention happened *because of* the silence of the mass media. Although it did not force open the mass media, it led to international media coverage.[65]

Finally, internet contention has contributed to an informational politics in China by making the internet a new means, stake, and arena of political struggle. It shows that as long as social injustices exist, it is always possible for people to enter cyberspace and protest with minimal temporal and spatial constraints. For the authorities, this creates a heightened sense of wariness of citizen resistance. For citizens, internet contention reveals new ways of expressing protest. In this sense, internet contention has reconfigured the relationship between citizens and state power.

YANFEI SUN
DINGXIN ZHAO

7 | Environmental Campaigns

In post-1989 China, environmental NGOs (ENGOs) are one of the most noticeable and vigorous forces in civil society.[1] They have proliferated across the nation, attracted mass participation, established translocal networks, and demonstrated considerable mobilization capacity.[2] Perhaps most remarkably, they have mounted several environmental campaigns with varying degrees of success.

Since their first appearance, ENGOs have garnered numerous international accolades and scholarly attention.[3] The international community and many scholars alike are eager to see the rise of a robust environmental movement in China to counterbalance environment-unfriendly economic forces, to cement a strong civil society that can curtail the reach of the authoritarian state, and to facilitate a possible democratic transition.[4]

An important part of the existing literature on Chinese ENGOs focuses on their relationship with the Chinese state, especially how much autonomy they actually have. Saich argues that although state control is visible, newly rising NGOs are able to employ strategies of negotiation, evasion, or feigned compliance to carve out a space for themselves.[5] Others tend to emphasize the existence of clear limits imposed on ENGOs, with the state setting both the terms of their existence and the extent of member activities.[6] Discussions along these lines continue a debate that began in the early 1990s concerning whether autonomous and semiautonomous intermediate associations and social forces in present-day China are elements of civil society or are corporatist.[7] Although the debate demonstrated how difficult it is to conceptualize civil society, it did not add much to our understanding of the Chinese environmental movement.

A more productive line of inquiry concerns how the structure of the Chinese state and its political processes have provided opportunities conducive to the rise of ENGOs. Saich argues that as the government has streamlined itself and divested itself of certain functions, it has needed the assistance of third-sector organizations to handle social problems.[8] Ho points out that China's grave environmental situation prompted the government to promulgate environmental laws and policies and to build environmental protection institutions, all of which boosted the legitimacy of ENGOs.[9]

This literature so far centers on the state and links up well with sociological treatments of the state and social movements. Following the publication of Skocpol's *States and Social Revolutions,* some scholars focused on how the nature, capacity, and practices of the state lead to the emergence, development, and consequences of movements.[10] But this statist approach has been critiqued for underplaying society's role and neglecting the interpenetration of state and society.[11] A state-society model, by taking into account the nature of the state, the society, and the linkages between them, offers a more promising framework for studying popular contention, including China's environmental movement.[12]

One basic problem in the existing literature on Chinese ENGOs is that both the state and civil society have been generally treated in undifferentiated terms. This chapter will show that it is necessary to disaggregate the state and civil society to arrive at an adequate explanation of the rise and development of the environmental movement. We will take into account the interests, ideology, resources, and power of actors in a multilayered and multidivisional state and an increasingly pluralistic society.

This study analyzes China's environmental movement, especially its more contentious elements, by examining the three best-known recent environmental campaigns: the effort to save the habitat of the snub-nosed monkey in Yunnan of 1995–1997; the campaign to save the Tibetan antelope in Qinghai of 1996–2000; and the campaign against the Nu River (Nujiang) dam project of 2003–2006. Each campaign was a landmark in the history of Chinese environmentalism. By analyzing these campaigns, this study aims to uncover some basic characteristics of China's environmental movement—its major actors, allies and foes, mobilization mechanisms, and developments in the repertoire of contention. In particular, we ask two questions: Under what circumstances did the movement become more contentious during the Nujiang campaign? And what influenced the outcomes of the movement's campaigns?

A Brief History

In the late 1980s and early 1990s, environmental awareness in China grew rapidly. The first flush of environmentalism was crystallized in the form of environmental NGOs.[13] The founding of Friends of Nature in 1993 was a groundbreaking event in this regard. Under the able leadership of Liang Congjie, a descendant of an illustrious family and a member of the National Committee of the Chinese People's Political Consultative Conference, Friends of Nature's major focus is environmental education and nature conservation. In 1996, Global Village of Beijing, another bellwether of the ENGO community, was launched, with a focus on recycling, sustainable energy, and environmental education. In the same year, a journalist, Wang Yongchen, started Green Earth Volunteers, a very loose organization with no formal membership. She also helped establish the Environmental Journalists' Salon, which held monthly events that brought government officials, experts on environmental issues, and journalists together. Wang's extensive personal network has been a crucial resource for the movement, and she has been a central figure in a series of antidam campaigns.

By the late 1990s, the environmental movement had entered a new stage of development. Most obvious, ENGOs proliferated nationwide. According to a national survey conducted by All-China Environmental Federation during July and December 2005, there were 2,768 ENGOs in China.[14] However, since this survey did not reach all unregistered ones, the real number is estimated to be considerably larger. They have now spread not only to metropolitan cities but also to small cities and the countryside. Almost every university has at least one environmental group. These student organizations hold lectures and exhibitions on campus and organize tree plant-ing and recycling activities, and excursions and camping. Some of these have even started to link up into regional networks and alli-ances.[15]

The spread of the internet has strengthened intergroup ties among ENGOs and facilitated the development of internet-based ones.[16] And specialization has occurred. Some ENGOs have chosen to focus on specific issue area(s) instead of general "environmental education." Advocacy has been growing, and some ENGOs have stepped into po-litically sensitive areas. For instance, the Center for Legal Assistance to Pollution Victims helps affected parties sue polluters. The Huai River Guardian (*Huaihe Weishi*) monitors illegal discharge of wastewater into the heavily polluted Huai River. Yu Xiaogang's Yunnan-based Green Watershed calls for implementation of environmental impact assess-ments when evaluating big dam projects. Concepts such as a citizens' rights to know, participatory rights, and environmental justice have appeared more and more frequently in the rhetoric of environmental-ists and increasingly frame China's environmental movement.

In the following analysis of the three cases mentioned above, we will treat the first two episodes relatively briefly, since they have been ex-amined by others.[17] We pay more attention to the more recent and more complicated Nujiang campaign.[18]

Saving the Snub-Nosed Monkey and the Tibetan Antelope

The campaign to save the snub-nosed monkey started in 1995 when wildlife photographer Xi Zhinong learned that Deqin County, Yun-nan, was planning to log over 100 square miles of pristine forest that made up about one-fifth of the endangered monkey's habitat. Xi sought help from Tang Xiyang, a pioneer conservationist. With Tang's advice and help, Xi wrote a petition to Song Jian, then state councilor and head of the State Environmental Protection Commission. Friends of Nature's involvement was crucial to the campaign from the outset. Because Friends of Nature had active members in many mainstream media outlets, the media also played a crucial role.[19] With extensive coverage, the issue drew public attention. Meanwhile, Liang Congjie, president of Friends of Nature, helped attract notice from Vice Premier Jiang Chunyun. At the same time, student green groups were also mobilized. Lectures about the monkey were arranged, and a candlelight vigil was held. In summer 1996, Tang Xiyang led an expedition team (partially supported by Friends of Nature) of 30 college students to Deqin. This expedition attracted enormous media attention and helped bring lasting public attention to the issue.

Top officials from the central government quickly responded to the petitions. They ordered the Yunnan provincial government to intervene, and logging was banned in the area. The central government also dispatched a work team to Yunnan to conduct an investigation. In the end, this poverty-stricken county received funds from the government as compensation for the losses caused by the logging ban. The fledging environmentalist community has scored its first major success: the habitat of the snub-nosed monkey was to be saved.

However, in 1998, environmentalists were tipped off that logging in Deqin continued. With the help of environmentalists, China Central Television sent undercover reporters to investigate the logging site. The ensuing media exposure sparked a national outcry. The outraged Premier Zhu Rongji intervened personally. The county leadership was reprimanded and disciplined: the head of Deqin County had to "confess his mistakes" to the Yunnan Forestry Department, and the deputy head of the county was removed.

Following this exhilarating start, the campaign to save the Tibetan antelope was another watershed for the environmental movement in China. Tibetan antelope roam the vast expanses of Tibet, Qinghai, and Xinjiang. Because of high demand in the West for shahtoosh, the wool made from the animal's undercoat, for shawls, Tibetan antelope had been poached to near extinction, despite trade bans and extensive legal protection.

The West Working Committee of Zhiduo County, Qinghai Province, was the only local force that actively sought to check poaching.[20] Its leader, Sonam Dorje, had been killed in a gunfight with poachers in 1994. In 1999, inspired by his martyrdom, environmentalist Yang Xin founded Green River, a Sichuan-based ENGO dedicated to the conservation of the headwater region of the Yangtze River. Friends of Nature's early involvement in 1996–1998 took the form of supporting the building of a station in Kekexili as a base to combat poachers. It became more involved in the campaign after

Zhawa Dorje, a brother-in-law of Sonam Dorje, came to Beijing at the invitation of Friends of Nature and the magazine *Green Weekend* in October 1998. Zhawa Dorje had reassembled the West Working Committee after Sonam Dorje's death and turned it into an armed antipoaching team, better known by its nickname, the Wild Yak Brigade. Friends of Nature arranged several campus lectures for Zhawa Dorje and introduced him to other ENGOs and journalists in Beijing. An ensuing flurry of sympathetic media reports portrayed the Brigade as an altruistic and heroic group that mounted regular patrols in desolate Kekexili, despite forbidding natural conditions and extreme financial straits. The Brigade emerged from these reports with a moral halo. Efforts to save the Tibetan antelope were quickly mobilized, and donations were channeled toward the Brigade.

The ENGOs also tried to win support from the central government. For instance, Yang Xin's project to protect the headwaters of the Yangtze and to build a Nature Preservation Station was applauded by the leaders of the State Environment Protection Administration (SEPA). Liang Congjie's proposal to coordinate the antipoaching efforts of Tibet, Qinghai, and Xinjiang was partly adopted by 1999.

The ENGOs focused on supporting the Brigade, which they believed was the only group that could effectively fight poaching. However, their high-profile endorsement of the Brigade led them into the muddy water of local politics. When the establishment of Kekexili National Natural Reserve and Management Bureau (hereafter referred to as the Kekexili Bureau) was approved in 1997 by the State Council, several local forces, including the Brigade, were contending for a handful of state-sponsored posts. Despite the impressive work done by the Brigade in fighting poachers, the Yushu prefectural government decided not to incorporate the team into the Kekexili Bureau. Promotion of the Brigade by Beijing ENGOs and the media impinged on the authority of the prefectural government and was resented by the Kekexili Bureau, the supposed official protector of the antelope and a rival of the Brigade. Ultimately, Yushu Prefecture moved to disband the Brigade in August 1999.

When news of the disbanding reached Beijing, Friends of Nature, together with 17 journalists who had reported on the Brigade, wrote a petition to Vice Premier Wen Jiabao, appealing for the decision to be revoked. Intervention from the central government halted the dissolution. However, at the end of 2000, after things quieted down, the

Yushu government disbanded the Brigade again, this time admitting most of its members to the Kekexili Bureau as a compromise.[21] Afterward, the disheartened Friends of Nature and other ENGOs gradually withdrew their attention and support from Kekexili. Still, despite the demise of the Brigade, the endangered antelope attracted lasting public attention and are now much better protected, thanks to the campaign staged by the ENGOs and their media allies.

These two cases reveal that the central and local governments often do not share the same attitude toward environmental protection and the environmental movement. The central government is increasingly environmentally conscious, and has tolerated and even encouraged the growth of ENGOs. Early on, the 1978 Constitution declared the state's commitment to "protect the environment and natural resources." Environmental protection, more recently, has been integrated into the central government's long-term planning, and the concept of sustainable development has been embraced. This trend toward safeguarding the environment is also reflected in the passage of laws and regulations and the establishment and strengthening of supporting institutions.[22] As environmental protection has been incorporated into the state agenda, legitimacy has been extended to social organizations that promote it. Except for worrying that ENGOs may elude state control and engage in true dissent, the central government has many reasons to welcome and support activities by ENGOs.

On the other hand, the relationship between local governments and ENGOs is often antagonistic. Many local governments in China, especially those in less developed hinterlands, work under serious financial constraints and tend to value economic development over environmental protection. In the snub-nosed monkey case, the ENGOs' interests in preserving the forests collided with the economic interests of the local county government, for which logging was a major source of revenue. Furthermore, Beijing ENGOs, with their powerful media allies, were seen as an external force that parachuted into the local scene and could upset the local power configuration. In the Tibetan antelope case, ENGOs became embroiled in local politics and were resented by the Yushu prefectural government.

The division between the central and local governments was adeptly exploited by the ENGOs in both campaigns. Petitions to top leadership became an institutionalized way for ENGOs to call for immediate intervention from above. Petitions by figures with social status and influence, like Tang Xiyang and Liang Congjie, or petitions with a significant number of signers carried considerable weight and at times prompted rapid resolution of the issues in question.

Seeking media coverage was also a major element of the repertoire of contention for Chinese ENGOs. The nascent ENGO community formed alliances with the media from the beginning. Some media-savvy ENGO founders either recruited journalists into their organizations or actively sought their cooperation. And the activities of ENGOs provided attractive material for good stories. Extensive and positive media coverage magnified the voice and power of green NGOs, and the ENGO-media alliance was a key to success for both advocacy campaigns.

Involving college students was another strategy. University students, due to their living arrangements and youthful enthusiasm, are a population with very high mobilization potential.[23] Lectures, exhibitions, petition signing, candlelight vigils, and expeditions were all organized with the assistance of student green groups, and attracted societal attention as well as further media coverage.

The repertoire of contention of ENGOs in these two campaigns was contained, rather than transgressive.[24] Activists did not intend to challenge the regime; instead they looked up to the central government as the ultimate authority and problem solver.[25] Their campaigns took organized and self-contained forms, very unlike the 1989 pro-democracy movement.[26] However, as a result of a series of anti-dam campaigns since 2003, the environmental movement has become emboldened and has sometimes taken a more contentious turn.[27] To date, the campaign against the Nujiang dam project has been the most influential and contentious case of environmental activism.

The Nujiang Campaign

The Nujiang, extending over 2,000 kilometers through Tibet and Yunnan and winding its way through Thailand and Burma, is one of China's major rivers. Its untapped hydroelectric power is among the most abundant in all of China. The river passes through a mountainous region with enormous biodiversity. In 2003, UNESCO designated parts of this region a World Natural Heritage Site.

In March 2003, Huaneng Power International, Inc. and the Yunnan provincial government signed an agreement on joint development of hydroelectric power in Yunnan. Huaneng is one of China's largest independent power producers and Li Xiaopeng, the son of former Premier Li Peng, serves as its Chairman. In August 2003, a proposal to build two reservoirs and 13 cascade dams on the middle and lower reaches of the Nujiang was submitted by the Nujiang Lisu Autonomous Prefecture of Yunnan Province to the National Development and Reform Commission (NDRC) for review.[28] The proposal was accepted by the NDRC and was submitted to the State Council for final approval.

However, a SEPA official who attended the NDRC meeting refused to give his endorsement, citing the lack of an environmental impact assessment, as mandated by the Environmental Impact Assessment Law (2002). But his dissent did not elicit an immediate response. During a break at the meeting, the official phoned Wang Yongchen and told her what had happened. Wang had played a central role in two previous antidam campaigns, and the phone call sparked her interest in protecting the Nujiang.

Moving quickly, SEPA sponsored a symposium at which scientists and experts voiced their objections to the Nujiang project. Through Wang Yongchen and her associates from the Environmental Journalists' Salon, these criticisms reached the wider public. The symposium thus precipitated a campaign to preserve the Nujiang and signaled the formation of a new coalition of environmental activists, journalists, scientists, and SEPA officials.

The Yunnan provincial government, one of the biggest beneficiaries of the Nujiang dam project, wasted no time in reacting. In response to SEPA's involvement, it ordered Yunnan Province to organize two meetings of local experts, where the presentations supported the dam project. In response, SEPA sponsored another two-day meeting in Yunnan, where debates between committed antidam Beijing experts and equally resolute pro-dam Yunnan experts became so contentious that at some moments they became confrontational and personal.

The Nujiang campaign represented a peak in the history of China's environmental movement. First, it was directed against a large hydroelectric project supported by a provincial government, powerful hydropower interests, and some branches of the central government. Unlike earlier environmental campaigns, this effort involved higher political risks. After all, only a decade before, opponents of the Three Georges Dam had been suppressed. Second, the campaign adopted more transgressive forms of collective action and novel framings. In addition to petitioning, seeking media coverage, and involving students, NGOs also tried to reach out to foreign NGOs and appealed to international organizations to apply pressure on the Chinese government. In November 2003, several Chinese ENGOs, including Green Earth Volunteers, Friends of Nature, and Green Watershed, traveled to Thailand to participate in the Second International Meeting of Dam-Affected People and Their Allies. At the request of the Chinese ENGOs, the conference issued a joint statement against the Nujiang project, signed by representatives from more than 60 countries. Chinese ENGOs also sent a petition to the UNESCO World Heritage Committee. In response, that Committee expressed its "grave concern" to Chinese authorities.[29]

Previous causes had been framed mostly as conservation issues. In the Nujiang effort, however, frames also embraced the issues of human rights, social justice, and good governance, all of which carried more political risk. In Yunnan, the most consistent and vocal critic of the Nujiang project was Green Watershed, founded in 2002 by Yu Xiaogang, who later won the 2006 Goldman Environmental Prize. Green Watershed insisted that local people should be included in the decision-making process for such projects. It worked hard to inform and empower local communities by organizing workshops to discuss the social impact of damming. Green Watershed even took a group of Nujiang villagers to the Manwan dam site, where villagers saw for themselves the dismal living conditions of relocated Manwan residents and were spurred to fight for their own rights.[30] In a public letter to the central government in August 2005, a group of ENGOs urged public disclosure of the environmental impact assessment of the Nujiang dams before the making of a final decision. Citing existing laws, they called for democratic decision making on hydropower development, keeping all stakeholders fully informed, and allowing broad participation.

Much more than the two previous campaigns, the Nujiang case approached nationwide political significance. And unlike those two cases, which were more or less successful, the Nujiang campaign had a mixed outcome, reflecting a different constellation of state and societal forces.

In early February 2004, Premier Wen Jiabao, in an unexpected decision, ordered the "suspension" of the Nujiang project. It has been reported that Wen said: "Large hydroelectric dam plans like this that have aroused a high level of societal concern and disagreement from the environmental protection side should be carefully reviewed and decided upon scientifically." Environmentalists were exhilarated by the news, hailing this as a victory for their side.

Yet just when environmentalists thought victory was theirs, pro-dam forces were preparing a counterattack. The premier's somewhat vague statement created opportunities for both the environmental movement and its opposition. Since the statement did not altogether reject the idea of a dam project, hydropower interests were able to interpret it as an opportunity to modify and resubmit the proposal. Their new plan addressed some of the most serious criticisms raised by environmentalists and emphasized the project's contribution to poverty alleviation and environmental protection.

In the counterattack, the pro-dam side tried to forge a coalition with forces in civil society. In April 2005, they arranged for a high-profile, 12-member group to visit the Nujiang, including the scientists He Zuoxiu and Fang Zhouzi. He Zuoxiu, a physicist and member of the prestigious Chinese Academy of Sciences, is also known as a crusader against paranormal claims and "unscientific" thinking. Fang Zhouzi, a United States–educated biologist, founded and controls the influential California-based website Xinyusi (*New Threads;* www.xys.org). Fang made his reputation by exposing pseudoscience, plagiarism, and corruption among China's academics, as well as criticizing Christianity and Falun Gong on his website.

Since the beginning of 2005, Fang Zhouzi and He Zuoxiu had sparred with environmentalists about "whether humankind should be in awe of nature."[31] In the three-month-long debate, Fang and He's camp accused their opponents of being hypocritical, irrational, benighted, superstitious, antiscience, antihuman, inflammatory, radical environmentalists, and bogus environmentalists; their opponents accused them of scientism and anthrocentrism. The debate polarized forces within the wider society, and pro-dam forces adroitly exploited this cleavage.

Fang and He's Yunnan trip was a start of the coalition between the two major foes of the ENGOs: the provincial government and the hydropower interests. The group delivered speeches at Yunnan University after the trip; this mimicked the ENGOs' efforts to win support among college students. At Yunnan University, Fang gave a scathing speech about antidam activists, lampooning their opposition to the Nujiang dam project as lacking scientific validity and condemning them for feeding public ignorance. When Fang posted a transcript of his speech on his website, it quickly spread and produced a firestorm of commentary. Fang and his followers continued to discredit and ridicule the environmentalists on Xinyusi.[32] They pointed out that the Nujiang already had a number of dams on it and the surrounding valley had suffered much ecological damage, and thus was hardly "pristine." Perhaps for the first time in the history of China's environmental movement, the ENGOs' credibility was subject to serious questioning. Fang's analytical rigor, aggressiveness, pungent rhetoric, reputation for independence, and effect on public opinion via Xinyusi made him an invaluable ally for pro-dam forces and an effective counterpoint to the mainstream media, which was overwhelmingly sympathetic to the environmentalists.

Petitioning high officials, a method employed effectively by ENGOs, was adopted by the pro-dam side as well. In May 2005, He Zuoxiu and a member of the Chinese Academy of Engineering coauthored and submitted a report to top state leaders endorsing the Nujiang project and denouncing the ENGOs.[33]

The pro-dam coalition also organized various conferences to champion the dam project and discredit the ENGOs and their claims. In October 2004, at an international symposium on hydropower and sustainable development sponsored by the United Nations Development Program, the World Bank, and the NDRC, the invited speakers, ranging from foreign delegates to local officials from the Nujiang region, spoke predominantly in favor of dam construction. Furthermore, Zhang Boting, the vice secretary-general of the Chinese Society for Hydroelectric Engineering, delivered a stinging attack on the ENGOs, charging them with impeding China's development and depriving local people of a chance to improve their standard of living. In October 2005, *China Investment,* a journal affiliated with the NDRC, sponsored another symposium where hydroelectric interests and their allies, including Fang Zhouzi and He Zuoxiu, dominated the meeting. Both the ENGOs and SEPA were roundly denounced.

Entering 2006, Chinese media reports on the Nujiang declined, as did oppositional voices emanating from SEPA and the ENGOs. The environmentalists believed that the issue was slipping beyond their reach. According to a report of the Hong Kong newspaper *Wenhui Po* on January 11, 2006, the environmental impact assessment for the Nujiang hydropower planning was completed and would soon go to the NDRC for approval.[34] It was reported that the review panel concluded that 4 out of the 13 proposed dam projects could go ahead. The newspaper also quoted a high-placed source who said that since the Nujiang was an international river, the environmental impact assessment was classified and could not be disclosed. This certainly disappointed the environmentalists. However, as of this writing (June 2007), this news report has not been confirmed or denied officially. Except for mentioning that there could be major adjustment of the original Nujiang dam project and the environmental impact assessment was still in process in June 2006, the government has been silent of late.

Explaining the Nujiang Controversy

Why was the Nujiang campaign, in comparison with the two previous ones, more contentious and harder to win? The answer lies in changing state-society relations.

The rising status and expanding power of SEPA and its support for ENGOs are crucial factors that explain the increasing audacity of ENGOs. The predecessor of SEPA was the Environmental Protection Office. Despite a few setbacks, the power of this office ascended steadily after its creation in the late 1970s.[35] In the early 1980s, it was granted the status of a bureau. In 1984, it was renamed the National Environmental Protection Bureau. In 1988, it was separated from the Ministry of Urban and Rural Construction and renamed the National Environmental Protection Agency, and its bureaucratic rank was raised to a half notch below a ministry. In 1998, when the number of ministry-level government bodies was reduced from 40 to 29, it was upgraded to the ministerial status and the name changed to the current one.

Along with institutional upgrading, the promulgation of environmental protection laws has greatly empowered SEPA. The Environmental Impact Assessment Law in particular has provided an important legal framework for SEPA to assert and shore up its authority. The law requires environmental assessment for all construction projects and encourages public participation in the impact assessment process. Beyond the Nujiang campaign, the law was cited at a public hearing in April 2005 on a plan to cover the bed of Lake Yuanmingyuan, in Yuanmingyuan Park in Beijing, with plastic sheeting, to prevent water seepage.[36] The new law has also affected framing within the environmental movement, which has come to focus on citizens' rights to know about and participate in decision making as stipulated in the law.

In addition, after Pan Yue joined SEPA as a vice minister in March 2003, SEPA's power expanded. Pan is a young, enterprising political reformer, and some have viewed the vicissitudes of his political life as a barometer of political reform in China. Ambitious, outspoken, and resolute, Pan has caused a stir in every post he has held. In January 2005, on behalf of SEPA and citing a failure to comply with the Environmental Impact Assessment Law, Pan suspended the construction of 30 large-scale projects, including a new hydropower plant in Yunnan. Again in 2006 and 2007, Pan wielded this law to launch two "environmental impact assessment storms."

At the same time, SEPA's authority has been constrained by its new, weak position within the bureaucracy, as well as its limited resources. It only has about 300 staff members. Its authority cannot even reliably penetrate local environmental protection bureaus, even though in theory they are subordinate to both SEPA and local governments. But since the bureaus rely on the latter for virtually all their funding, they tend to be more responsive to local governments than to SEPA.[37] That is why on the Nujiang dam project, the Yunnan provincial environmental protection bureau heeded the Yunnan government, not SEPA.

Facing these constraints, SEPA has been compelled to look outside the government for allies, and ENGOs have become a natural partner for SEPA, for several reasons. They have an impressively large membership and a crosscountry network that can be mobilized. They enjoy sizable moral capital, owing to their image as independent groups that work for the public good and represent the grassroots. The ENGOs' intimate relationship with the media also gave them

considerable sway with society at large. Moreover, they have more leeway than SEPA to adopt a critical stance toward state-sponsored projects. Finally, some figures in the green community have access to
important political resources. For example, Liang Congjie, in his capacity as a member of the National Committee of the Chinese
People's Political Consultative Conference, once wrote a letter to the
State Council arguing that SEPA should be included in the leading
group of the "the Great Western Development" campaign.[38]

While SEPA and ENGOs cooperated only occasionally in the two
earlier cases, the Nujiang campaign signaled the formation of an
abiding coalition. It was midwifed by Pan Yue, who from the start
sought a closer relationship with the ENGOs. He publicly called the
ENGO community a "government ally" and, among other things, organized training workshops for student green groups from 157 universities.

The ENGO community was more than willing to respond to Pan's
gestures. In January 2005, three days after SEPA announced the suspension of the construction of 30 large-scale projects, 56 ENGOs
issued a joint statement, cited by more than 20 major media outlets,
hailing the decision and proclaiming their solidarity with SEPA.[39]
Although the Nujiang campaign eventually faded away, the SEPA-
ENGO coalition is still in place. In the environmental impact assessment hearing on the plan to cover the bed of Lake Yuanmingyuan
with plastic sheeting, in April 2005, SEPA provided a venue for
ENGO members to participate in decision making. Right after the
first public hearing, training workshops for ENGOs were held to improve their presentation and debating skills at public hearings. Much
of the training was offered by department heads from SEPA.[40]

The alliance with SEPA imparted legitimacy to the ENGOs and emboldened them to stage bolder actions. It was mainly SEPA's backing
that enabled the ENGOs to challenge the hydropower Goliath head
on during the Nujiang campaign. Why, then, did the ENGOs, with
strong support from a central state actor, experience more frustra-
tions in the Nujiang campaign? This was the result of a counterattack
and the even stronger coalition of the local government, business interests, and several influential intellectuals, as well as the top leadership's decision-making rationale.

In the Nujiang campaign, ENGOs faced a powerful foe, the provincial government in partnership with the mighty hydropower interests, which could quickly react to challenges from environmentalists. This countermovement exploited fissures within civil society and formed a coalition with the ENGOs' critics. It emulated the tactics of ENGOs, including petitioning the top leadership, winning over students, magnifying its voice through the media, and using experts, international organizations, and local grassroots voices to lend legitimacy to its aims. In response to the environmentalists' critique, it also adjusted its framings by emphasizing the dams' benefits to environmental protection and poverty alleviation. In the contestation, the resources and mobilizing capacities of its network outweighed those of the ENGOs.

But the outcome of this episode of contention was ultimately determined by the top leadership. Due to the routinization of state rule and fiscal decentralization, the top leadership increasingly has restrained itself from direct intervention in local government operations. In today's China, when local governments or some branches of the central government make decisions, as long as they act within their jurisdictions and follow legitimate procedures, top leaders will find it hard to overturn them, especially decisions made by powerful provincial governments. The top leadership tends to offer support to ENGOs when there is no or little opposition to an environmental campaign. However, when ENGOs face strong criticisms, the top leadership commonly withdraws support partially or completely, and lets social and bureaucratic conflicts play themselves out. In the monkey case, the ENGOs, with the support of their media allies and access to the top leadership, far surpassed the power of their opposition—a county government. By obtaining an edict from the central government, environmentalists won the battle without much effort. In the antelope case, although the ENGOs helped attract societal attention and funding, their effort to preserve and strengthen the Wild Yak Brigade was thwarted by the prefectural government. Although the ENGOs won the first round, successfully halting the prefecture's decision to dissolve the Brigade by securing the central government's decision in the Brigade's favor, they could not prevent the Brigade's eventual demise. The prefectural government in the antelope case was a more forceful antagonist than the county government in the monkey case. In the Nujiang case, top leaders supported the environmental campaign when the SEPA-ENGO alliance took the offensive, but when the hydropower interests staged a forceful counterattack, the central government backed off and accepted compromises.

Our analysis suggests that post-1989 China is beginning to see truly vibrant political interaction between state and society. Although such interaction is also taking place in other issue areas, so far, nationwide contentious mobilization is especially prominent in the environmental sphere.

Our analysis has centered on two questions: Under what circumstances did the movement become more contentious? And what factors have affected the results of environmental campaigns? The key to the answers lies in the nature of the state, civil society, and the state-society relationship. An evolving state-society relationship led ENGOs to adopt moderate, self-contained means to tackle politically safe issues (for example, protection of endangered species). However, further changes in the state-society relationship, especially the boost the ENGOs received from SEPA and other agencies, stimulated the ENGOs to take up more sensitive issues (antidam issues) and to adopt more radical, confrontational means. In a similar vein, we hold that the campaigns' results are largely attributable to state-society power configurations. In the end, the outcomes were determined by the top leadership, who made their decision on the basis of the power balance of the contending sides. In the Nujiang case, one coalition of state actors and civil society actors contended with another.

One might suggest that it was not the dynamics of the state-society relationship but the nature of the issues that made the three campaigns act and end differently. That is, issues like protection of endangered species can gather unequivocal public sympathy and are more likely to win endorsement of the top leadership, whereas issues like dam construction tend to arouse controversy and trigger conflict, and favorable decisions on them are harder to secure from the central government. Other factors than the state-society relationship, of course, influence the dynamics and results of contention. However, the state-society relationship is key for three reasons.

First of all, how to define an issue is a subject of contestation, and how a definition is perceived by the public is also partly a result of contestation within the state-society power configuration. In the monkey case, the local county government might have argued that logging would not damage the monkeys' habitat and that the environmentalists were raising the animal rights above human rights of the local population. However, this definition would not have succeeded, because the county government did not have institutions and resources to generate effective frames for it, and did not possess the means to promulgate the frame and shape public opinion. In an environmental campaign and its opposition, framing is crucial and subject to adaptation and alteration. Environmentalists initially framed the Nujiang campaign as a conservation issue (to protect the "pristine" river). Later they tended to stress social justice and participatory decision making. In response, the pro-dam side shifted its framing from energy-generating capacity to poverty alleviation and environmental protection. In other words, it is the power to frame and the framing of the issue rather than the issue per se that matters here.

Second, more often than not the nature of the issue has little predictive power as to whether a campaign will arise and how contentious it will be. An example is the plan of the authorities at Yuanmingyuan Park in Beijing in 2006 to lay plastic sheets at the bottom of Yuanmingyuan Lake to prevent water seepage. Even such a small issue with minimal relevance to public welfare triggered bitter conflict between environmentalists and the park administration.

Third, the nature of the issue alone does not determine the outcome of a campaign. The Three Gorges controversy did not gain wide support, but the Nujiang campaign did, and achieved at least a partial success. The divergent fates of these causes are not a result of a difference in issues but of a changed pattern of state-society relations.

What implications does our study of environmental campaigns have for studies of contentious politics in contemporary China, and perhaps social movements in general? We suggest that to apply a state-society relations model, as a first step, the state and civil society should not be treated as monolithic entities with fixed interests and modes of action. Instead we must disaggregate. This is not new advice. Mills and Domhoff see states as composed of diverse institutions that are conquered by power elites and class fractions.[41] Skocpol recognizes the unevenness of capacity and autonomy across state agencies.[42] Mann's "polymorphous" theory of the state takes into account the multiplicity of state institutions and their functions.[43] That cleavages in elite politics facilitate the rise and intensification of social movements is well established.[44] Meyer's recent efforts to bring clarity and analytical rigor to the concept of political opportunity can be viewed along these lines, as can recent work by O'Brien and Li in China studies.[45]

In authoritarian regimes, the divergent interests of societal actors have often been overlooked. Civil society has been perceived as in united opposition to the state, and a strong civil society has been expected to challenge authoritarian rule. This is not necessarily the case. In China, the societal forces unleashed during the 1980s at times were highly rebellious, as attested by the 1989 Pro-Democracy Movement.[46] However, in the late 1990s, when Chinese civil society further differentiated into groups with often conflicting interests and ideas, societal forces started to cancel each other out, and this has enhanced the political stability of the regime. This mechanism is a familiar one to sociologists.[47]

How far should the state and the civil society be disaggregated? In other words, how cohesive or differentiated are the state and civil society? This depends on the historical context and the cases at hand. In the case of China, state institutions are becoming more differentiated in terms of function, interest, and ideology, and civil society is increasingly cacophonous, with different constituencies having divergent views and interests. More and more, when a cause and campaign arises, an opposition will be assembled and mobilized.

Given these developments, contentious politics in contemporary China can mean a change from a scenario of civil society against the state to a scenario of one state-society coalition against another. Future research on contention in China might benefit from examining the formation of coalitions and countercoalitions and how they do battle.

8 | Disruptive Collective Action in the Reform Era

China has witnessed a rapid increase in the number of acts of collective resistance in recent years. From 1993 to 2005, the number of such incidents increased tenfold, from 8,700 to 87,000, and some of them involved disruptive tactics or even violence and were deemed "mass incidents" (*quntixing shijian*) or "social unrest" by the government.[1] According to the Ministry of Public Security, instances of the latter include those actions that violate the law or government regulations, disrupt social order, threaten public security or citizens' personal security, or damage public or private property. Disruptive action comes in a number of forms, including collective petitions, protests, sit-ins, gatherings, demonstrations, traffic blockades, office blockades, attacks on state agencies, and confrontations with officials or the police.[2] In 2003, for example, there were 3,100 episodes of blocking highways, roads, and railways nationwide.[3]

Disruptive actions are mainly used to attract attention. They interfere with the routine activities of targets and bystanders. They also enlarge the scope of conflict and can place issues on the political agenda. As Tarrow suggests, "by blocking traffic or interrupting public business, protestors inconvenience citizens, pose a risk to law and order and draw the state into a conflict."[4] Hence, disruptive actions are "outside of normal politics," and "against normal politics," in the sense that people transgress permissible modes of political action.[5]

The relationship between disruptive tactics, including violence, and success is not straightforward, however.[6] Gamson has shown that those who employ violence have a higher-than-average rate of success, but that success is conditional on a number of factors, in particular the legitimacy of the tactics employed.[7] Tarrow notes that one serious limitation of violence is that it reduces uncertainty because of its legitimacy-damaging effect: "where violence occurs or is even likely, this gives authorities a mandate for repression and turns non-violent sympathizers away."[8] Gamson also argues that under some circumstances, violence "merely hastens and insures its failure because its actions increase the hostility around it and invite the legitimate action of authorities against it."[9] Disruptive tactics thus pose a dilemma; as della Porta writes, "the nonviolent demonstrators need more courage; the militants have to be wiser."[10] Police may also try to stir up disorder and violence so that repression can be employed or intensified.

In state-citizen interaction in China, participants turn to disruptive tactics for two main reasons: first, in response to the use of force by local officials or business people supported by local governments, and second, because they have exhausted approved but ineffective channels of participation. Disruptive tactics thus represent a tactical escalation.[11] In either situation, many see such action as morally justifiable. But in a political system where local officials are not institutionally accountable to the people, such legitimacy neither guarantees success nor necessarily reduces risks.

The legitimacy of disruptive tactics is important in China, but the effectiveness of disruption is largely determined by whether the action is disclosed by the media, involves casualties, and has a large number of participants. As most instances of disruption are not reported by the media and do not involve numerous casualties, the number of participants is often the most crucial factor in the likelihood of success. A combination of many participants and the use of disruptive tactics generates serious pressure on local officials because it tends to (or threatens to) trigger intervention from above. Disruptive acts, especially violence, mounted only by a small number of participants are much more likely to be repressed or ignored.

Current Modes of Resistance in China

Since the late 1980s, reform and other changes in China have threatened the interests of a vast number of people. China has multiple channels for political participation, including elections, petitions, lawsuits, reports to the media, and the use of personal networks, as in other socialist regimes.[12] But the availability of channels does not at all mean that they are effective. Due to factors such as accessibility, cost, and needed knowledge, some channels of participation are more frequently employed than others. In recent years, appealing to state authorities through petitions in person, reporting to the media, and filing lawsuits have been the three most common methods to combat misconduct by local officials or business people closely aligned with the government.[13] But each of the modes has limitations that say much about the conditions for successful resistance in China.

Legal channels have come to be an increasingly important mode of conflict resolution in China.[14] For example, since the enactment of the Administrative Litigation Law (1990), which allows government agencies to be sued, it has been frequently used by citizens to defend their rights against abuses by state agencies. From 1996 to 2002, an average of 90,550 administrative suits were filed annually, as opposed to 10,003 in 1990.[15] From 1990 to 2001, litigants won 31.3 percent of the total number of lawsuits they filed.[16] But "the bird of rule by law" has remained in "the cage of the party-state."[17] Citizens have encountered great difficulties suing state agencies, both in getting cases into court and in having favorable decisions executed.[18] Over the years, the number of administrative litigation cases has never exceeded 2 percent of the total lawsuits accepted by Chinese courts. Indeed, the many problems with the legal system have made it a focus of complaints. For example, 10,000 people approached the Central Discipline Inspection Commission with petitions in just two months in 2003. About 40 percent of them complained about local police departments, courts, and procurators, and 33 percent reported problems with local governments.[19]

A second important mode of action is relaying grievances to the media, which at times lend significant help. For example, a survey of 661 journalists found that more than 7 percent reported that all the problems they had reported were addressed, about 33 percent reported a majority, more than 32 percent reported a small portion, and 13 percent reported none.[20] Media commercialization in China has created incentives for the media to "expand the scope of critical reporting, to challenge propaganda department content regulations, and to influence court decision making."[21] However, although government departments in charge of the media are facing more challenges than ever, the media still operates under serious constraints and is highly selective in airing popular grievances. For example, the program *Focus,* produced by Chinese Central Television, is influential in the sense that the problems it uncovers are almost always immediately addressed. It is thus frequently approached by people seeking justice. In the early 2000s, it received about 300 letters and 200 telephone calls every day. But only one out of 10,000 callers, for example, could find a place on the program. As a result, the number of grievances that were investigated and broadcast was negligible.[22]

Recourse to the law and media appeals are hardly rare. But appealing to upper-level authorities (i.e., writing letters or making visits in person) remains the most commonly used mode of action by citizens.[23] For example, a survey of about 2,000 citizens in six cities in 2000 found that appealing to state agencies (71 percent) was the dominant means for citizens to address problems, followed by seeking out media attention (10 percent) and the use of law (8 percent).[24] To be sure, the wide use of petitions is not unique to China. Inga Markovits argued that in the former socialist countries of eastern Europe, even if the authorities had endorsed judicial review without qualification, and even if socialist judges had been eager to censor abuses of government power, it is doubtful that ordinary citizens would have made much use of the right to go to court. "Instead of suing, socialist citizens prefer to raise their objections to administrative decisions through complaints."[25]

As in other socialist countries, however, appeals or petitions are mostly ineffective in China. For example, according to a survey of 632 villagers who lodged petitions in Beijing, each person approached six offices on average, with a maximum of 18. But only about 0.2 percent of them reported that their petitions received a satisfactory response. This finding may be open to question because successful petitioners are probably excluded from the sample (i.e., they went home after receiving redress). In addition, there are different types of petitions, and their effectiveness varies.[26] But that thousands or even tens of thousands of people go to Beijing every year and make appeals for months or years without success points to the serious limitations of this mechanism.[27] The paltry effectiveness of petitions (when not combined with collective action) has also been reflected in data on repeat petitions. For example, of the more than 52,850 letters the complaints bureau of the National People's Congress received in 2003, 37 percent were repeats.[28] The root cause of petitioning again and again is undoubtedly that complaints (or instructions on how to resolve a complaint) had been ignored.[29]

In 2004, when the central government was considering revising the 1995 regulation on "letters and visits," a heated debate broke out among Chinese scholars over whether the system should be scrapped. Those who supported abolition argued that the petition system was basically useless. It not only wasted complainants' time, money, and energy but also damaged the legitimacy of the central government, because most petitioners who approached higher-level authorities did not receive meaningful help and ended up profoundly disappointed.[30]

Frustration and failures have often led to tactical escalation in the United States and elsewhere.[31] As O'Brien and Li have shown, this dynamic is also at work in rural China.[32] Although tactical escalation in China need not entail disruptive action, as noted, citizens often will make a ruckus when they have exhausted the authorized ways to make their grievances known. Some disgruntled citizens believe that disruption "is the only way to solve problems like ours."[33] The mode of disruptive action can vary. Collective petitions are perhaps most typical. For example, in Fujian Province in 1999, 74 percent (or 611) of the 827 instances of social unrest took the form of collective petitions, 6 percent (or 49) were strikes, and the remaining were demonstrations, gatherings, sit-ins, or riots. In Qinghai Province between 1998 and 1999, more than 63 percent (or 188) of the 297 instances of disruptive action took the form of collective petitions or appeals, and 17.5 percent (or 52) were gatherings.[34]

Effectiveness of Disruptive Action

As most of such action in China has been directed against local governments, its effectiveness depends on the pressure it generates on local officials. It is well recognized that there is a significant divide be-

Table 8.1 Disruptive action and its effectiveness (N = 74)

Intervention by	Cases	Results of action	Cases
The central government	5	Concessions	9
Provincial authority only	10	Concessions with discipline	10
None (from above)	59	Suppression	55

Source: Author's collection of 74 cases, mainly from Chinese newspapers, magazines, and court reports.

tween the central government and local officials in attitudes toward citizens who mount resistance. The central government is tolerant of some "rightful resistance" because it can uncover problems with policy implementation at the local level.[35] Moreover, compared with local governments, Beijing is more concerned with regime legitimacy. Therefore, the effectiveness of disruption is determined by whether action is likely to draw attention from the central government or other upper-level local authorities (see Chen, chapter 2).

Needless to say, intervention from above is unpredictable, because higher-level officials are only likely to intervene when they feel the regime's legitimacy and social stability are at stake. I have studied the rationale behind intervention from above (i.e., by central and provincial governments) by examining 74 cases of disruptive action I collected mainly from Chinese sources. These cases can by no means be taken as representative.[36] But they do include episodes in which the authorities interacted with local officials and citizens, and thereby provide important clues to what makes disruption successful or not. Among the 74 cases (Table 8.1), 19 were successful in the sense that participants obtained concessions, including incidents in which concessions were made but some participants were punished (i.e., concessions with discipline). Among the 74 cases, the central government intervened in 5 and provincial governments intervened in 10.

The Politics of Intervention

The central and provincial governments intervened in these 15 cases largely because contention was disclosed by the media, involved serious casualties, or mobilized a large number of participants. By contrast, the 59 cases that failed to receive attention from above tended to be small in scale (i.e., involving at most 100 to 200 participants), did not involve casualties, or were directed solely against local governments. These cases were exclusively handled by local officialdom.

The central and provincial governments are highly likely to intervene when a case involves casualties *and* is disclosed by the media. For example, in Dingzhou city (a county-level city) in Hebei Province, the local government constructed a power plant that needed a parcel of land to store its coal ash.[37] The construction of the ash storage facility was contracted to a businessman who had close ties with the local government, which appropriated the land and paid its owners nominal compensation. In March 2004, when villagers learned that they had been seriously undercompensated for their land, they began to petition different levels of government but were ignored. A few villagers were sentenced to jail for resisting the land appropriation. By July 2004, the city government and the power plant had made more than 10 attempts to use the police to clear the site of protesters. But they met strong resistance. Villagers put up dozens of tents on the land to prevent ground breaking, and assigned 100 to 200 villagers to patrol every night. This resistance irritated local officials and the contractor. Early on June 11, 2005, more than 300 thugs suddenly attacked the tent dwellers, killing 6 and wounding another 48. One person managed to videotape the fighting at the cost of a broken arm. The five minutes of footage, broadcast worldwide on the internet and on foreign television stations, became compelling evidence of excessive force and local misconduct.

The casualties and media coverage generated serious pressure on local authorities, including the provincial government. The provincial public security bureau formed a task force to look into the case, and it quickly found that the contractor had hired the thugs. The provincial police department then detained 106 toughs, who participated in the attack. On June 13, two days after the event, provincial authorities in Hebei removed the city party secretary and the mayor. On December 27, the suspects were tried. Four men who had organized the attack were sentenced to death; three were sentenced to the death penalty with a reprieve; and another six, including the party secretary and the contractor, were sentenced to life in prison. The party secretary was accused of participating in planning the attack (though he had not intended to inflict fatal injuries on the villagers). In the end, the provincial government reversed the decision to use the land for the power plant.[38]

This case, a particularly well-known one, is not typical. In fact, media exposure of ongoing protests is rare. Some cases have come to light because they are first disclosed by media overseas; others have been disclosed by the media within China, because new technology, particularly the internet and cell phones, makes it difficult for the government to cover them up. Still others have been disclosed because they have involved only lower-level officials (i.e., normally below the city level), and the media have reacted faster than the state agencies responsible for management of the media.

Nevertheless, media exposure is not the only impetus for intervention from central or other upper-level governments. Incidents of large-scale resistance can also trigger it, because they are seen as serious threats to social stability. In a high-profile episode in Sichuan Province in October 2004, tens of thousand of villagers in Hanyuan County protested against low compensation for their farmland and homes in the wake of the construction of a dam. The primary grievance was local misappropriation of compensation funds. On average, the central government had provided about 30,000 yuan (about $4,000) for each villager, but many rural households had only received a few thousand yuan. After repeated, fruitless petitions to higher-level authorities, tens of thousands of local residents approached the construction site on the night of October 27, 2004, and attempted to halt construction. The government sent about 1,500 police officers to disperse the protesters. Violent confrontations occurred, resulting in casualties on both sides. Because of the large number of protesters involved, the government ultimately sent in more than 10,000 militiamen to restore order.

Reportedly, a provincial party secretary who went to the site himself was surrounded for hours. After the incident ended, the central government did not punish the protesters; instead, it enjoined the local government to address the issues raised. The central government also dispatched a work team headed by a State Council official to the county, where the team announced the central government's decision to consider the event a "large-scale gathering of migrants who lacked knowledge of the true situation." This phrasing essentially exempted most of the participants from responsibility. Meanwhile, the province issued a public letter that promised to increase compensation and to relocate affected homes. In addition, top county leaders, including the party secretary, were removed.[39]

In another case in Zhejiang Province, Dongyang city set up an industrial park in one of its townships in 2001.[40] The chemical factories in the park produced eye-watering pollution that threatened villagers' health and damaged their farmland. They appealed to local and central authorities repeatedly but to no effect. In 2001, more than 10 villagers were arrested by the local authorities for attacking several factories in the park. After four years of fruitless effort, villagers built tents at the industrial park's entrance on March 20, 2005, and a number of elderly protesters set up camp in the tents in an effort to embarrass the factories into stopping production. In short order, more than 100 policemen and government officials descended on the camp and dismantled and torched the tents. But more tents were built the next day, and about 200 elderly villagers kept a 24-hour vigil in the tent city and blocked entry into the industrial park for two weeks.

Early on the morning of April 10, the city government sent in about 3,500 police officers and government officials to disperse the villagers and dismantle the tent city. After a rumor circulated that two old women had been killed, many villagers were enraged. At the industrial park, thousands of people clashed with the police and government officials, beating them, overturning police cars, and smashing dozens of buses that had ferried them there. Local officials and police did not dare use further force and fled the scene. In the end, more than 140 people ended up in the hospital, a majority of them police and local officials, including a deputy city mayor. Within days, 26 tents reappeared, blocking the industrial park for another month and keeping the factories closed. After this series of confrontations, which also caught the attention of provincial leaders, the local government was eager to end the impasse, and 6 of the 13 factories were ordered to relocate. In the wake of this episode, the city party secretary and the mayor were removed, and several other officials were subject to party or administrative discipline.

These examples of intervention point to the possibility of successful elite-backed "rightful resistance" in China.[41] Tolerating abusive officials not only damages the legitimacy of higher-level authorities who are responsible for supervising local officials but also leads to social instability. A constraint imposed by the political opportunity structure, in other words, has shaped local officials' behavior, in the sense that the possibility of intervention from above has produced concessions before intervention occurs or as a result of it.

Concessions without Intervention

Among the 74 cases, local governments made concessions without intervention from above on eight occasions, largely because of the large number of participants involved. In four of these cases, the number of participants exceeded 5,000, and the largest episode involved 20,000 people. Another two of the eight actions mobilized 3,000 or more participants. Another involved upward of 2,500 rural households, and in another only about 200 villagers appealed to a city government, complaining about a corrupt village party secretary. These examples do not mean that small-scale resistance never succeeds, only that the odds are long because both the central and local governments feel less pressure.[42] Indeed, among the 74 cases, an action with more than 5,000 participants never failed. This does not imply that this is a threshold that guarantees victory; instead, it proves the logic of the often-heard remark "A big disturbance leads to a big solution" *(da nao da jiejue)*.[43]

Disruptive action places two kinds of pressure on local governments: it threatens to trigger intervention from above, and it foments disorder. A common mode of action directed at municipal or county governments is to block traffic, including roads, highways, railways, bridges, and government office compounds. For example, in Changchun, the capital of Jilin Province, there were over 300 instances of collective action with 100 or more participants in 2003. More than 200 of these were directed at party or government agencies, and blocking office compounds and traffic was the major method used.[44]

Although not all such episodes are successful, sizable ones have better prospects. In October 2004, thousands of retired workers from several textile factories in Anhui Province took to the streets for three days to protest their low pensions. Thousands of sympathizers joined them and formed a kilometer-long demonstration that blocked traffic throughout the city. The police were initially deployed but were then withdrawn because the government worried that any repression might incite a riot. After three days of protesters blockading traffic, the local government eventually agreed to increase pensions by about 50 yuan per month. In this case, the government showed tolerance because many participants were elderly, and repression would have put it in a morally difficult position and could well have led to a riot.[45]

Groups that are more able to cause disruption are more likely to achieve their aims.[46] Collective action by taxi drivers in a number of cities is a good example of this. In recent years, there have been many disputes between local governments and taxi drivers. The major source of conflict is regulation of the management of cabs, including the number of years a license is valid, the cost of a license, and various fees imposed on drivers. Taxi drivers in a number of cities have used legal channels to pursue their interests, but because of local officials' influence over the courts, they seldom win lawsuits.[47]

Although the drivers are not always in the right, violations of their rights do occur. When lawsuits prove ineffective, they often use other modes of contention, such as strikes or traffic blockades. A high-profile case in Ningxia Hui Autonomous Region was successful. On July 28, 2004, the city government of Yinchuan announced a new regulation shortening the duration of licenses issued to drivers. The city had about 4,840 registered vehicles, 94 percent of them taxis. The number of employees in this line of work exceeded 10,000, and many of them were laid-off workers and villagers who had lost their farmland. If the new regulation was enforced, these displaced persons would likely fail to recover the money they had spent purchasing their vehicles and licenses.

On the morning of July 29, 2004, more than 20 taxi drivers gathered in front of the city government's main office building, holding copies of a newspaper carrying the new regulation and declaring a strike. Shortly thereafter, the number of protesters increased to about 400. That afternoon, about 300 taxi drivers marched to the autonomous region's (i.e., provincial) government offices. The next morning, large-scale disruption took place. Thousands of taxi drivers paralyzed traffic in the city, in several ways. First, most of them joined the strike that had started up. Second, hundreds of taxi drivers massed on the streets to prevent other vehicles from transporting passengers. Still others parked their vehicles blocking busy intersections. Some also pressured fellow drivers who had failed to go along with the resistance.[48]

The effect was immediate. Traffic in the city came to a halt. Surprised by the collective action, the city government first mobilized the police to tow away vehicles obstructing traffic. Second, it issued an urgent notice that it would postpone enacting the new regulation. The next day, the mayor delivered a speech on television and apologized for the disruption to daily life. The city government also called on district governments to make 50 vehicles available for passenger transport every day. In addition, the city government promised that any taxi driver who came to work would receive a 100-yuan bonus each day. But most refused to resume working because they believed "postponed enactment is like a postponed 'death penalty.'" As a result of increasing pressure and the province's dissatisfaction with the city's handling of the issue, the municipal authorities eventually "surrendered," and the new regulation was revoked. But the taxi drivers' victory was not costless. About 130 participants were briefly detained, and four were formally arrested.

All these cases suggest that disruption plays a larger role in agenda setting than other modes of collective action like petitions or lawsuits. Disruption is more effective because the pressure it generates on local officials is direct and cannot be ignored. Chinese citizens often encounter serious obstacles when using approved procedures (e.g., petitions) to defend their interests. Disruptive acts circumvent these channels and leave limited or little room for those in power to ignore citizens' grievances. Such action often gains publicity and prevents officials from pretending they do not know of a problem. It also poses a challenge to both officials who ignore citizens' rights and their superiors. Depending on the scale of such action, local governments and higher levels often find it advisable to react quickly in order to avoid intervention from above. Hence, in China, the power of disruption, especially large actions, lies in the fact that it alters interactions between citizens and local officials, making the local officials more impatient than the protesters to end an impasse.

Existing research on the use of disruption has generated mixed findings about its effectiveness. Giugni concludes: "the effectiveness of disruptive tactics and violence is likely to vary according to the circumstance under which they are adopted."[49] Gamson suggests that disruption is effective when it is used against weak parties.[50] In China, as the cases presented show, the effectiveness of disruptive acts does not lie in local governments' weakness but in that it causes chaos and signals to upper-level authorities that local officials have abused their power or failed to perform their duties.[51] In this way, disruption and the prospect of third-party intervention constrains local officials.

Risks of Disruptive Action

While disruption can be an important way to achieve a desired outcome, it is not always feasible. First, not all disgruntled citizens can mount large-scale resistance; they cannot always mobilize a large number of participants. Second, staging disruptive action entails unavoidable risks. In the 74 cases I examined, 269 people were jailed for up to 15 years, with one being executed; 308 were detained briefly; and another 21 were arrested, some of whom would later be tried.

Intervention from above is not only conditional but also limited, in the sense that it does not protect protest leaders from local punishment.[52] This is understandable, because caving in completely would make the local government too vulnerable to future challenges. Tarrow writes: "one of the most remarkable characteristics of collective action is that it expands the opportunities of others. Protesting groups put issues on the agenda with which other people identify and demonstrate the utility of collective action that others can copy or innovate upon."[53] By punishing organizers, a local government shows that victory can be very costly, at least for those who lead actions, and thereby reduces this demonstration effect. In the 2005 Hanyuan case, 28 participants were tried in local courts and found guilty, and one was sentenced to death for killing a police officer.[54] In the Huaxi episode, eight villagers were jailed from eight months to five years.[55] As O'Brien and Li have observed, higher-level authorities may be "quite happy to see them [protest leaders] jailed" when they are seen as threats to local stability.[56]

Suppression without concessions even more clearly illustrates a local government's determination to safeguard its authority and image. In 38 (or 68.5 percent) of the 55 failed cases, activists or leaders were punished because they had staged repeated actions. For example, in Nanhai city in Guangdong Province, because of disputes with local cadres over village financial affairs, activists organized villagers to block a road twice. They also led more than 400 community members in forcing their way into a township compound, shutting the government down for three hours. Finally, the activists inspired more than

300 villagers to block the gate of a factory notorious for its pollution. Distressed by this wave of protest, local authorities accused the four key activists of disrupting social order and put them behind bars for 4 to 11 years.[57]

Limits on Repression

The many incidents of collective resistance that occur every year, despite frequent suppression, demonstrate that repression has not stopped disruptive action. Political opportunity theorists have argued that repression generally "works"; but it does not always deter resistance. Even anticipated repression may fail to deter protests when participants are ignorant of the true risks or define risks optimistically.[58] In China, O'Brien and Li find, "defeat does not . . . cause all rightful resisters to lapse into despair and passivity."[59] Repression may also lead to renewed commitment when activists have little choice but to continue their resistance.[60] At other times, protesters may also misperceive the opportunity structure and overestimate their likelihood of succeeding.[61]

Collective action is sensitive to threats as well as opportunities. As McAdam suggests, "in polities where there is some expectation of state responsiveness and few formal barriers to mobilization, we should expect perceived threats to group interests to serve, along with expanding opportunities, as two distinct precipitants of collective action."[62] In China, it is very common for citizens to take action to *defend* rights that have been impinged on. As long as the central-local divide remains, "rightful resistance" will continue.[63]

Repression may also fail to deter resistance because many such actions do not need identifiable leaders. In defensive or reactive episodes, a strong consensus that they have been wronged may be sufficient to mobilize participants, as long as information dissemination is possible. As Piven and Cloward explain, "riots require little more by way of organization than numbers, propinquity, and some communication."[64] Some actions occur in reaction to a poster, news on the internet, or a cell phone call. Some are initiated without much mobilization or are mobilized anonymously. For example, taxi drivers in Hefei, the capital city of Anhui Province, organized a highly effective strike against fines imposed by the local police. The strike notice was issued by the "Taxi Association of Hefei," an organization that did not exist.[65]

New technology has also facilitated mobilization. The minister of public security acknowledged in 2005 that "the development of information technology, while facilitating social and economic development, has also posed serious pressures for maintaining social stability."[66] For example, in August 2005, when citizens in a county-level city in Hubei Province learned that their city was to be turned into a district, they launched an attack on the municipal government. On August 5, one person posted news of the demonstration on the internet. The next day, about 20,000 people participated in a demonstration, assaulting the city government, destroying property, and wounding some police officers. The planned reclassification was soon abandoned. Not surprisingly, however, 10 protesters were later sentenced to jail for up to five years.[67]

Disruptive actions are difficult to prevent, in part because they may escalate from peaceful protest unexpectedly. It is not rare for instances of nonviolent resistance, such as petitions, to turn confrontational because of disappointment or frustration with a lack of any response or of a meaningful response from the authorities. An important characteristic of tactical escalation is that in many cases, new modes of action or tactics are not consciously chosen or decided on beforehand; instead, they appear almost spontaneously in an ongoing process of action and reaction. For example, on September 12, 2002, several thousand villagers in Guangxi approached municipal authorities to present a petition regarding difficulties growing sugarcane. Failing to receive any response, some activists blocked traffic at the city center. They later obstructed the railway between Guizhou and Guangxi, stopping traffic for eight hours. Villagers also laid waste to the office compounds of the city government and the city party committee, damaging 22 cars.[68] Disruptive tactics, it is clear, sometimes emerge out of "a momentary passion."[69]

This chapter has examined how disruptive collective action in China can, at times, succeed. It shows that the legitimacy of disruptive action can be an important factor affecting the chance of prevailing, but that legitimacy alone is far from enough. The cases I presented demonstrate that the number of participants, media exposure, and the occurrence of casualties are all factors that strongly affect the likelihood of success. These considerations are important because of the political opportunity structure in China.[70] Opportunities are produced, in the main, by the central-local divide, and they do not necessarily hinge on changes in the political system or further reform.[71] Local officials have always been accountable to upper-level authorities, and maintaining social stability is an important responsibility they cannot shirk.[72] Mishandling disruptive action thus implies failure to maintain local stability. A large amount of participants, media exposure, and casualties increases the chance of redress, because it increases the possibility of intervention from above.

Evidence from China confirms that both opportunities and threats can lead to collective action. Activists appear to be relatively rational entrepreneurs awaiting signals from the state and the larger society about what claims to lodge and how.[73] Gamson and Meyer suggest that activists in general are often unduly optimistic about opportunities, and do not necessarily calculate with any rigor the likely prospects for successfully mobilizing or generating policy reform; they just keep trying.[74] This may also be true for some activists in China. But because many episodes of popular resistance in China are defensive in nature, participants and activists are often left with few other choices, in the sense that not acting means accepting major losses or an egregious injustice. A combination of the belief in the legitimacy of "rightful resistance" and a threat to one's interests implies that protest, including disruptive modes, will persist so long as citizens' rights are ignored—although success, as always, will remain conditional.

It is against this background that the central party-state has recently made "building a harmonious society" a top priority. Nevertheless, this does not necessarily mean that citizens who stage resistance now have a greater chance of success. The pressure of maintaining social stability faced by local governments, which are responsible for dealing with most instances of poplar resistance, may drive them to maintain the practice of knee-jerk suppression.[75] Therefore, setting up the goal of "building a harmonious society" alone is far from adequate for preventing popular contention, including disruptive incidents. Instead, many other measures, in particular those involving strengthening political and legal institutions and restraining state power, will have to be introduced in order to achieve this goal.

9 | Manufacturing Dissent in Transnational China

In November 2004, the *Epoch Times*, an overseas Chinese newspaper with close links to the outlawed spiritual group commonly known as the Falun Gong, published a series of editorials on its website entitled *Nine Commentaries on the Communist Party*, "in order to fully expose how this largest cult in history has embodied the wickedness of all times and places." Addressing "those who are still deceived by the Chinese Communist Party," the editorial board aimed to convince its readers to "purge its poison from their spirits, extricate their minds from its evil control, free themselves from the shackles of terror, and abandon for good all illusions about it." Beginning in December, the *Epoch Times* and its affiliates distributed the *Nine Commentaries* by email to an estimated 2.3 million email users in mainland China, where its website is blocked, and created a public forum on the internet in which individuals could renounce their membership in the CCP and its affiliated organizations.[1] According to the *Epoch Times*, to date, over 15 million people have participated in this movement; one report found that most of the resignations posted during the first five months of the campaign were effected via online proxy services, and therefore presumably originated on the Chinese mainland.[2]

One of the earliest names to appear on the list was that of Meng Weizai, a former high-ranking Propaganda Department official. In an explanatory statement that accompanied his resignation, Meng purportedly declared that since becoming a Falun Gong practitioner, he had been repeatedly harassed by Chinese authorities. Announcing "I must make a choice between the Communist Party and my life. Now for myself, I declare that I am leaving the Communist Party to live as a Chinese with a clean conscience," he urged others to follow his example. Two days later, on December 8, 2004, he allegedly issued a "final declaration" reconfirming his resignation, adding that, due to threats he had received from public security agents, he would remain silent for the foreseeable future.

The following day, the state-run Xinhua News Agency released a "solemn declaration" authorized by Meng in which he expressed shock over the reports of his resignation. In a videotaped statement before a group of Chinese reporters, Meng described himself as a loyal member who joined the CCP on the front lines of the Korean battlefield in 1953, following in the footsteps of his father, a revolutionary martyr killed during the War of Resistance against Japan. Dismissing the news of his resignation as "pure fabrication" and "malicious rumor mongering," Meng affirmed: "I, Meng Weizai, was a CCP member, am a CCP member and will be a CCP member until I die. I will never betray the great Chinese Communist Party!"[3]

Surprisingly, Meng's declaration had no discernible impact on the mounting media frenzy. One day later, three overseas Chinese websites published yet another statement purportedly authored by Meng in which he lambasted the Xinhua document as a blatant forgery and vowed that he would "never pay homage to the evil Karl Marx."[4] Ignoring Meng's earlier videotaped denial before the Chinese press, one Voice of America reporter commented that since Meng had not responded personally to the allegations, the outside world would never know the truth of the matter.[5] During a December 21 forum at the National Press Club, Washington, D.C., hosted by the *Epoch Times,* opinion editor Stephen Gregory claimed that the party leadership was nothing less than "panicked" by the resignation movement, and feared a "chain reaction . . . a meltdown that can't be controlled."[6] Veteran dissident Liu Xiaobo remarked to the *South China Morning Post* that whether Meng had quit the party could be easily verified in a country with freedom of speech. The real problem for the party, Liu observed, was that the official media had declared cyberspace an ideological battleground, and had no choice but to lock horns with overseas websites over the matter.[7]

During the New Year holiday, several overseas Chinese websites posted yet another essay ostensibly penned by Meng in which he claimed that 50 high-ranking cadres had joined him in the movement to "renounce the Party in order to save the nation." An investigation launched by the Hong Kong–based *Phoenix Weekly (Fenghuang zhoukan)* in January 2005 quickly determined that the 50 names had been lifted from a petition circulated 10 years earlier by the "Left Coalition of Writers" condemning the release of Li Zhisui's *Private Life of Chairman Mao,* several of whom had since passed away. The reappearance of their names on the resignation list was, in the words of the *Phoenix Weekly* reporter, "laughable."[8] Xinhua has since ceased commenting on the matter, but the *Epoch Times* and its affiliated organizations maintain a running count of the resignations on their websites, and regularly mark important milestones by organizing rallies and other events to publicize the success of their campaign.[9] In a candid March 2005 message to conservative blogger Daniel W. Drezner, Stephen Gregory said he hoped "to avoid the suspicion [he was] attempting to hype a story" by openly acknowledging that the resignations count included the names of many who were not actual party members, anonymous resignations, and even posthumous renunciations posted by the surviving family members of party members. Nevertheless, despite these significant caveats, Gregory trumpeted the renunciation movement as "the most important story in China today," adding, "and no one outside the *Epoch Times* is covering [it]."[10]

The murky case of Meng Weizai sheds light on two prominent developments in the study of popular contention in recent years: transnational protest movements and the internet. The increasing amount of horizontal integration of forces—nation-states, government officials, and nonstate actors of various kinds—in the wake of globalization, and the solidification of vertical links between local, national, and international in recent decades has created new opportunity structures in which transnational activism has become not only more frequent but also more sustained.[11] At the same time, the spread and development of the internet has facilitated transnational political action by reducing the cost and increasing the effectiveness of communication both within and across national borders, thereby triggering rapid and dramatic shifts in the scale of contention in a manner not possible previously.[12] In China, the spread of the internet alongside the suppression of new quasi-religious groups has given rise to a new form of organization I call the "cybersect."[13] Such groups continue to serve as nodes of transnational political contention, both online and offline. Banned by mainland authorities during the late 1990s, cybersects originally turned to the internet as a tool for connecting exiled leaders with rank-and-file members on the Chinese mainland during the initial phases of repression. However, as the crackdown developed into a broader ideological campaign against what the Chinese government called "heretical superstitious groups and practices," those banned groups that had most successfully made the leap to cyberspace evolved into far-flung multinational conglomerates incorporating media enterprises, public relations firms, and commercial operations beneath a loose umbrella of shifting entrepreneurial, political, and spiritual interests. Courting the support of foreign governments, international nongovernmental organizations (NGOs), transnational advocacy networks, and the international media, these cybersects have continued to apply external pressure on the Chinese government, hoping to generate what Keck and Sikkink have termed "boomerangs" of transnational support, with varying degrees of success.[14] As the Meng Weizai incident demonstrates, such groups and their affiliates sometimes succeed in provoking a public response from Chinese authorities. On the other hand, as the same incident also suggests, on occasion, such activities can and do backfire, not only weakening the credibility of movement activists but also potentially tarnishing the reputations of the NGOs, transnational advocacy networks, and other actors that champion these causes.[15]

I propose that behind these two potential outcomes—"boomerang" and "backfire"—lies a more fundamental insight into the highly competitive dynamics shaping contemporary transnational activism. The arsenal of aggressively promotional strategies pursued by cybersects banned in China has long included not only the cultivation of the press, both domestic and foreign, but the creation of new media as well. The largest transnational cybersects are closely associated not only with traditional newspapers or newsletters that can be counted on to report stories supportive of their agendas but they also own controlling interests in independent television and radio stations, whose programming can be beamed (with some difficulty) directly into mainland China. By engineering protest spectacles and staging high-profile events that are effectively framed, promoted, and spun by their own media outlets, these banned cybersects are attempting to go beyond the "marketing of rebellion" to international NGOs and supporters, and are, in some instances, virtually "manufacturing dissent"—mobilizing not only their loyal members but also their privately owned media companies to pursue their aims and delegitimize their opponents.[16]

Although underground presses and dissident media are by no means new phenomena, particularly in hard authoritarian regimes, the pattern I describe differs from earlier incarnations in form as well as intent. Historically, alternative or underground media primarily operated within national borders, serving as a vehicle for the expression of repressed voices and counterhegemonic views in the face of severe political repression. For example, Soviet *samizdat* (literally, "self-publication") originated as a mechanism for the reproduction and circulation of banned literary materials, an attempt to give public voice to the rich and varied texts that fell outside the state's monopoly on publishing. As messages became increasingly political in the 1960s and 1970s, *samizdat* writers continued to maintain that their critiques were both legal and justifiable within the Soviet tradition.[17] This scenario is not unlike the "rightful resistance" O'Brien and Li have found in contemporary rural China.[18]

By contrast, today's Chinese cybersects deploy media strategies that transcend the "venue shopping" and "information politics" practiced by similar groups, insofar as they blend seemingly objective news with promotional messages as a strategy of legitimation. Much of their reportage aims to build a record of public recognition and certification for movement elites and their allies, and to discredit perceived opponents, skillfully synthesizing traditional "news" items and partisan advocacy to legitimate and magnify the scope and importance of movement activities.[19] In so doing, today's cybersects are effectively conjoining the "internet to mass media" and "mass media to internet" trajectories described by Guobin Yang (chapter 6), creating a self-perpetuating news cycle in cyberspace. Movement-allied media outlets like the *Epoch Times* help to launch and publicize protests, and then report favorably on the significance of event outcomes, amplifying the effect of dissident activities in the echo chamber of the global media. Like the "cyberboosterism" of small state actors, which blends propaganda, statistical information, and promotional material on websites designed to stimulate public interest and attract investment, these engineered media spectacles depend for their success on the ability of movement elites to conflate the actual with the virtual in a manner favorable to movement goals.[20]

In their often cited work *Manufacturing Consent: The Political Economy of the Mass Media,* Herman and Chomsky postulate that the imbrication of the modern mass media with socioeconomic elites in ownership, management, and advertising effectively delimits its ability to serve as an independent voice in democratic capitalist societies. According to their "propaganda model," the modern mass media promote, suppress, legitimize, and endorse information in a way that serves dominant elites and is ideologically serviceable to corporate and state interests, effectively "manufacturing" or "engineering" popular consent for particular courses of action that favor elite interests.[21] Similarly, by providing alternative media that are friendly to dissident voices, the media-savvy movement entrepreneurs behind China's transnational cybersects frame a unique blend of selective news coverage, promotional material, and scathing political critiques with the aim of building popular support for their cause and of delegitimizing Chinese authorities, using tactics in many ways similar to those deployed against them in the state-controlled Chinese press.

Transnational Networks and the Internet

The key features of transnational activism—diffusion of social movements across borders, international mobilization, and the borrowing of modular forms and frames for collective action—are not new. But the process of globalization, as manifested in increasing volume and speed of flows across borders, has greatly facilitated transnational contention.[22] Recent advances in communications technologies like the internet provide important resources for the new generation of transnational activists by virtually guaranteeing social movements a relatively inexpensive, rapid, and reliable means of international communication. Clearly, as Diani observes, the internet can transform "sets of geographically dispersed aggrieved individuals into a densely connected aggrieved population" that is more capable of launching and sustaining coordinated collective action.[23]

Some have argued that the internet should not merely be seen as a tool of communication but should be analyzed as a form of social organization in its own right. The internet, according to Castells, is not "simply a technology: it is a communication media, and it is the material infrastructure of a given organizational form: the network." Older, hierarchical, and bureaucratic forms, supported by a rapidly expanding technological infrastructure that supports interactive media, are being rapidly replaced and outpaced by more heterarchical and collaborative forms. "Networks constitute the new social morphology of our societies."[24] Other observers celebrate the network as a new/old organizational form that hearkens back to a time "before simple human relationships became obscured by hierarchy and bureaucracy." At the same time, it is said, these new networks manifest a utility that make it possible for them to "leap forward" into the future "with globe-encompassing capability that subsumes the enduring aspects of authority and bureaucracy."[25] According to Keck and Sikkink, for activists and citizens living and operating in repressive contexts, networks may prove an invaluable resource for pressing claims against otherwise unresponsive state agents. Domestic groups can activate networks and thereby "bypass their state and directly search out international allies to try to bring pressure on their states from outside." These "international contacts can amplify the demands of domestic groups, pry open space for new issues, and then echo back their demands into the domestic arena," creating a "boomerang effect" that ultimately forces change back home. Insofar as "information binds network members together and is essential for network effectiveness," recent advances in communication technologies—cell phones, fax machines, and the internet—have contributed greatly, it is said, to the efficiency of transnational advocacy networks in pressing claims.[26]

Access to the internet proved invaluable to the leaders and members of a host of banned quasi-spiritual groups during the crackdown against "evil heretical sects" launched by the Chinese government during the 1990s. A string of arrests, investigations, and critical articles published in the state-run press prompted the leaders of several popular Qigong sects to flee the mainland. However, the concurrent development and spread of the internet inside China gave the beleaguered groups a virtual forum through which to maintain contact. Exiled leaders continued to issue statements and directives and to provide frequent counsel to their followers; rank-and-file practitioners shared their experiences and received and offered support to others online. Over time, what began as loose aggregations of websites maintained by pockets of practitioners evolved into an increasingly centralized and highly polished internet presence that was policed and managed by public relations professionals based overseas. Increasingly relying on the internet for text distribution, recruitment, and information sharing, the most successful of these banned groups became cybersects: dispersed small gatherings of practitioners that seek to remain anonymous domestically while maintaining links to a global network of believers who share a set of practices and texts and a common devotion to a leader. Overseas chapters provide funding and support; domestic cells occasionally distribute tracts, participate in acts of resistance, and share information on the internal situation with outsiders. Collectively, members within and across national borders construct viable virtual communities that interweave spiritual faith and political practice via email and online chatrooms and message boards.[27] The accessibility of new information technologies both inside and outside China in the 1990s proved key to overcoming the bifurcation between clandestine pockets of domestic practitioners and a web of support groups based overseas and made possible this new organizational form.

A second factor that proved central to the ability of some of these sects to survive a crackdown was the considerable material resources at their disposal. After the Chinese state erected further barriers to the registration of new social organizations in the wake of the 1989 student demonstrations, the popular Qigong sects that emerged in the 1990s had few options but to incorporate on the mainland as profit-making or nonprofit enterprises. The skillful marketing and media manipulation strategies these spiritual entrepreneurs developed in China's highly competitive Qigong market during those years have served them well.[28] Like the "sacred companies" or "marketed social movements" that have emerged in contexts other than China, well-endowed syncretic sects had an organizational hybridity that proved highly adaptable to the demands of both virtual and transnational environments.[29] With the resources and wherewithal to lobby representatives of foreign governments, transnational Chinese cybersects have emerged as savvy players within the larger network of overseas Chinese dissidents, and in the halls of power of Western democracies.

Over time, the three banned groups that were most successful in making the leap to cyberspace—Guanyin Famen/Quan Yin, Zhonghua Yansheng Yizhi Gong (hereafter Zhong Gong), and Falun Dafa, the group more commonly referred to as Falun Gong—honed their media strategies, hiring public relations firms, media consultants, and lobbyists to polish and package their message. These three cybersects are closely associated with media outlets that broadcast their respective agendas, and they also own controlling interests in independent television and radio stations within the "global diasporic Chinese mediasphere."[30] Suma Ching Hai International, the corporate entity behind Guanyin Famen/Quan Yin, has been affiliated with World Peace Media, Oceans of Love Entertainment, Supreme Master Television, and several cable television series. Zhong Gong is associated with the International Zhonggong Headquarters, Inc., the Alliance Against Persecution, and the Tianhua Cultural Studies Center. The New York–based Falun Dafa Information Center, established in 1999, has close organizational links to various media units staffed largely by Falun Gong practitioners, including the *Epoch Times*, New Tang Dynasty Television, World Falun Dafa Radio, Sound of Hope Radio, and several others. These media companies produce informational and promotional materials designed to raise international awareness of the repression suffered by practitioners in China, to undermine the negative propaganda circulated by the state-run Chinese press, and to provide information about their beliefs and practices to the wider public.

Yet their careful cultivation of a "boomerang" effect, "which curves around local state indifference and repression to put foreign pressure on local policy elites," comes, not infrequently, at a cost.[31] These banned sects' bids for transnational support have resulted in increased domestic and international scrutiny of their internal affairs and public relations tactics, and have occasionally produced a backlash of negative media attention. In contrast to the transformative backfire generated by repression, which can produce a "take-off" in popular mobilization, backlash undermines the credibility of movement organizers and their capacity to influence established media, politicians, and the public at large.[32] Although movement organizers' efforts to court media attention have been well documented in the literature on social movements, surprisingly little attention has been paid to the potential for promotional activities to rebound in this way. As the following three cases demonstrate, if new digital media has enabled repressed groups to have more access to transnational audiences, it has also made their organization, beliefs, and tactics more vulnerable to surveillance and occasionally public exposure by reporters, investigators, or anonymous legions of fact-checking digerati. In all three of these cases, the hoped-for boomerangs of support missed their mark and backfired, to varying degrees, in the form of negative media attention.

Guanyin Famen/Quan Yin

The Supreme Master Ching Hai World Society (Qinghai Wushang Shijie Hui) was established in Taiwan in 1986 as a religious society with Buddhist leanings, associated with the Center for Meditation on the Immeasurable Light (Wuliang Guang Jingzuo Zhongxin). Supreme Master Suma Ching Hai, the female spiritual leader of the movement, was born in 1950 in Quang Ngai, Vietnam, but left at age 22 to study in England, eventually becoming an interpreter for the Red Cross. Following a brief marriage, she later moved to India to devote herself to the study of Sant Mat Buddhism, and then Surat Shabd Yoga under Thakar Singh, before entering a Tibetan Buddhist nunnery, where she remained for nearly a year.

Her recognition as a spiritual leader came suddenly in 1982, when she tried to buy a copy of the Hindu sacred work the *Bhagavad-Gita* from a small shop along the Ganges. The shopkeepers denied having copies in stock, but she continued to insist she had seen it there. An extensive search uncovered a copy of the volume locked away in a sealed box; word quickly spread that Ching Hai had an unusually well-developed third eye. The following year, she left India for Taiwan, and began to teach Sound Current Yoga to small groups of students. In 1986, she founded the Immeasurable Light Meditation

Center and the Way of Sound Contemplation (Quan Yin) in Miaoli, Taiwan. Two years later, following a dispute with a local Buddhist society in Malaysia on the eve of a speaking engagement, she publicly disavowed any formal connection with established Buddhism and adopted the distinctly secular appearance she maintains today.[33] Her highly syncretic message and set of practices, designed to help followers "discover" and "awaken the Divine Presence within," involves vegetarianism, daily meditation on the Inner Light and Sound, and the observation of Five Precepts—injunctions against taking the lives of sentient beings, lying, stealing, sexual misconduct, and the use of intoxicants.[34]

Quan Yin was introduced on the Chinese mainland in 1992, where it is commonly known as Guanyin Famen, and quietly spread for several years. In July 1996, two years before the onset of a campaign to stamp out "heretical sects," authorities in Sichuan's Jiangyou city discovered a list of several thousand practitioners in seven different provinces that included many CCP members and some high-ranking cadres. Following an investigation into the sect, its beliefs, and activities, party authorities concluded that the organization was fundamentally anticommunist and labeled it a "reactionary religious organization." By July 1999, when the ban against such groups was promulgated into law, Guanyin Famen/Quan Yin claimed an estimated 500,000 followers in 20 provinces and cities.[35]

There is limited, anecdotal evidence that some mainland chapters have been successful in maintaining their links to the their leader despite the ban. In 1998, nearly two years after the group was branded an "evil heretical sect," a group of "fellow initiates" visited Shanxi to distribute flood relief in the aftermath of a disaster; a May 2000 "dharma meeting" presided over by the Supreme Master in Hong Kong's Elisabeth Stadium attracted 3,000 followers, including several hundred from Fujian, Guangdong, Hunan, and elsewhere on the mainland.[36] Eighteen months later, at a retreat in Youngdong, Korea, the Supreme Master greeted a group of Chinese disciples "who had longed very much to see Her" and comforted them by acknowledging the hardships they had endured.[37] On returning to the mainland, at least one member of the group claimed to have been met in rural Hebei by a group of over 100 local practitioners eager to hear his account of the retreat.[38] According to association news posted on the group's website, Guanyin Famen/Quan Yin initiates on the Chinese mainland have received informational flyers "designed by Master personally" and distributed them locally as recently as early 2006.[39]

The group's reliance on the internet to communicate across national boundaries is one key to its survival. The sect currently maintains versions of its website in at least 17 different languages, but the main pages—and the sites with the most content—remain those in English, traditional Chinese, and Vietnamese. The websites offer in-house news magazines, RealAudio and downloadable MP3 versions of radio broadcasts, and online WindowsMedia versions of Supreme Master television programs for those without access to cable stations. Seminars and lectures can be downloaded in Chinese in MP3 format, viewed online, or even downloaded as podcasts, which cannot be filtered for objectionable content.[40]

Much of the media produced by Suma Ching Hai International is heavily self-referential and promotional, and aims to build a public record of recognition for group activities. In December 1998, the organization staged a concert to benefit several prominent children's foundations in the United States; highlights of the event were captured in a coffee-table book, *One World of Peace Through Music*. Like Falun Gong's Li Hongzhi, Supreme Master Ching Hai has had local authorities in the United States, Taiwan, and elsewhere declare particular dates "Supreme Master Ching Hai Day." The website displays letters of appreciation she has received for her charitable contributions and works, including one purporting to be from the "China Communist City Council of Chifeng and City Government of Chifeng" thanking her for her flood relief efforts in Shanxi Province in 1998.[41]

The source of the vast financial assets supporting the group's charitable efforts as well as its media empire is a mystery. Like the syncretic Qigong sects that emerged in the 1980s and 1990s, the organization adopted the structure of a business enterprise early on; in the wake of growing repression, some chapters may have continued to operate more openly as commercial organizations, concealing their relationship with the World Society. In January 2002, the State Security Defense Section of Wuhan reported that the manager of the Wuhan Zhongzhi Electric Testing Equipment Company used the company as a cover to "use business to support heresies" associated with Guanyin Famen/Quan Yin. The enterprise allegedly supported 30 practitioners and sect members who masqueraded as employees and business associates. Following an eight-month-long investigation, the manager of the enterprise was charged with using the company's offices and buildings as "retreat sites," organizing "initiations" and "screenings" to recruit members, and illegally printing and distributing more than 6,000 copies of "heretical texts."[42] He allegedly also established a "secret stronghold" in Hubei and set up branch companies in seven cities, including Guangzhou, Shenyang, and Chengdu. When apprehended, he had in his possession 1,410 "heretical publications" describing the "Quanyin Method," 290 audiovisual products, nine mimeograph machines, and a large quantity of unnamed "heretical objects."[43]

Although it is unlikely that such clandestine business activities in China are capable of generating significant wealth, the entrepreneurial orientation of the sect and its leader are apparent on the sect's main website, which links prominently to the "Celestial Shop," as well as the sect's publishing company. Items available for purchase through the website include a line of "Celestial" apparel and jewelry designed by the Supreme Master, and an assortment of other items that included, as of September 2006, "Supreme Kitchen Fortune Cookies: Food for the Soul," and a line of table lamps in six different designs (Enlightenment, Love, Vitality, Perfection, Heavenly Rain, and Cooling). She is rumored to have once sold her used sweat socks for $1,100 to one happy disciple, who defended the purchase by saying, "When the Master leaves the physical world, at least I will have her socks."[44]

The organization's extensive financial dealings became embroiled in political scandal following the Supreme Master's apparent attempt to seek transnational support. In 1995, with the government in China already shifting toward restricting new syncretic sects, the Suma Ching Hai International organization redoubled its efforts to mobilize resources across the globe. In one effort that backfired, the Supreme Master began encouraging her followers to "do all they could" to support then U.S. president Bill Clinton, who was facing legal challenges stemming from the Whitewater investigation. During a 1995 lecture tour, the Supreme Master ostensibly solicited checks and money orders totaling over $880,000. Charlie Yah Lin Trie, an Arkansas businessman and longtime friend of Clinton, who had visited the sect's main temple in central Taiwan and been initiated into the group, personally delivered the funds to the executive director of the Presidential Legal Defense Fund. However, the donations were refused when it was discovered that the bulk of them were made in sequentially numbered postal money orders, in the names of sect followers who apparently lacked the financial resources to make such sizable donations.[45] Investigators quickly determined that the handwriting on the checks and money orders was the same, and that the nominal donors had been reimbursed by Ng Lapseng, a tycoon from Macao and business partner of Charlie Trie.[46]

Instead of the desired boomerang of transnational support, these activities resulted in an extensive investigation and a congressional subpoena, as well as a welter of negative press about the Supreme Master and her financial dealings. Hailed by the Western press as the "Immaterial Girl: Part Buddha, Part Madonna," for her flamboyant dress, the "Buddhist Martha . . . [a] merchandizing mystic from Taiwan," and "God, Inc.," Suma Ching Hai quickly became the object of a media frenzy.[47] In the end, the backfire reverberated for well over a year, and deepened popular suspicions regarding the fundraising practices of the Clinton administration. The Supreme Master's disastrous attempt to garner transnational support for herself and her followers culminated in a campaign finance scandal involving individuals with links to organized crime in Asia and at least one Chinese official who channeled large sums of money to the Democratic National Committee.[48]

International Zhong Gong Headquarters, Inc.

One the most popular syncretic Qigong sects of the 1980s and 1990s, Zhong Gong was established in 1988 by Zhang Hongbao, a former commander of a local militia and local-level party cadre from rural Heilongjiang who returned to school to study economic management in Beijing. On completing his studies, Zhang established the Haidian Qigong Science Research Institute and a Chinese-American joint venture enterprise, the Beijing International Qigong Service Company, and began to publicly promote what he called Zhonghua Yangsheng Yizhi Gong (Zhong Gong) or Practice of Life Preservation and Wisdom Accretion.

His two organizations formed the foundation of what eventually became an impressive set of interlocked enterprises, the engine of which was a Qigong practice. In the aftermath of the 1989 Tiananmen Square demonstrations, Zhang retreated to a remote base area in Sichuan, where he reorganized his followers as employees of a sprawling web of private enterprises owned by a parent firm, the Qilin Group. When a Beijing daily reported that his Beijing-based International Qigong Service Enterprise had been shut down pending an investigation into possible criminal activities, Zhang hired the team of lawyers who had defended Mao's widow during the Gang of Four trial and wrested a public apology from the paper. A five-year string of unsuccessful legal actions against the government followed, during which Zhang nonetheless managed to elude arrest.[49]

Overtly political and distinctly entrepreneurial, the Zhong Gong grew from Zhang's assertion that the realms of thought and matter existed in dialectical tension. Zhang proposed that "the power of thought" (*yinianli*) has a quantifiable material existence that, properly tapped, is capable of transforming common yang-realm matter.[50] At its height, Zhang Hongbao's enterprise group administered a diversified network of entities, including over 3,000 schools and nearly 100,000 training offices; Taiweike, a health products company that marketed mineral water, yoga clothing, meditation cushions, and textbooks; eight resorts, with hotels, stores, car rental businesses, restaurants, and on-site security services; six travel agencies; a scientific research institute with several affiliated hospitals; and a set of specialized educational institutions that included the Chongqing International Life Science Technology University, Traditional Chinese Culture University, a medical school, and associated elementary, junior high, and senior high schools.[51] A January 2000 report estimated that Zhong Gong–linked enterprises employed 400,000 people in all.[52]

In response to the July 1999 ban on "heretical sects," Zhang Hongbao launched a campaign called Action 99-8 campaign, so-named because he and his followers staged protests throughout August 1999. In this campaign, he encouraged his followers to distribute texts accusing Jiang Zemin of pursuing "stability above all" in order to perpetuate his own power at all costs. Shortly thereafter, Zhang and an associate escaped to Thailand, and then traveled on to Guam, where both applied for political asylum in the United States. Attempting to garner transnational support and international media attention, Zhang launched a hunger strike from a detention center in Guam and won

the backing of several overseas Chinese dissident organizations, including the Free China Movement, the Chinese Democracy Party,
and the Joint Conference of Chinese Overseas Democracy Movement.[53] After being granted political asylum, Zhang and his associate
used $2 million from Zhong Gong–affiliated enterprises to establish
the Chinese Anti–Political Persecution Alliance, vowing to push for
the release of political dissidents from mainland Chinese jails. On
March 3, 2003, the alliance composed a letter of appeal, addressed to
the National People's Congress and Chinese People's Political Consultative Conference, calling for an end to political persecution in
China. On the same date, International Zhong Gong Headquarters
submitted a petition to the same two bodies demanding the immediate release of all detained Zhong Gong practitioners and the return
of all confiscated properties to International Zhong Gong Headquarters, with an estimated value of 800 million yuan ($96.6 million).

The earliest Zhong Gong websites appeared in 2000; they initially
served either as electronic bulletin boards frequented largely by
movement representatives or as repositories for the writings of Zhang
Hongbao. Following the founding of the Chinese Anti–Political Persecution Alliance, however, the website content diversified to include
more information about overseas Chinese dissident networks and activities, and links to human rights groups. In November 2002, Zhang
announced the formation of the China Shadow Government, based
in Washington, D.C.: "an enterprising group engaged in political culture" that proposed "to run a political operation as a business administration."[54] By 2004, the group's main website offered mirroring sites
in six different languages. Information posted on the group's current
website details a complex legal and financial struggle within the
Zhong Gong organization that originated, in part, from the removal
of $1.5 million out of the Chinese Anti–Political Persecution Alliance
by a former associate of Zhang. Zhang was further beset by criminal
charges filed by his housekeeper, who accused him of beating her
and locking her in a room because he believed she was mismanaging
workers who were completing construction on his Pasadena home.[55]

By 2003, the group's chief website was increasingly dominated by
news of Zhang's mounting legal troubles and the deterioration of
his personal relationship with his former associate. Facing more than
20 separate lawsuits, in April Zhang Hongbao again dipped into

Zhong Gong funds to form the China Federation Foundation, with dissident Peng Ming at the helm. However, their attempt to mobilize the broader community of overseas dissidents backfired when Peng Ming described the China Federation Foundation to an Associated Press reporter as an organization that "seeks the forceful overthrow of China's communist government and establishment of a democracy."[56] Peng's remarks provoked a bitter split in the overseas Chinese dissident community in North America, prompting members of the China Support Network to publicly denounce Peng as a "stray extremist" and the new China Federation Foundation a "discredited splinter group that is without a reputation or a track record."[57] This clash plunged Zhang Hongbao and his associates into a new wave of crossclaims and countersuits involving various members of the Chinese Anti–Political Persecution Alliance, the China Federation Foundation, and the Free China Movement.[58] A year later, Peng Ming was arrested by Myanmar police, extradited, and tried in China for having established and operated a terrorist training base, and for organizing kidnappings in Wuhan, Changsha, and Beijing to fund his operations. He was subsequently sentenced to life in prison.[59]

On July 31, 2006, while scouting locations for a new base in Arizona, Zhang Hongbao was killed when his car was struck by a tractor trailer. An official announcement appeared on the website exactly one month later. Within days, a coalition of his organizations announced the formation of a committee to investigate "the truth of the accident," but other central players in the overseas democracy movement wondered whether Zhang's death might trigger a backlash of fractious squabbles within the activist community over Zhang's assets and legacy.[60] A September 7 *Epoch Times* article suggested that Zhang, who once served as a senior consultant to the Chinese military, may have been murdered by party agents for disclosing Chinese military secrets.[61]

Falun Dafa

Li Hongzhi, a former trumpet player in the People's Liberation Army and a clerk at a cereals processing factory in Changchun, began his involvement with the Qigong movement as a follower of Li Weidong's Chanmi Gong in 1988. He then studied Yu Guangshen's Jiugong

Bagua Gong, a Qigong practice similar to the one Li subsequently introduced to the public in 1992.[62] Word of the practice began to spread, first in Changchun and outlying areas. The following year, Li and a handful of disciples attended the second Oriental Health Expo in Beijing, where they offered on-the-spot diagnosis and treatment. Li later recounted that his treatments proved so effective that the Falun Gong booth was soon swamped with people. The organizer of the event described Li Hongzhi as "the most popular Qigong master" at the Expo and bestowed the highest honor of the event, the Advancing Marginal Sciences Award, on Falun Gong.[63] By 1996, it claimed millions of followers throughout mainland China.

Like other Qigong sects of the 1980s and 1990s, Falun Gong was initially tolerated and even sanctioned by Chinese authorities, and maintained linkages with various state- and party-connected organizations and enterprises. Li's Beijing-based Falun Dafa Research Society registered with the China Qigong Research Society. Initially, beneath the umbrella of the research society, "main stations" were founded at the provincial, region, and municipal levels, with subordinate guidance stations established at the county level and in urban districts within cities. At the lowest level, practice sites and study groups were established in groups of villages in rural areas and housing and work units in cities. This organizational structure was not dissimilar to those of other large, nationwide Qigong sects, like Zhong Gong; however, early on in their institutional history, Falun Gong organizations channeled considerable administrative and material resources toward public relations and media management. The Beijing headquarters supervised a translation committee, a material service committee that managed document distribution, and various liaison personnel who responded to questions concerning doctrinal and practical meditation techniques. The main stations, located in Beijing and Shanghai, also had three functional committees that oversaw doctrine and method, logistics and operations, and propaganda. The earliest main station, established in Changchun by Li Hongzhi himself, was organized into two divisions and one office in late 1993. The duties of the Changchun General Office included liaising with outside organizations, disseminating directives from the main station committee, and receiving, managing and distributing Falun Gong publications and paraphernalia.[64]

Clearly, in sheer economic terms, Falun Gong was enormously successful in mainland China. Li's magnum opus, *Zhuan Falun* (Turn the dharma wheel), became a runaway bestseller by 1996. Official Chinese sources maintain that from 1992 to 1994, Li Hongzhi personally collected at least 1.78 million yuan in seminar fees; however, Falun Gong activists hasten to point out that the China Qigong Scientific Research Society and their local branches that hosted the training seminars received 40 percent of the admission receipts.[65] When Chinese authorities banned Falun Gong publications in 1996, sales continued underground through agents purportedly authorized by Li himself. For example, between the imposition of the 1996 ban and April 1999, the director of Falun Gong's Wuhan chapter purportedly sold millions of Falun Gong books and audiovisual products, as well as tens of thousands of exercise accessories, badges, pictures, posters, and banners, with sales totaling an estimated $11 million.[66]

This financial success—much of which enriched individuals and groups outside of the sect, as well as those within—afforded considerable leverage to Falun Gong activists intent on protecting the group's reputation. As is well known, between April 1998 and mid-1999, Falun Gong practitioners initiated more than 300 actions, frequently involving more than 1,000 participants, protesting negative media representation. Strategies ranged from doing Falun Gong exercises in front of news organizations to harassing editors and reporters, by phone or in person in their places of work or homes.[67] Not infrequently, these tactics worked. When He Zuoxiu, a member of the prestigious Chinese Academy of Sciences and Falun Gong's chief critic in Beijing, sought to publish an article entitled "I Do Not Approve of Teenagers Practicing Qigong," the only venue he could find was a popular science journal affiliated with Tianjin Normal University.[68] Nevertheless, in the week that followed, literally thousands of practitioners descended on the offices both of the publication and the Tianjin municipal government, leading to a spate of arrests. Before the Tianjin incident had been resolved, over 10,000 Falun Gong activists gathered in front of Zhongnanhai, the gated residential compound of the Beijing elite, shortly before dawn on April 25, 1999. The demonstration, the largest such public gathering since the crackdown of June 4, 1989, continued for 13 hours and led the authorities to initiate more serious measures to contain and then eliminate the group.[69]

Foreign media reported the April 25 demonstration and smaller, scattered protests that followed the July 1999 ban on "evil heretical sects," but coverage dwindled afterward. Falun Gong practitioners and activists have engaged in a variety of activities designed to keep the group's name and plight in the international media. In response to "media fatigue," activists have taken to staging news conferences and protest spectacles in major U.S. cities. In addition, practitioners in the United States have pursued Chinese officials, for example, filing civil actions against former Beijing mayor Liu Qi and Xia Deren, deputy governor of Liaoning, seeking compensation for violations of international law, and publicly confronted Chinese officials visiting overseas, as when *Epoch Times* reporter Wang Wenyi heckled President Hu Jintao for three minutes during a 2006 White House appearance.[70] Other recent attempts to garner media attention have included an unsuccessful letter-writing campaign to have Li Hongzhi nominated for the Nobel Peace Prize, and numerous efforts to encourage local authorities in the United States to declare "Falun Dafa" or "Li Hongzhi" days. Such activities have resulted in some media coverage and have kept Falun Gong at least on the edges of the public radar screen in the West.

However, motivated by both the difficulty of obtaining regular access to foreign media and its concerns that Chinese authorities have been extending their control over Chinese language media outlets abroad, the Falun Dafa organization has established its own web of media outlets.[71] These include World Falun Dafa Radio, which broadcasts shortwave radio programming that is capable of reaching central and northern China, and Fang Guangming TV, a television station also established in 2001 that broadcasts by satellite from Los Angeles. In February 2002, Falun Gong supporters established New York-based New Tang Dynasty Television, which broadcasts via satellite 24 hours a day. In March 2004, New Tang began beaming unencrypted programming via two new satellites into Asia and Europe. Relying on members across the globe to serve as unsalaried producers and stringers, both outlets feature stories related to Falun Gong activities worldwide, as well as news, music, and other types of programming. In February 2002, Falun Gong activists hacked into the television cables serving the northeastern city of Anshan and managed to broadcast for several minutes. A few weeks later, activists in

Changchun apparently hacked into that city's cable network and broadcast nearly 20 minutes of video footage from a documentary by Fang Guangming that casts doubt on official Chinese accounts of a self-immolation incident.[72] The New York–based *Epoch Times* was established in August 2000; the newspaper's website (www.epochtimes .com) and the Epoch Times group of newspapers quickly became one of the most popular Chinese-language news websites available, and with its free local editions in more than 30 states, one of the largest overseas Chinese news outlets in the world. Local franchises choose content from the *Epoch Times* website, which offers coverage of Falun Gong–related activities and events, and add local material. While both New Tang and the *Epoch Times* publicly deny being Falun Gong–related media, tax records reveal that top Falun Gong spokesmen serve as either directors or as chairmen of the board.[73] Nonetheless, the corporate director of the English-language edition of the *Epoch Times*, Levi Browde, recently said that characterizations of such media organizations as mere mouthpieces of Falun Gong are not merely inaccurate but assist the CCP in preventing reporters from attending events to which they have been invited.[74]

Yet incidents like the April 2006 heckling of Hu Jintao by an *Epoch Times* reporter who was issued a one-day press pass, casts doubt on such claims. An *Epoch Times* spokesperson described the reporter as a medical doctor who was "very overstressed" by her work on a series of articles related to organ harvesting.[75] The tirade succeeded in raising the media profile of a story that the *Epoch Times* had begun reporting the month before, that of the alleged existence of a concentration camp for Falun Gong practitioners that routinely harvested and sold the organs of inmates. Shortly after a former Chinese journalist working for a television station in Japan proclaimed the camp's existence, Falun Gong representatives pressed U.S. State Department officials to investigate. Two teams of American officials visited the facility on two occasions, once unannounced, but "found no evidence" that the site was anything other than "a normal public hospital."[76] Amnesty International and United Nations officials have also been asked to investigate. A eight-week-long investigation conducted by two prominent Canadian officials who were not granted visas to enter China concluded that the allegations were most likely true.[77] However, veteran dissident Harry Wu, who spent 15 years gathering evidence on the harvesting of organs from executed Chinese prisoners, publicly expressed his suspicions that the claims were fabricated, based on the testimony of only two witnesses, neither of whom was reliable.[78] Wu has since released an essay detailing his experiences investigating the Falun Gong death camp claims in which he describes being threatened by senior Falun Gong representatives who counseled him to keep his reservations to himself.[79] Rather than heed this advice, Wu shared his concerns in writing with a member of the U.S. Congress, whose staff leaked the letter to high-ranking Falun Gong representatives in the United States. Shortly thereafter, Falun Gong–related media outlets, including Secret China and the *Epoch Times,* began a coordinated smear campaign against Harry Wu, publishing accusations that he was a "butcher," a "Chinese Communist senior-level spy," and had "betrayed his conscience and the conscience of the Chinese people" in order to secure his own release from a Chinese prison in 1995.[80]

In May 2006, the outspoken dissident and former Beijing University journalism professor Jiao Guobiao published an essay in the overseas Chinese *Apple Daily (Pingguo Ribao)* entitled "Breaking through the Mainland Internet Blockade," in which he lauded the unbalanced and highly partisan journalistic tactics of Falun Gong–related media like Radio Free Asia. Arguing that there is no attempt at balance on the mainland, Jiao proposed that even if Falun Gong outlets published only negative information highly critical of the CCP, the weight of their attacks could never begin to counterbalance the positive propaganda the party publishes about itself. To a Radio Free Asia reporter who claimed that the Falun Gong media were viewed with contempt by the Washington press corps because of lack of balance, Jiao retorted that the Washington press corps was comprised of "dogmatists" and "pedants who don't understand China" or the principle of journalistic "balance": "What the mainland Chinese public lacks is negative information about mainland China. . . . Balance does not mean that all media entities have to achieve a God-like balance, but that the media can balance the principles of freedom, equality and legality together. . . . Balance is the result of the collective imbalances of all."[81]

Boomerang, Backfire, or Spectacle?

The widespread availability of new technologies like the internet has transformed contentious claims making, not only by reducing costs and increasing the reliability of communications across geographical and temporal barriers but also by spawning new organizational forms. The web-based digital tools that enable internet users to access text, audio, visual, and other forms of information in an encompassing, interactive environment have forged transnational communities that share quasi-spiritual practices and common political agendas. The transnational cybersects described in the preceding pages began as syncretic Qigong sects targeted for elimination but now participate to varying degrees in complex digital ecologies that incorporate the internet, websites, electronic bulletin boards, email, and SMS (short message service) messaging, all of which allow participants to communicate in entirely new ways. At the core of these advances in recombinant communication technology is a new dynamic, which Bach and Stark have called "link, search and interact," that permits users to "link social structures (who knows who) and knowledge networks (who knows what)."[82] The vehicle of interactive digital media has brought together pockets of underground Qigong practitioners with their exiled leaders and new chapters formed abroad, and linked shared grievances to those of other overseas Chinese dissidents in a manner that would not have been possible only a few decades ago. The role of the internet and other new communication technologies in shifting the scale of these collective grievances cannot be understated. Underground practitioners within China share information about the extent and nature of repression with those based abroad. Overseas supporters provide funding, lobby NGOs and other transnational activists, and actively court international media attention in hopes of triggering a "boomerang" effect that could affect domestic reforms.

However, beneath the impressive façade of elaborately designed websites, rousing political manifestoes, and vast webrings (a collection of websites joined together, generally with a common navigation bar), lurks the troubling question of how to assess the operational strength and credibility of network linkages forged in virtual environments. If the internet is capable of providing resource-poor groups and actors with a virtual soapbox from which to trumpet their respective causes, it is equally capable of spinning vast webs that are more virtual than real, an endless parade of "dot-causes" that deploy "credibility-enhancing tactics" in a competitive struggle for the media spotlight.[83] The brave new world of "global civil society," as Bob notes, is a "Darwinian arena in which the successful prosper but the weak wither."[84] The most successful cybersects have evolved into multinational conglomerates that incorporate media enterprises, public relations firms, and commercial operations beneath an umbrella of shifting entrepreneurial and spiritual interests. Yet along with the partisan news reports and promotional information they provide, these transnational media machines have navigated—sometimes poorly—a narrow course between marketing their local rebellions and becoming subject to the dissecting lenses of the mass media and the general public. All too often, rather than triggering "boomerangs" of transnational support, their promotional strategies have backfired, bringing a hail of negative press, inflaming internecine rivalries, and inviting charges of misrepresentation from the very audiences they seek to cultivate. In such incidents, the negative fallout has threatened to affect not only core members but also transnational dissident networks, NGO activists, and politicians who have lent their support.

Potentially more disturbing is the insight that these media machines, originally designed to communicate movement goals both within and outside the movement, are equally capable of engineering spectacles of protest, manufacturing virtual dissent that amplifies the impact of extremist views held by relatively small constituencies, and spinning vast conspiracy theories. As Stewart has noted, "the Internet was made for conspiracy theory: it *is* a conspiracy theory: one thing leads to another, always another link leading you deeper into no thing and no place."[85] Nor are such phenomena restricted to Chinese cybersects: alternative digitally based media have emerged as one of the defining reportorial hallmarks of popular contention in the information age. In March 2002, the Italian branch of the alternative media outlet Indymedia organized a march entitled Reclaim Your Media, cosponsored by Radio Onda Rossa. The demonstration's placards bore the slogan "Don't hate the media! Become the media!"[86]

In an era in which all subjects of struggle also strive to become subjects of information, it becomes increasingly difficult to divine the boundaries between the representation of dissent and actual measurable popular support. The advent of the so-called information age has brought an explosion of "manufactured dissent" in a variety of forms, including the creation and sponsorship of faux "grassroots" campaigns by government and corporate actors seeking to protect their interests.[87] Pseudo-consumer rights groups have been fabricated by powerful lobbyists acting on behalf of well-heeled clients.[88] And fake international NGOs have been established with invented histories of conferences, reports, and proposals.[89] The ease with which the internet permits users to fashion virtual identities has given rise to a host of collective disinformation strategies, including "astroturfing" (efforts by a small group of activists or actors to convey the impression that a particular agenda is supported by a grassroots movement), "sock-puppeting" (the activation of multiple separate user accounts by an existing registered member of a virtual community), and even "wikiturfing" (posting a Wikipedia entry for a particular organization, catchphrase, or activity to suggest that it has already attained a level of broad recognition).[90] The deployment of these and similar tactics in online activism confounds the efforts of even the most astute observers of contentious politics to discern the differences between genuine and manufactured forms of dissent and between mainstream and marginal activism.

Yet this problem, too, is not entirely new in the study of social movements. As Tilly has noted, the image of a social movement as a permanent and stable group with a collective commitment to a unitary political agenda has always been an exercise in "mystification." "In real social movements, involvement ebbs and flows, coalitions form and dissolve, fictitious organizations loom up and fade away, would-be leaders compete for recognition as the representatives of unorganized constituencies, leaders make deals with police and politicians." Movement leaders and entrepreneurs generally "seek to control and disguise" internal divisions and shifting levels of popular support for their particular agendas. The dilemma this poses for students of social movements, Tilly observes, is whether to "follow the interest, the population, the belief, or the program" to understand and evaluate a trajectory of contention.[91]

As in the cases of the three Chinese cybersects I have discussed, more often than not, the internet proves an uncannily effective medium for making such claims appear credible, by seeming to link broad coalitions of actors behind a virtual united front, and amplifying the impact that smaller and marginal groups have on the political process. For these groups, cyberspace offers new possibilities for framing and pressing transnational collective claims in the face of repression at home, but, because of the heterarchical participation it inspires, does so at enhanced risk of scrutiny by movement activists, mainstream participants, and erstwhile transnational supporters. Virtual reality therefore provides fertile new ground for testing theories of contentious politics, but not one entirely unrelated to the problems and dynamics that shape earlier forms of mobilization.

10 | Permanent Rebellion? Continuities and Discontinuities in Chinese Protest

Writing in the 1850s, in the midst of the tumultuous Taiping Uprising, the English sinologist Thomas Taylor Meadows opined that "of all nations that have attained a certain degree of civilization, the Chinese are the least revolutionary and the most rebellious."[1] Although Meadows was struck by the extraordinary record of popular unrest throughout the two-millennium history of imperial China, culminating with the Taipings, he saw this protest as directed toward replacing particular rulers (rebellion) rather than reconstituting the entire political system (revolution). As he explained the distinction, "revolutionary movements are against principles, rebellions against men . . . there has been but one great political revolution in China, when the centralized form of government was substituted for the feudal, about 2,000 years ago."[2]

Later generations of scholars would debate the question of whether the Taipings that so absorbed Meadows's attention were better understood as rebels or as revolutionaries.[3] But no one could deny that China later underwent a series of momentous revolutions: Sun Yat-sen's Revolution of 1911, which toppled the 2,000-year-old imperial system; Chiang Kai-shek's Revolution of 1927, which routed the warlords and unified the country; and Mao Zedong's Revolution of 1949, which expelled the Nationalists and established the People's Republic of China. Some would even include Mao's "Great Proletarian Cultural Revolution" of 1966–1976 and Deng Xiaoping's "Opening and Reform" of 1979–1989 on the list of "revolutions" that fundamentally altered China's political principles.[4]

Today China is again gripped by all manner of popular protest. Like rebels of yore, contemporary protesters often aim their fire at individual officials—especially grassroots cadres who are blamed for excessive peasant burdens, illegal land sales, and other forms of egregious misrule. And unlike China's twentieth-century revolutionaries, current Chinese protesters generally refrain from attacking the political system as a whole.

The Limits of Contemporary Protest

Analysts of the contemporary Chinese scene, like Thomas Meadows in his day, are struck by the limited nature of the rampant protest they observe. Perry and Selden, in an earlier volume on conflict in China, stress that "for all the popular anguish and the variety and depth of contemporary protest, to date no significant organizational focus, whether enshrined in a political party or social movement, has emerged at the national, regional or even local level to challenge Communist Party leadership."[5] The authors of a study of recent tax protests in the Chinese countryside attribute their unrevolutionary character to the absence of crossregional and crossclass connections: "the literature on revolution emphasizes the forging of urban-rural linkages as a key to success. In the Chinese Communist revolution, urban intellectuals and students went to the countryside to mobilize peasants, providing leadership, organization, coordination, and a vision that linked parochial rural grievances to broader, national, and even international goals. Such links were absent in the 1990s."[6]

Despite its remarkable frequency, then, contention in contemporary China remains limited in size, scale, and scope. With few exceptions, the social composition, territorial reach, and endurance of individual protests have all been highly circumscribed. Even the notable exceptions, for example the student movement of 1989 or the Falun Gong demonstrations of 1999, have raised only modest demands—seeking greater inclusion and recognition from the party-state authorities, rather than clamoring for an end to the communist system. Should we therefore conclude, a la Meadows, that China (following an aberrant twentieth-century detour) is once again "the least revolutionary and the most rebellious" nation on earth?

To be sure, there are many similarities between contemporary Chinese protests and earlier patterns of rebellion. The vegetarianism and meditation regimens of new quasi-religious groups, described by Patricia Thornton (chapter 9), for example, recall the practices of many rebellious sects in centuries past.[7] Even their transnational linkages have precedents in the redemptive societies of an earlier era.[8] The taxi drivers protesting municipal licensing regulations, discussed by Yongshun Cai (chapter 8), bear more than a passing resemblance to the feisty rickshaw pullers of Republican-period Beijing.[9] The petitioning of higher-level officials and visits to the capital undertaken by disgruntled workers and environmentalists (as well as by their opponents), noted by Feng Chen (chapter 4) and Yanfei Sun and Dingxin Zhao (chapter 7), can be connected to a long tradition of Chinese remonstrance.[10] The use of cultural performances as recruitment sites for contemporary Christians, discussed by Carsten Vala and Kevin O'Brien (chapter 5), is reminiscent of the catalytic role of local operas and temple fairs in the emergence of the Boxer Uprising.[11] The striking regional differences in protest culture and orientation, observed by William Hurst (chapter 3), have long fascinated students of "traditional" Chinese rebellion as well.[12] One could go on at some length in this vein, highlighting numerous continuities in protest patterns from imperial times to the present.

When we move beyond surface analogies to plumb the deeper political ramifications of contemporary Chinese protest, however, the differences with earlier prototypes—rebellious and revolutionary alike—become readily apparent.[13] Even if the rebellions that attracted Meadows's attention were primarily intended to replace the ruling elite rather than to overhaul basic political principles, their consequences were often monumental. The massive Red Turban Army of the mid–fourteenth century, inspired by White Lotus millenarianism and led by the peasant rebel Zhu Yuanzhang, routed the Mongol Yuan Dynasty and replaced it with the Han Chinese Ming Dynasty.[14] The mid-nineteenth-century quasi-Christian Taipings, although eventually vanquished, nevertheless mobilized millions of followers, established their own "Heavenly Capital" in Nanjing, and for a decade exercised control over a large portion of the Chinese heartland. The

Taiping upheaval proved to be the costliest civil war in world history, resulting in the deaths of some 25 million people. Its bloody suppression contributed to a major devolution of state power in late imperial China, a development that paved the way for the Republican Revolution of 1911.[15]

The weak and decentralized polity that emerged from that revolution, combined with new cultural and ideological influences from abroad, generated a vibrant civic awareness and activism that some scholars have characterized as a Chinese "public sphere" or "civil society."[16] However we choose to characterize the Republican era, it was unquestionably a time of extraordinary political ferment. The CCP, born in the midst of this upheaval, took advantage of state weakness to forge new alliances among previously separated social elements. Under the banner of Chinese nationalism, communist revolutionaries built a powerful movement that included intellectuals, workers, peasants, and national bourgeoisie. During the Japanese invasion (1937–1945), the communists' Red Army recruited more than a million men to defend the homeland.[17] More important, they constructed rural base areas across the countryside, infiltrated labor unions in all the major cities, and established crossclass patriotic associations that set the organizational stage for their rapid victory in the civil war against the Nationalists (1945–1949).[18] Today's scattered protests obviously do not begin to approach these imperial or Republican precedents in terms of either ambition or outcomes.

The Maoist Imprint

Why the difference? The primary answer lies in the fundamental restructuring of state-society relations that took place on the heels of the communist revolution, in the early years of Mao Zedong's rule. Having discovered firsthand the recipe for revolutionary success, which involved mixing previously isolated social elements, Mao lost little time in ensuring that his formula would not be repeated. In less than a decade after the founding of the People's Republic in 1949, agriculture had been collectivized, industry nationalized, severe mobility restrictions imposed on the entire population, and a variety of highly effective political controls instituted down to the grassroots level. These political controls included the assignment of class labels (which operated as caste-like designations passed down from one generation to the next), the implementation of household registration and personnel dossiers (which facilitated police surveillance and limited both geographical and political movement), and the frequent convening of political study groups, criticism sessions, mass campaigns, and other state-directed activities that demanded whole-hearted—yet segregated and orchestrated—participation from all citizens.[19]

It was not that Mao sought to end mass involvement in political demonstrations; quite the opposite. The stringent controls of the Maoist era did not inhibit the Chinese populace from engaging in periodic, widespread, and occasionally very large-scale expressions of militancy. Chairman Mao's incendiary injunctions to "let a hundred flowers bloom," "bombard the headquarters," and "carry on the revolution" helped inspire an impressive level of popular activism. Encouraged by Mao's insistence that "to rebel is justified," the resulting protests sometimes exceeded his own expectations and desires. In short, this was hardly a "totalitarian" system in which overweening state power atomized and paralyzed society, rendering its members incapable of independent collective action. On the contrary, frequent popular action—sometimes going beyond the confines of state-directed limits—was a distinctive feature of Mao's China.[20]

The same Maoist institutions that divided the populace by work unit, class label, residential category, record of political activism, and the like served also as lines of mobilization (and demobilization) in times of political ferment. Huge as the mass movements of Mao's day were, their internal organization tended to replicate state-imposed cleavages. In the Hundred Flowers Movement of 1956–1957, for example, intellectuals and workers were both active in voicing criticisms of "bureaucratism," but their protests remained notably isolated from each other, with students and teachers generally remaining on their own university campuses and workers in their own factories. Occupational and territorial segregation was further reinforced in the "Anti-Rightist" suppression campaign that followed, when the state meted out different punishments to campus and factory dissidents.[21] A similar pattern can be seen toward the close of the Maoist period, during the April Fifth Movement of 1976, when participation was again clearly segmented along lines of *danwei* (state work units).

As the political scientist Sebastian Heilmann observes of this historic protest against the radical excesses of the Cultural Revolution, "it was the work units that served as centers of coordination and self-organization during the April Fifth Movement, which simultaneously revealed the dilemma of *danwei*-based 'cellular protest': mobilization was facilitated by easy communication within the *danwei,* but the establishment of more comprehensive organizational forms was impeded by its segregation from society at large."[22]

The dual effect of Maoist institutions—at once energizing and isolating—is apparent in contemporary protest patterns as well.[23] Thus Feng Chen (chapter 4) notes that today's labor disputes, while widespread and increasing in frequency, are almost always confined to workers at a single factory. The contrast with the precommunist era, before the imposition of the *danwei* system, is stark. During the May Thirtieth Movement of 1925, for example, the city of Shanghai was paralyzed by strikes that occurred simultaneously at more than 100 factories.[24] That general strike, coordinated by politicized young intellectuals (in both the Communist and Nationalist parties) and sustained financially by generous contributions from the Shanghai Chamber of Commerce, drew its strength not only from the participation of factory workers but also that of students, businessmen, and the general public.[25] These days, as Chen emphasizes, workers seldom enjoy the benefit of alliances with intellectuals. Even during the "democracy" protests of 1989, Teresa Wright reminds us (chapter 1), students self-consciously isolated themselves from other elements of society in order to reduce the likelihood of repression.

Despite considerable journalistic and scholarly attention to the reemergence of "civil society" in post-Mao China, social organizations remain highly constrained.[26] Autonomous labor unions, peasant associations, and student associations—to say nothing of political parties—are illegal, and the various NGOs that have excited so much interest among foreign observers are hamstrung by strict government regulations. Again the contrast with the *pre*-Maoist era is instructive, in that the communists' revolutionary drive to power in the 1920s–1940s was fueled by precisely these kinds of independent and overlapping organizations.[27]

Continuities with the Maoist period are ideational and behavioral, as well as organizational. What scholars call collective action frames and protest repertoires adopted by today's protesters reveal the indelible imprint of the preceding era.[28] Protests by the downtrodden, discussed in the chapters by Yongshun Cai, Guobin Yang, and William Hurst among others, often employ anachronistic Maoist language of egalitarianism and class struggle. The actions as well as the words of these protesters recall scenes from the Cultural Revolution. For example, the blocking of transportation routes, highlighted by Cai (chapter 8), is reminiscent of the famous Anting Incident of November 1966, when radical workers from Shanghai made a (successful) bid for the central government's attention and support in their rebellion against municipal authorities.[29]

Present-day parallels to Mao's Cultural Revolution are hardly accidental. As Chen points out (chapter 4), contemporary labor leaders learned their protest methods in the course of the struggles of that tumultuous decade. And such continuities extend beyond the realm of labor disputes. Many of the most influential intellectuals in the 1989 "democracy movement" cut their political teeth as Red Guards in the mid-1960s.[30] The special role of trusted friendships in facilitating protest under authoritarian conditions, underscored in Wright's analysis of the 1989 movement (chapter 1), was a prominent feature of Red Guard factionalism as well.[31] In short, the mass campaigns of Mao's day served as a kind of basic training camp—in tactics and in battle slogans—for subsequent expressions of dissent.

Of course, protesters are not the only people to have gleaned valuable lessons from the Maoist past. Government leaders, mindful of the CCP's own revolutionary history, are well aware of the continued benefits of maintaining state control of the divisive institutions and repressive tactics introduced during Mao's rule. Although Maoist institutions have undergone substantial transformation in the reform era, earlier practices retain significant power.[32] Today, for example, urban registrations may be purchased by the well-to-do as well as inherited, but they remain a crucial means for gaining access to educational opportunity. Jobs are now often procured via market mechanisms rather than by state fiat, yet personnel dossiers continue to play a role in promotions, sensitive assignments, and the like. In other words, the state still wields key levers for dividing and ruling the populace, in ordinary times and in moments of crisis.[33]

New Features of Contemporary Protest

Recent years have also witnessed significant departures from earlier patterns. Some of these developments have clear parallels in pre-Maoist patterns of popular protest; others are quite unprecedented.

Perhaps the most obvious new feature of contemporary protest is the use of cutting-edge electronic technology to facilitate communications among protesters, as well as to publicize their plight to prospective supporters in the media and international community. Fax machines, cell phones, text messaging, camcorders, email, websites, and the like provide effective new weapons in the protesters' arsenal (see chapters 6, 8, and 9). These means of communication are not only instantaneous, but also allow dissidents to bypass state-designated geographical and occupational barriers "virtually." Having witnessed the power of internet technology to assemble with lightning speed a surprisingly heterogeneous gathering of Falun Gong demonstrators in April 1999, public security agencies are investing considerable energy in maintaining tight control over these potentially subversive media.[34] Yet this is surely a Sisyphean struggle. These technologies that allow protesters to network swiftly and effectively at home and abroad present a significant transnational challenge for the state security system.

Another new feature is the prominent role played by lawyers in framing protesters' grievances. Once decried as bourgeois elements, professional lawyers virtually disappeared in Mao's China.[35] The rapid resurgence of the legal profession in recent years, together with the post-Mao state's vigorous efforts to promote public obedience to laws and regulations, has encouraged new alliances between protesters and legal specialists. Human rights lawyers (a number of whom are recent converts to Christianity) have been responsible for persuading protesters to frame their economic grievances as a matter of "rights protection" *(weiquan)*. The result in some instances has been a dramatic escalation of demands as well as rhetoric.[36] In March 2006, the standing committee of the All-China Lawyers' Association (a government-approved agency) adopted new regulations designed to restrict lawyers' involvement in popular protests. These guidelines require lawyers who accept "mass cases" (i.e., those involving 10 or more plaintiffs) to submit to close government supervision, and warn lawyers against collecting mass petitions or discussing cases with overseas organizations or the media.[37]

The participation of intellectuals (such as human rights lawyers) in the protests of farmers or workers is especially worrisome to the Chinese authorities, aware as they are of the explosive role that cross-class coalitions played in their own revolutionary history. But it is difficult to bar professional lawyers from involvement in such cases at the same time that the state trumpets the importance of processing grievances through legal channels. And lawyers are not the only intellectuals entering the fray these days. Sun and Zhao (chapter 7) point to the leadership of "celebrity intellectuals" in China's growing environmental movement; protests against pollution and other ill effects of unbridled industrial growth are often instigated by journalists and other well-known intellectuals with substantial international connections.

Future Prospects: Rebellion or Revolution?

Although widespread concern and complaints about environmental degradation are a relatively recent phenomenon, the catalytic role of cosmopolitan intellectuals in stimulating popular protest in China is not. Sun Yat-sen's leadership of the 1911 Revolution or Chen Duxiu and Li Dazhao's founding of the Chinese Communist Party come readily to mind. The ties to Honolulu, Tokyo, Paris, and Moscow enjoyed by these earlier "celebrity intellectuals" provided crucial ideological and financial resources for mounting a revolutionary challenge to the Chinese state.[38]

While the scale of contemporary Chinese protest pales against the massive upheavals of the revolutionary (and rebellious) past, are there indications that the current unrest may harbor the seeds of a fatal threat to the communist political system? This question is of course impossible to answer with a high degree of confidence, inasmuch as successful revolutions not only require skillful leadership, appealing ideas, and conducive structural conditions; but also are the product of accidental triggers that cannot be predicted in advance.[39] The chapters in this volume point to a number of developments that could, over the long run, contribute to a revolutionary situation: increasing violence (on the part of state and society alike) (chapter 8);

new values (from Christianity to environmentalism) (chapter 5 and 7); a rise in transnational activism (chapter 9), and more. Even so, it seems safe to say that as long as the communist party-state retains its impressive capacity to fragment society in such a way that crossclass and crossterritorial coalitions remain difficult and dangerous to undertake, the likelihood of a serious revolutionary challenge from below is slim.

It is certainly conceivable that new advances in communications technology coupled with the escalating mobility of the population, both domestically and internationally, will eventually cripple the state's coercive controls. In that case, a precipitous decline in the economy or a sudden rise in religious or secessionist sentiment—among many other possible scenarios—could presage a revolutionary upsurge as unsettling as those that rocked China in the twentieth century. But absent a major deterioration in the state's ability to fragment its citizenry, popular protest actually may work to *extend*, rather than to extinguish, the lifespan of the regime.

Thomas Meadows offered the following explanation for the remarkable longevity of the imperial system: "In China . . . it is precisely the right to rebel that has been a chief element of a national stability, unparalleled in the world's history."[40] While one would be foolhardy to forecast for the current political order anything approaching the lifespan enjoyed by the imperial system, nevertheless it does appear that contemporary patterns of protest—still animated by a widespread appreciation of "the right to rebel"—are more system-supportive than system-subversive.[41]

Lacking elections and other democratic channels for conveying popular interests and grievances, protest in China provides valuable information to higher political authorities about pressing grassroots concerns.[42] Furthermore, the issues that motivate widespread protests sometimes lead to substantive policy reform. The central government's historic abolition of the 2,600-year-old agricultural tax in January 2006, for example, came in response to a raft of rural tax riots—sparked by local officials' imposition of "unfair burdens"—that had engulfed the inland provinces in the 1990s.[43] Similarly, the newly enacted property rights law, which establishes villagers' rights to the ownership and benefits of collective landholdings, is a reaction to the recent surge in violent land disputes—triggered by the sales of village lands by local officials—that have swept the coastal provinces.[44]

So long as higher authorities respond judiciously to these outpourings of popular discontent, directed for the most part against grassroots officials, China indeed seems poised to reclaim its ancient reputation as "the least revolutionary and the most rebellious" of nations. Rebellions "against men" encourage elite turnover, and thus may contribute to the invigoration and perpetuation of the extant political system.

If handled skillfully by state authorities, protests may even enhance regime legitimacy. Meadows believed that the frequent rebellions for which imperial China was renowned were an indication of popular *acceptance* of the political regime rather than of *alienation*. As he saw it, the imperial Chinese political system was to be understood not as despised "despotism" but as an "autocracy existing in virtue of the acquiescence of the people."[45] Here the parallel to the contemporary scene seems striking. Political scientist Andrew Nathan, a harsh critic of the regime, acknowledges that "one of the puzzles of the post-Tiananmen period has been the regime's apparent ability to rehabilitate its legitimacy (defined as the public's belief that the regime is lawful and should be obeyed). . . . There is much evidence from both quantitative and qualitative studies to suggest that expressions of dissatisfaction, including widely reported worker and peasant demonstrations, are usually directed at lower-level authorities, while the regime as a whole continues to enjoy high levels of acceptance."[46]

The genius of the Chinese political order—whether in imperial times, in Mao's day, or today—has been its capacity to sustain (and on occasion even to stimulate) massive popular protest without jeopardizing the fundamental underpinnings of the system. So long as Chinese popular protests target "men" rather than "principles," a revolutionary challenge to the legitimacy of the regime remains unlikely. Yet it seems appropriate to close this brief historical overview on a note of caution: it was, after all, just on the threshold of China's eventful revolutionary century that Meadows penned his treatise; historically grounded forecasts, in China as elsewhere, have a way of being overtaken by history itself.

Notes

Prologue

I am grateful to Kevin O'Brien, who inveigled me into taking part in the conference that led to this volume, and to Elizabeth Perry and Mark Selden for comments on an earlier version of this chapter. I also want to thank David S. Meyer, who shared my awkward dilemma of speaking about China to a room full of China specialists at that conference.

1. Lucien Bianco, *Origins of the Chinese Revolution* (Stanford, Calif.: Stanford University Press, 1967); Elizabeth J. Perry, *Rebels and Revolutionaries in North China, 1845–1945* (Stanford, Calif.: Stanford University Press, 1980); Mark Selden, *The Yenan Way in Revolutionary China* (Cambridge, Mass.: Harvard University Press, 1971).

2. Barrington Moore Jr., *The Social Origins of Dictatorship and Democracy: Lord and Peasant in the Making of the Modern World* (Boston: Beacon Press, 1966); Eric R. Wolf, *Peasant Wars of the Twentieth Century* (New York: Harper, 1971); Jack A. Goldstone, *Revolution and Rebellion in the Early Modern World* (Berkeley: University of California Press, 1991); Theda Skocpol, *States and Social Revolutions* (New York: Cambridge University Press, 1979).

3. Charles Tilly, *From Mobilization to Revolution* (Reading, Mass.: Addison-Wesley, 1978); Ted Robert Gurr, *Why Men Rebel* (Princeton, N.J.: Princeton University Press, 1970). A useful handbook on the study of protest events is Dieter Rucht, Ruud Koopmans, and Friedhelm Neidhardt, eds., *Acts of Dissent: New Developments in the Study of Protest* (Lanham, Md.: Rowman and Littlefield, 1999).

4. Especially in the work of Elizabeth J. Perry. For a recent example, see her *Patrolling the Revolution: Worker Militias, Citizenship and the Modern Chinese State* (Lanham, Md.: Rowman and Littlefield, 2006).

5. For a careful analysis of what is still a controversial development, see Pierre Landry and Yanqi Tong, "Disputing the Authoritarian State in China," paper presented at the annual meeting of the American Political Science Association, September 1, 2005, Washington, D.C. www.allacademic.com/meta/p40460index.html.

6. Kevin J. O'Brien and Lianjiang Li, "Popular Contention and Its Impact in Rural China," *Comparative Political Studies* 38,3 (April 2005): 235–259.

7. For an effort to connect political economy and contention, see Ching Kwan Lee and Mark Selden, "China's Durable Inequality: Legacies of Revolution and Pitfalls of Reform," japanfocus.org/products/details/2329 (accessed May 26, 2007).

8. For a good example of a deprivation-based analysis of protest, see Ethan Michelson, "Deprivation, Discontent and Disobedience in Rural China: Collective Learning in Southeast Henan," unpublished paper, Indiana University Department of Sociology, March 2007.

9. A topic that cries out for analysis is the relationship between the rapid growth of internet-based mobilization and the current policy of tight control of the internet. If online mobilization is unstoppable, as many observers in the West seem to think, China's attempts to use it for sanctioned purposes but clamp down on its use for mobilization will be a crucial test case.

10. Three useful collections are Marco Giugni, Doug McAdam, and Charles Tilly, eds., *From Contention to Democracy* (Lanham, Md.: Rowman and Littlefield, 1998), the same editors' *How Social Movements Matter* (Minneapolis: University of Minnesota Press, 1999), and David S. Meyer, Valerie Jenness, and Helen Ingram, eds., *Routing the Opposition: Social Movements, Public Policy and Democracy* (Minneapolis: University of Minnesota Press, 2005).

11. For studies that focus on links between internationalization and transnational social movements, see Robert O'Brien, Anne Marie Goetz, Jan Aart Scholte, and Marc Williams, *Contesting Global Governance: Multilateral Economic Institutions and Global Social Movements* (Cambridge: Cambridge University Press, 2000), and Sidney Tarrow, *The New Transnational Activism* (New York: Cambridge University Press, 2005).

12. See Sally Engle Merry, "Transnational Human Rights and Local Activism: Mapping the Middle," *American Anthropologist* 108 (2006): 38–41; Rachel E. Stern, "Unpacking Adaptation: The Female Inheritance Movement in Hong Kong," *Mobilization* 10,3 (October 2005): 421–440.

13. Tilly, *From Mobilization;* Frances Fox Piven and Richard Cloward, *Poor People's Movements: Why They Succeed, How They Fail* (New York: Vintage Books, 1977). Two studies that synthesize this tradition are Doug McAdam, John McCarthy, and Mayer N. Zald, eds., *Comparative Perspectives on Social Movements* (New York: Cambridge University Press, 1996), and Sidney Tarrow, *Power in Movement: Social Movements and Contentious Politics* (New York: Cambridge University Press, 1998).

14. In the Western tradition, this approach was generally known as the "collective behavior" approach. For a review and critique, see Doug McAdam, *The Political Process and the Development of Black Insurgency* (1982; reprint, Chicago: University of Chicago Press, 1999).

15. For an attempt to do this comparatively, including some discussion of China,

see Doug McAdam, Sidney Tarrow, and Charles Tilly, *Dynamics of Contention* (New York: Cambridge University Press, 2001).

Introduction

1. Doug McAdam, "Conceptual Origins, Current Problems, Future Directions," in Doug McAdam, John D. McCarthy, and Mayer N. Zald, eds., *Comparative Perspectives on Social Movements* (New York: Cambridge University Press, 1996), xiii. See also Maryjane Osa and Cristina Corduneanu-Huci, "Running Uphill: Political Opportunity in Non-Democracies," *Comparative Sociology* 2,4 (2003): 606; Carrie Rosefky Wickham, *Mobilizing Islam: Religion, Activism, and Political Change in Egypt* (New York: Columbia University Press, 2002), 5; Quintan Wiktorowicz, "Introduction: Islamic Activism and Social Movement Theory," in Wiktorowicz, ed., *Islamic Activism* (Bloomington: Indiana University Press, 2004), 4.

2. See Charles Kurzman, "Structural Opportunity and Perceived Opportunity in Social-Movement Theory: The Iranian Revolution of 1979," *American Sociological Review* 61,1 (1996): 153–170; Anthony Oberschall, "Opportunities and Framing in the Eastern European Revolts of 1989," and Elena Zdravomyslova, "Opportunities and Framing in the Transition to Democracy," both in McAdam, McCarthy, and Zald, *Comparative Perspectives on Social Movements;* Charles D. Brockett, *Political Movements and Violence in Central America* (New York: Cambridge University Press, 2005).

3. Charles Tilly and Sidney Tarrow, *Contentious Politics* (Boulder, Colo.: Paradigm, 2007), 196. But see Kurt Schock, "People Power and Political Opportunities: Social Movement Mobilization and Outcomes in the Philippines and in Burma," *Social Problems* 46,3 (1999): 355–375; Doowon Suh, "How Do Political Opportunities Matter for Social Movements? Political Opportunity, Misframing, Pseudosuccess, and Pseudofailure," *Sociological Quarterly* 43,2 (2001): 437–460; Vince Boudreau, *Resisting Dictatorship* (New York: Cambridge University Press, 2004).

4. Joseph Esherick and Jeffrey N. Wasserstrom, "Acting Out Democracy: Political Theater in Modern China," *Journal of Asian Studies* 49,4 (1990): 835–866; Daniel Kelliher, "Keeping Democracy Safe from the Masses: Intellectuals and Elitism in the Chinese Protest Movement," *Comparative Politics* 25,4 (July 1993): 379–396; Elizabeth J. Perry, "Casting a Chinese 'Democracy' Movement: The Roles of Students, Workers, and Entrepreneurs," in Jeffrey N. Wasserstrom and Elizabeth J. Perry, eds., *Popular Protest and Political Culture in Modern China*, 2nd ed. (Boulder, Colo.: Westview, 1994): 74–92; Teresa Wright, "State Repression and Student Protest in Contemporary China," *China Quarterly* 157 (1999): 142–172; Dingxin Zhao, *The Power of Tiananmen* (Chicago: University of Chicago Press, 2001).

5. Craig Calhoun, *Neither Gods nor Emperors* (Berkeley: University of California

Press, 1994); Jiping Zuo and Robert D. Benford, "Mobilization Processes and the 1989 Democracy Movement," *Sociological Quarterly* 36,1 (1995): 131–156; Doug McAdam, Sidney Tarrow, and Charles Tilly, *Dynamics of Contention* (New York: Cambridge University Press, 2001), 215–225.

6. Zhongyang Zhengfawei Yanjiushi, *Weihu shehui wending diaoyan wenji* (Collected essays on maintaining social stability) (Beijing: Zhongguo falü chubanshe, 2001); Kevin J. O'Brien, "Collective Action in the Chinese Countryside," *China Journal* 48 (2002): 139–154; Thomas P. Bernstein and Xiaobo Lü, *Taxation without Representation in Contemporary China* (New York: Cambridge University Press, 2003); Murray Scot Tanner, "China Rethinks Unrest," *Washington Quarterly* 27,3 (2004): 137–156; Carl F. Minzner, "Xinfang: An Alternative to Formal Chinese Legal Institutions," *Stanford Journal of International Law* 42 (2006): 103–179. In 2006, there was apparently a downturn in collective incidents, partly because the term was redefined, partly for unknown reasons.

7. "Faculty in Political Science," polisci.berkeley.edu/faculty/bio/permanent/OBrien,K/syllabi/ps244d-fl05.pdf (accessed June 29, 2007).

8. Patricia Thornton, "Framing Dissent in Contemporary China: Irony, Ambiguity and Metonymy," *China Quarterly* 171 (2002): 661–681; Feng Chen, "Industrial Restructuring and Workers' Resistance in China," *Modern China* 29,2 (2003): 237–262; Andrew C. Mertha, *Water Warriors: Citizen Action and Policy Change* (Ithaca, N.Y.: Cornell University Press, 2008).

9. Wright, "State Repression and Student Protest."

10. Dingxin Zhao, "Ecologies of Social Movements: Student Mobilization during the 1989 Prodemocracy Movement in Beijing," *American Journal of Sociology* 103,6 (1998): 1493–1529; Yongshun Cai, "The Resistance of Chinese Laid-Off Workers in the Reform Period," *China Quarterly* 172 (2002): 327–344.

11. Elizabeth J. Perry, *Challenging the Mandate of Heaven* (Armonk, N.Y.: Sharpe, 2003); Xi Chen, "Between Defiance and Obedience: Protest Opportunism in China," in Elizabeth J. Perry and Merle Goldman, eds., *Grassroots Political Reform in Contemporary China* (Cambridge, Mass.: Harvard University Press, 2007), 253–281.

12. William Hurst, "Understanding Contentious Collective Action by Chinese Laid-Off Workers: The Importance of Regional Political Economy," *Studies in Comparative International Development* 39,2 (2002): 94–120; Kevin J. O'Brien and Lianjiang Li, *Rightful Resistance in Rural China* (New York: Cambridge University Press, 2006).

13. Ronald R. Aminzade et al., *Silence and Voice in the Study of Contentious Politics* (New York: Cambridge University Press, 2001).

14. Elizabeth J. Perry, "Moving the Masses: Emotion Work in the Chinese Revolution," *Mobilization* 7,2 (2002): 111–128; Peter Hays Gries, "Tears of Rage: Chinese Nationalist Reactions to the Belgrade Embassy Bombing," *China Journal*

46 (2003): 267–295; Guobin Yang, "Emotional Events and the Transformation of Collective Action," in Helena Flam and Debra King, eds., *Emotions and Social Movements* (London: Routledge, 2005): 79–95.

Feng Chen, "Subsistence Crises, Managerial Corruption and Labor Protests in China," *China Journal* 44 (2000): 41–63; William Hurst and Kevin J. O'Brien, "China's Contentious Pensioners," *China Quarterly* 170 (2002): 345–360; Ethan Michelson, "Climbing the Dispute Pagoda: Grievances and Appeals to the Official Justice System in Rural China," *American Sociological Review* 72 (June 2007): 459–485.

Bernstein and Lü, *Taxation without Representation;* Cai, "Resistance of Chinese Laid-Off Workers"; Fayong Shi and Yongshun Cai, "Disaggregating the State: Networks and Collective Action in Shanghai," *China Quarterly* 186 (June 2006): 314–332; Lianjiang Li and Kevin J. O'Brien, "Protest Leadership in Rural China," *China Quarterly* 193 (March 2008): 1–23.

15. The structurally inclined include Charles Tilly, *From Mobilization to Revolution* (Reading, Mass.: Addison-Wesley, 1978); Sidney Tarrow, *Power in Movement* (New York: Cambridge University Press, 1998); McAdam, Tarrow, and Tilly, *Dynamics.* The culturally minded include James M. Jasper, *The Art of Moral Protest* (Chicago: University of Chicago Press, 1997); Jeff Goodwin and James M. Jasper, "Caught in a Winding, Snarling Vine: The Structural Bias of Political Process Theory," *Sociological Forum* 14,1 (1999): 27–53.

16. The Berkeley conference was not the first to address these issues. The Weatherhead Center for International Affairs at Harvard University convened a conference in 2000 entitled "Contentious Politics in the 'Developing' World: Theory, Culture, and History."

17. "Windows of opportunity for mobilization and policy reform need not be either open or closed, but may be partly opened, and opportunities may vary across political issues and constituencies over time." Traci M. Sawyers and David S. Meyer, "Missed Opportunities: Social Movement Abeyance and Public Policy," *Social Problems* 46,2 (1999): 189. "What provokes mobilization for one movement or constituency may depress mobilization of another, and be completely irrelevant to a third." David S. Meyer and Debra C. Minkoff, "Conceptualizing Political Opportunity," *Social Forces* 82,4 (2004): 1461.

18. Jeffery N. Wasserstrom, "Student Protests in Fin-de-Siècle China," *New Left Review* 237 (1999): 56.

19. Perry, *Challenging the Mandate,* xiii–xiv.

20. O'Brien and Li, *Rightful Resistance,* 66, 51.

21. Joel S. Migdal, *State-in-Society* (New York: Cambridge University Press, 2001). See also Neil J. Diamant, Stanley B. Lubman, and Kevin J. O'Brien, "Law and Society in the People's Republic of China," in Diamant, Lubman, and O'Brien, eds., *Engaging the Law in China* (Stanford, Calif.: Stanford University Press, 2005), 19.

22. Shi and Cai, "Disaggregating the State."

23. O'Brien and Li, *Rightful Resistance,* 66.

24. Thomas R. Rochon, *Culture Moves* (Princeton, N.J.: Princeton University Press, 1998), 237.

25. McAdam, "Conceptual Origins," 37; David S. Meyer, "Protest and Political Opportunities," *Annual Review of Sociology* 30 (2004): 140; Brockett, *Political Movements and Violence,* 15.

26. Tarrow, *Power in Movement,* 73.

27. Meyer, "Protest and Political Opportunities," 140–141.

28. Tarrow, *Power in Movement,* 73–76. See also Hank Johnston, "'Let's Get Small': The Dynamics of (Small) Contention in Repressive States," *Mobilization* 11,2 (2006): 197.

29. McAdam, "Conceptual Origins," 24; Theda Skocpol, *States and Social Revolutions* (New York: Cambridge University Press, 1979).

30. Tilly and Tarrow, *Contentious Politics,* 57.

31. Ibid., 57.

32. At the Berkeley conference, David Meyer posed a timely question about internet contention: "Is a single website the tip of an iceberg or just an ice cube?" Sidney Tarrow also wondered about the relationship between online and offline activity in China, especially whether talking among internet activists led to challenging the authorities.

33. McAdam, "Conceptual Origins," 34.

34. Sidney Tarrow, *The New Transnational Activism* (New York: Cambridge University Press, 2005), 160. See also Margaret E. Keck and Kathryn Sikkink, *Activists beyond Borders* (Ithaca, N.Y.: Cornell University Press, 1998); Sanjeev Khagram, *Dams and Development* (Ithaca, N.Y.: Cornell University Press, 2004).

35. Tarrow, *New Transnational Activism,* 156–158.

36. For a different perspective on the Chinese movement, see Perry, "Casting a Chinese 'Democracy' Movement," and Kelliher, "Keeping Democracy Safe."

37. Zuo and Benford, "Mobilizing Processes"; Quintan Wiktorowicz, "The Salafi Movement in Jordan," *International Journal of Middle East Studies* 32,2 (2000): 219–240; Osa and Corduneanu-Huci, "Running Uphill"; Wickham, *Mobilizing Islam;* Diane Singerman, "The Networked World of Islamist Social Movements," in Wiktorowicz, *Islamic Activism,* 143–163.

38. The cultural meanings encoded in networks and the messages transmitted across them may be more important than the networks themselves. See Jasper, *Art of Moral Protest,* 76; Anne Mische, "Cross-talk in Movements: Reconceiving the Culture-Network Link," in Mario Diani and Doug McAdam, eds., *Social Movements and Networks* (Oxford: Oxford University Press, 2003): 258–259.

39. For research that points in this direction, see Zhao, "Ecologies of Social Movements," 1512; Sharon Erickson Nepstad and Christian Smith, "Rethinking Recruitment to High-Risk/Cost Activism: The Case of Nicaragua Exchange," *Mobilization* 4,1 (1999): 33–34; Florence Passy, "Social Networks Matter. But How?" in Diani and McAdam, *Social Movements and Networks,* 33, 41.

40. Wiktorowicz, "The Salafi Movement," 233. See also William H. Sewell Jr., "Space in Contentious Politics," in Aminzade et al., *Silence and Voice,* 89–125.

41. Zhao, "Ecologies of Social Movements," 1509.

42. See William A. Gamson, "Safe Spaces and Social Movements," *Perspectives on Social Problems* 8 (1996): 27.

43. Sewell, "Space," 68–70. Eric L. Hirsch, "Protest Movements and Urban Theory," in Ray Hutchinson, ed., *Urban Sociology in Transition* (Greenwich, Conn.: JAI Press, 1993): 159–180.

44. Ties to criminal organizations can also facilitate mobilization by protesters or religious believers. See Jae Ho Chung, Hongyi Lai, and Ming Xia, "Mounting Challenges to Governance in China: Surveying Collective Protestors, Religious Sects, and Criminal Organizations," *China Journal* 56 (July 2006): 1–32.

45. See also Marc J. Blecher, "Hegemony and Workers' Politics in China," *China Quarterly* 170 (2002): 283–303.

46. At the Berkeley conference, Sidney Tarrow suggested a more elegant, extended version of this metaphor. "The lesson of the [American] civil rights movement is that the symbols of revolt are not drawn like musty costumes from a cultural closet and arrayed before the public. Nor are new meanings unrolled out of whole cloth. . . . Frames are woven from a blend of inherited and invented fibers into collective action frames in confrontation with opponents and elites." See also Tarrow, *Power in Movement,* 118; Hank Johnston and John A. Noakes, *Frames of Protest* (Lanham, Md.: Rowman and Littlefield, 2005), 9.

47. James C. Scott, *Domination and the Arts of Resistance* (New Haven, Conn.: Yale University Press, 1990).

48. Wiktorowicz, "Introduction," 18. See also O'Brien and Li, *Rightful Resistance.*

49. Research on homeowner's activism is starting to fill this gap. See Shi and Cai, "Disaggregating the State"; You-tien Hsing, "Urban Protests and Mobilization in Inner-City Beijing," paper presented at the conference entitled "Reclaiming Chinese Society," University of California, Berkeley, October 27–28, 2006; Benjamin Read, "Assessing Variation in Civil Society Organizations: China's Homeowner Associations in Comparative Perspective," *Comparative Political Studies* 41,9 (September 2008); Yongshun Cai, "China's Moderate Middle Class: The Case of Homeowners' Resistance," *Asian Survey* 45,5 (September–October 2005): 777–799; Luigi Tomba, "Residential Space and Collective Interest Formation in Beijing's Housing Disputes," *China Quarterly* 184 (December 2005): 934–951.

50. For explanation and use of these terms, see McAdam, Tarrow, and Tilly, *Dynamics of Contention,* 7–9; Kevin J. O'Brien, "Neither Transgressive nor Contained: Boundary-Spanning Contention in China," *Mobilization* 8,3 (2003): 51–64; Johnston, "'Let's Get Small.'"

51. Zhiping Li, "Zai gongzhong weiquan shijian zhong shou jianshi de gongzhong canyu yu huanjing yingxiang pingjia zhidu: Yi Shenzhen xibu tongdao cejiexian gongcheng shijian weili (Upholding the public rights of public par-

ticipation and environmental impact assessment: The example of the Shenzhen Western Corridor Project), unpublished manuscript.

52. For activism by lawyers and pressures they face to make a living, see Ethan Michelson, "The Practice of Law as an Obstacle to Justice: Chinese Lawyers at Work," *Law and Society Review* 40,1 (2006): 1–38, and David Kelly, "Citizen Movements and China's Public Intellectuals in the Hu-Wen Era," *Pacific Affairs* 79,2 (2006): 83–204.

53. Eva Pils, "Asking the Tiger for His Skin: Rights Activism in China," *Fordham International Law Journal* 30 (2007), 1209–1287, and "Rule by Law," *New York Times,* February 25, 2007.

54. Keck and Sikkink, *Activists beyond Borders.*

55. For a description of one such program, see Becky Shelley, "Political Globalisation and the Politics of International Non-governmental Organisations: The Case of Village Democracy in China," *Australian Journal of Political Science* 35,2 (2005): 225–238.

56. A partial list of American organizations funding programs focused on building civil society or the rule of law includes: the Ford Foundation, the International Republican Institute, the Carter Center, the National Democratic Institute, the National Endowment for Democracy, the Open Society Institute, the Asia Foundation, and the Rockefeller Brothers' Fund. There are also European, Australian, Canadian, and Japanese organizations (and government affiliates) administering programs. See Anthony Spires, "Influences from Abroad: The Impact of Global Civil Society on Chinese Civil Society," paper presented at the International Contemporary China Studies Conference, University of Hong Kong, January 2007.

57. Pauline Jones Luong and Erika Weinthal, "The NGO Paradox: Democratic Goals and Non-democratic Outcomes in Kazakhstan," *Europe-Asia Studies* 51,7 (1999): 1267–1284; Laura A. Henry, "The Greening of Grassroots Democracy? The Russian Environmental Movement, Foreign Aid, and Democratization," in Berkeley Program in Soviet and Post-Soviet Studies Working Paper Series (Berkeley: University of California Press, 2001).

58. Between 2002 and 2005, U.S. private foundations issued over $280 million in China-targeted grants. Spires, "Influences from Abroad," 11.

59. Monique Deveaux, "Comments," *Current Anthropology* 46,3 (2005): 402–403. But also see Millie Thayer, "Negotiating the Global: Northeast Brazilian Women's Movements and the Transnational Feminist Public" (Ph.D. diss., University of California, Berkeley, 2004); Clifford Bob, *The Marketing of Rebellion* (New York: Cambridge University Press, 2005).

60. James Ferguson, "Seeing Like an Oil Company: Space, Security and Global Capital in Neoliberal Africa," *American Anthropologist* 107,3 (2005): 380.

61. Murray Scot Tanner, "Rethinking Law Enforcement and Society: Changing Police Analyses of Social Unrest," in Diamant, Lubman, and O'Brien, *Engaging the Law in China,* 193–212.

62. Tanner, "China Rethinks Unrest," 144.
63. Jonathan Hassid, "An Uncertain Business: Controlling the Chinese Media," *Asian Survey* 48,3 (May–June 2008).
64. See Jennifer Earl, "Tanks, Tear Gas, and Taxes: Toward a Theory of Movement Repression," *Sociological Theory* 21,1 (2003): 44–68; also *Mobilization* 11,2 (2006) special issue devoted to repression and the social control of protest.
65. Patricia M. Thornton, "Insinuation, Insult, and Invective: The Threshold of Power and Protest in Modern China," *Comparative Studies in Society and History* 44,3 (July 2002): 597–619. Hurst and O'Brien, "China's Contentious Pensioners."

1. Student Movements in China and Taiwan

1. Doug McAdam, Sidney Tarrow, and Charles Tilly, "Toward an Integrated Perspective on Social Movements and Revolution," in Mark Irving Lichbach and Alan S. Zuckerman, eds., *Comparative Politics: Rationality, Culture, and Structure* (Cambridge: Cambridge University Press, 1997), 142.
2. See Peter Eisinger, "The Conditions of Protest Behavior in American Cities," *American Political Science Review* 67,1 (1973): 11–28; Charles Tilly, *From Mobilization to Revolution* (Reading, Mass.: Addison-Wesley, 1978), and Doug McAdam, *Political Process and the Origins of Black Insurgency* (Chicago: University of Chicago Press, 1982).
3. David Meyer, "Protest and Political Opportunities," *Annual Review of Sociology* 30 (2004): 128.
4. William Gamson and David Meyer, "Framing Political Opportunity," in Doug McAdam, John McCarthy, and Mayer Zald, eds., *Comparative Perspectives on Social Movements* (New York: Cambridge University Press, 1996), 275–290; Jeff Goodwin and James E. Jasper, eds., *The Social Movements Reader: Cases and Concepts* (New York: Blackwell, 2003); Meyer, "Protest and Political Opportunities."
5. Doug McAdam, "Conceptual Origins, Current Problems, Future Directions," in McAdam, McCarthy, and Zald, *Comparative Perspectives on Social Movements,* 31.
6. Meyer, "Protest and Political Opportunities," 136.
7. Ibid., 137.
8. Ibid., 136.
9. Charles Kurzman, "Structural Opportunity and Perceived Opportunity in Social-Movement Theory: The Iranian Revolution of 1979," *American Sociological Review* 61,1 (1996): 153–170; Doug McAdam, Sidney Tarrow, and Charles Tilly, "Comparative Perspectives on Contentious Politics," in Mark Lichbach and Alan Zuckerman, eds., *Rationality, Culture, and Structure: Advancing Theory in Comparative Politics* (Cambridge: Cambridge University Press, forthcoming), 14; Kevin J. O'Brien and Lianjiang Li, *Rightful Resistance in Rural China* (Cambridge: Cambridge University Press, 2006).

10. Charles Brockett, "The Structure of Political Opportunities and Peasant Mobilization in Central America," *Comparative Politics* 23,3 (1991): 253–274; Lynn Kamensita, "The Process of Political Marginalization: East German Social Movements after the Wall," *Comparative Politics* 30,3 (1998): 313–333; Karl-Dieter Opp and Christiane Gern, "Dissident Groups, Personal Networks, and Spontaneous Cooperation: The East-German Revolution of 1989," *American Sociological Review* 58,5 (1993): 659–680; Michael Bratton and Nicolas van de Walle, "Popular Protest and Political Reform in Africa," *Comparative Politics* 24,4 (1992): 419–442; Donatella della Porta, *Social Movements, Political Violence and the State* (Cambridge: Cambridge University Press, 1995); Sharon Erickson Nepstad and Christian Smith, "Rethinking Recruitment to High-Risk/Cost Activism: The Case of Nicaragua Exchange," *Mobilization* 4,1 (1999): 40–51; Peter Houtzager and Marcus Kurtz, "The Institutional Roots of Popular Mobilization: State Transformation and Rural Politics in Brazil and Chile, 1960–1995," *Comparative Studies in Society and History* 42,2 (2000): 394–424; Kurt Schock, "People Power and Political Opportunities: Social Movement Mobilization and Outcomes in the Philippines and Burma," *Social Problems* 46,3 (1999): 355–375; Kurt Schock, *Unarmed Insurrections: People Power Movements in Nondemocracies* (Minneapolis: University of Minnesota Press , 2005); Helena Flam, "Anxiety and the Successful Oppositional Construction of Social Reality: The Case of the KOR," *Mobilization* 1,1 (1996): 103–121; E. Pierre Deess, "Collective Life and Social Change in the GDR," *Mobilization* 2,2 (1997): 207–225; Maryjane Osa and Cristina Corduneanu-Huci, "Running Uphill: Political Opportunity in Non-Democracies," *Comparative Sociology* 2,4 (2003): 605–629; O'Brien and Li, *Rightful Resistance,* chap. 2.
11. Schock, *Unarmed Insurrections,* 362, 370; Osa and Cordureanu-Huci, "Running Uphill," 612, 620, 622.
12. Schock, *Unarmed Insurrections,* 362, 370.
13. Ibid., 362, 368; Osa and Cordureanu-Huci, "Running Uphill," 620.
14. McAdam, Tarrow, and Tilly, "Comparative Perspectives," 13.
15. Brockett, "Structure of Political Opportunities."
16. Osa and Cordureanu, "Running Uphill"; Paul Almeida, "Opportunity Organizations and Threat-Induced Contention: Protest Waves in Authoritarian Settings," *American Journal of Sociology* 109,2 (2003): 345–400; Karl-Dieter Opp and Wolfgang Roehl, "Repression, Micromobilization, and Political Protest," *Social Forces* 69,2 (1990): 521–547; Schock, *Unarmed Insurrections.*
17. Almeida, "Opportunity Organizations."
18. O'Brien and Li, *Rightful Resistance,* chap. 2.
19. Almeida, "Opportunity Organizations."
20. Kevin J. O'Brien and Lianjiang Li, "Accommodating 'Democracy' in a One-Party State: Introducing Village Elections in China," *China Quarterly* 162 (June 2000): 465–489.

21. Tun-jen Cheng, "Democratizing the Quasi-Leninist Regime in Taiwan," *World Politics* 41,4 (1989): 471–499.

22. Lee Chin-chuan, "Sparking a Fire: The Press and the Ferment of Democratic Change in Taiwan," *Journalism Monographs* 138 (April 1993): 1–39.

23. Ruth Hayhoe, *China's Universities and the Open Door* (New York: Sharpe, 1989), 43.

24. Ibid., 31; Erwin H. Epstein and Wei-fan Kuo, "Higher Education," in Douglas C. Smith, ed., *The Confucian Continuum: Educational Modernization in Taiwan* (New York: Praeger, 1991), 182; Piyun Deng, *Bashi niandai* (The eighties) (Taipei: Taiwan Yanjiu Jijinhui, 1990), 4.

25. Hayhoe, *China's Universities,* 30; Ronald Price, "Moral-Political Education and Modernization," in Ruth Hayhoe, ed., *Education and Modernization: The Chinese Experience* (New York: Pergamon Press, 1992), 219; Epstein and Kuo, "Higher Education," 190.

26. Epstein and Kuo, "Higher Education," 198, 200.

27. Orville Schell, *Mandate of Heaven* (New York: Simon and Schuster, 1994), 186–227; Hongda Harry Wu, *Laogai: The Chinese Gulag* (Boulder, Colo.: Westview, 1992), 1–53.

28. See John Kaplan, *The Court Martial of the Kaohsiung Defendants* (Berkeley: Institute of East Asian Studies, 1981). In the early 1980s, individuals were assassinated by groups associated with the KMT.

29. Theda Skocpol, *States and Social Revolutions: A Comparative Analysis of France, Russia and China* (Cambridge: Cambridge University Press, 1979); Peter Gourevitch, "The Second Image Reversed: The International Sources of Domestic Politics, *International Organization* 32,4 (1978): 161–185; David Meyer, "Political Opportunity and Nested Institutions," *Social Movement Studies* 2,1 (2003): 19.

30. For China, see especially Dingxin Zhao, *The Power of Tiananmen* (Chicago: University of Chicago Press, 2001), 241, 308–319.

31. The source of the data in the following account is approximately 40 personal interviews I conducted with major student and intellectual leaders from all factions in both movements. The mainland Chinese case study also draws on data found in a little-consulted transcript of a conference held in Paris in 1991 where 17 key student and intellectual leaders discussed in detail their thoughts and behavior in 1989: [German Rhine Writers' Association 1989 Student Research Group, *Huigu yu fansi* (Review and reflect) (Essen, Germany: German Rhine Writers' Association, 1993). I also consulted all the major primary and secondary written sources on each movement, the best of which include: Zhao, *Power of Tiananmen;* Craig Calhoun, *Neither Gods nor Emperors* (Berkeley: University of California Press, 1994); Jonathan Unger, ed., *The Pro-democracy Protests in China: Reports from the Provinces* (Armonk, N.Y.: Sharpe, 1991); Tony Saich, ed., *Perspectives on the Chinese People's Movement: Spring 1989* (Armonk, N.Y.: Sharpe, 1990); Elizabeth Perry and Jeffrey Wasserstrom, eds., *Popular Protest and Political Culture in Modern China: Learning from*

1989 (Boulder, Colo.: Westview Press, 1994); Han Minzhu and Hua Sheng, eds., *Cries for Democracy: Writings and Speeches from the 1989 Chinese Democracy Movement* (Princeton, N.J.: Princeton University Press, 1990); Michel Oksenberg, Lawrence R. Sullivan, and Marc Lambert, eds., *Beijing Spring, 1989: Confrontation and Conflict, The Basic Documents* (Armonk, N.Y.: Sharpe, 1990); Piyun Deng, *Bashi niandai;* Yun Fan, ed., *Xin sheng dai de ziwo zhuixun* (Self-reflections on the new era) (Taipei: Taiwan yanjiu jijinhui, 1991); and Jinshan He, Hongzhi Guan, Lijia Zhuang, and Chengqi Guo, *Taipei xueyun* (Taipei student movement) (Taipei: Zhongguo shibao chubanshe, 1990).

32. German Rhine Writers' Association, *Huigu yu fansi,* 3.
33. Ibid.
34. Ibid., 21.
35. Ibid., 26.
36. Ibid., 22.
37. Ibid., 26.
38. Ibid., 26.
39. Ibid., 31.
40. Ibid., 25, 37.
41. Oksenberg, Sullivan, and Lambert, eds., *Beijing Spring,* 207–208.
42. German Rhine Writers' Association, *Huigu yu fansi,* 44.
43. Ibid., 123.
44. Ibid., 89.
45. Ibid., 93.
46. Ibid., 94–95.
47. Ibid., 95.
48. Ibid., 90.
49. Ibid., 136.
50. Ibid., 223.
51. Ibid., 238–239.
52. Jinshan He et al., *Taipei xueyun,* 36.
53. Yun Fan Yun, *Xin sheng dai,* 404.
54. Piyun Deng, *Bashi niandai,* 304.
55. Yun Fan Yun, *Xin sheng dai,* 410.
56. Editorial department, "Da zongtong miandui daxuesheng, zongtongfu biancheng tanpanchang" (President faces students, presidential house becomes site of negotiations), Xin Xinwen (Journalist), March 26–April 1, 1990, 72.
57. Andrew Walder and Gong Xiaoxia, "Workers in the Tiananmen Protests: The Politics of the Beijing Workers' Autonomous Federation," *Australian Journal of Chinese Affairs* 29 (1993): 7.
58. Ibid.
59. Indeed, only a few days after the public establishment of the Beijing Workers'

Autonomous Federation, one of its founding members was kidnapped on the streets of Beijing and detained without explanation. In the days and weeks that followed, other worker activists were similarly harassed.

60. Guillermo O'Donnell, "La Cosecha del Miedo," *Nexos* (Mexico City) 6 (1983): 51–60; Brockett, "Structure of Political Opportunities"; Opp and Gern, "Dissident Groups"; Bratton and van de Walle, "Popular Protest and Political Reform."

61. Juan E. Corradi, Patricia Weiss Fagen, and Manuel Antonio Garreton, eds., *Fear at the Edge: State Terror and Resistance in Latin America* (Berkeley: University of California Press, 1992), 2.

62. Ibid.

63. Ibid.

64. Norbert Lechner, "Some People Die of Fear: Fear as a Political Problem," in Corradi, Fagen, and Garreton, *Fear at the Edge*, 29.

65. Fagen, "Repression and State Security," in Corradi, Fagen, and Garreton, *Fear at the Edge*, 67.

66. Maria Helena Moreira Alves, "Cultures of Fear, Cultures of Resistance," in Corradi, Fagen, and Garreton, *Fear at the Edge*, 190.

67. Carrie Rosefsky Wickham, *Mobilizing Islam: Religion, Activism, and Political Change in Egypt* (New York: Columbia University Press, 2002); Almeida, "Opportunity Organizations," 349.

68. I am grateful to David Meyer for this insight.

69. David Snow, Louis Zurcher, and Sheldon Eckland-Olson, "Social Networks and Social Movements: A Microstructural Approach to Differential Recruitment," *American Sociological Review* 45,5 (1980): 787–801; Doug McAdam, "Recruitment to High-Risk Activism: The Case of Freedom Summer," *American Journal of Sociology* 92 (July 1986): 64–90; William Gamson, *The Strategy of Social Protest*, 2nd ed. (Belmont, Calif.: Wadsworth, 1990); see also chapter 5 here.

70. Opp and Gern, "Dissident Groups," 673–674.

71. Almeida, "Opportunity Organizations." Vincent Boudreau, *Resisting Dictatorship: Repression and Protest in Southeast Asia* (Cambridge: Cambridge University Press, 2004).

72. I am grateful to Kevin O'Brien for this insight.

73. Calhoun, *Neither Gods nor Emperors*, 183.

74. Juan E. Corradi, "Fear of the State, Fear of Society," in Corradi, Fagen, and Garreton, *Fear at the Edge*, 279.

75. Javier Martinez, "Fear of the State, Fear of Society: On the Opposition Protests in Chile," in Corradi, Fagen, and Garreton, *Fear at the Edge*, 146.

76. Kurzman, "Structural Opportunity," 161.

77. Wonmo Dong, "Student Activism and the Presidential Politics of 1987 in

South Korea," in Ilpyong J. Kim and Young Whan Kihl, eds., *Political Change in South Korea* (New York: Korean Professors' World Peace Academy, 1988), 175.

78. Josef Silverstein, "Students in Southeast Asian Politics," *Pacific Affairs* 49,2 (1979): 211.

79. Carina Perelli, "Youth, Politics, and Dictatorship in Uruguay," in Corradi, Fagen, and Garreton, *Fear at the Edge*, 239.

80. Opp and Roehl, "Repression"; Kamenitsa, "Process of Political Marginalization."

81. Brockett, "Structure of Political Opportunities," 262.

82. Bratton and van de Walle, "Popular Protest and Political Reform," 430.

83. Kamenitsa, "Process of Political Marginalization," 315.

84. Ross Prizzia and Narong Sinsawasdi, *Thailand: Student Activism and Political Change* (Bangkok: Allied Printers, 1974), 52.

85. Ibid., 56.

86. Silverstein, "Students," 202.

87. Ibid., 204.

2. Collective Petitioning and Institutional Conversion

1. Elizabeth J. Perry, *Challenging the Mandate of Heaven: Social Protest and State Power in China* (Armonk, N.Y.: Sharpe, 2002), xxi.

2. Andrew Walder, "Collective Protest and the Waning of the Communist State in China," in Michael Hanagan, Leslie Page Moch, and Wayne te Brake, eds., *Challenging Authority: The Historical Study of Contentious Politics* (Minneapolis: University of Minnesota Press, 1998), 71.

3. Kathleen Thelen, "How Institutions Evolve: Insights from Comparative Historical Analysis," in James Mahoney and Dietrich Rueschemeyer, eds., *Comparative Historical Analysis in the Social Sciences* (Cambridge: Cambridge University Press, 2003), 228.

4. Guillermo Donnell and Philippe Schmitter, *Transitions from Authoritarian Rule: Tentative Conclusions about Uncertain Democracies* (Baltimore: Johns Hopkins University Press, 1986), 49.

5. This is why many disruptive protest events have been classified as "unusual petitioning" (*yichang shangfang*).

6. When discussing the structure of the *xinfang* system, a distinction between *xinfang* agencies and the *xinfang* system must be made. *Xinfang* agencies are usually called *xinfang* bureaus or *xinfang* offices. They exist at party committees and at the county government and above. They are answerable to both upper-level *xinfang* agencies and to leaders at their own level. Besides this hierarchy, many smaller *xinfang* agencies exist, for example in people's congresses, the People's Political Consultative Conference, the courts, the procuratorate, state-owned enterprises, and universities. Compared to *xin-*

fang agencies, the *xinfang* system is broader and includes three components: (1) *xinfang* bureaus, (2) party-state leaders, and (3) other agencies that are routinely involved in handling petitions. This chapter concentrates on the *xinfang* system.

7. Yongshun Cai, "Managed Participation in China," *Political Science Quarterly* 119,3 (Fall 2004): 425–451.

8. Sidney Tarrow, *Power in Movement* (New York: Cambridge University Press, 1998).

9. Doug McAdam, "Conceptual Origins, Current Problems, Future Directions," in Doug McAdam, John D. McCarthy, and Mayer N. Zald, eds., *Comparative Perspectives on Social Movements: Political Opportunities, Mobilizing Structures, and Cultural Framings* (New York: Cambridge University Press, 1996), 27.

10. David Meyer, "Protest and Political Opportunities," *Annual Review of Sociology* 30 (2004): 134–135.

11. Tarrow, *Power in Movement,* 71.

12. Ira Katznelson, "Periodization and Preferences," in Mahoney and Rueschemeyer, *Comparative Historical Analysis.*

13. Thelen, "How Institutions Evolve," 224–225.

14. Elizabeth J. Perry, *Patrolling the Revolution: Worker Militias, Citizenship, and the Modern Chinese State* (Lanham, Md.: Rowman and Littlefield, 2006). In this work she used the term *institutional inversion*, which is essentially the same as institutional conversion.

15. X. L. Ding, "Institutional Amphibiousness and the Transition from Communism: The Case of China," *British Journal of Political Science* 24 (1994): 293–318.

16. Ibid., 298.

17. Walder, "Collective Protest and the Waning of the Communist State," 71.

18. Jonathan Unger and Anita Chan, "China, Corporatism, and the East Asian Model," *Australian Journal of Chinese Affairs* 33 (January 1995): 37.

19. Elizabeth J. Perry, "Casting a 'Democracy' Movement: The Roles of Students, Workers, and Entrepreneurs," in Jeffery N. Wasserstrom and Elizabeth J. Perry, eds., *Popular Protest and Political Culture in Modern China* (Boulder, Colo.: Westview, 1992), 159.

20. Jeremy Brooke Straughn, "'Taking the State at Its Word': The Arts of Consentful Contention in the German Democratic Republic," *American Journal of Sociology* 110,6 (May 2005): 1602.

21. Doug McAdam, Sidney Tarrow, and Charles Tilly, *Dynamics of Contention* (New York: Cambridge University Press, 2001), 47.

22. Ibid., 47.

23. Ding, "Institutional Amphibiousness," 306.

24. Kevin J. O'Brien and Lianjiang Li, *Rightful Resistance in Rural China* (New York: Cambridge University Press, 2006), 10.

25. Steven Pfaff and Guobin Yang, "Double-Edged Ritual and the Symbolic Re-

sources of Collective Action: Political Commemorations and the Mobilization of Protest in 1989," *Theory and Society* 30 (2001): 550.

26. Kevin J. O'Brien, "Rightful Resistance," *World Politics* 49,1 (October 1996): 43.

27. Doug McAdam, *Political Process and the Development of Black Insurgency, 1930–1970* (Chicago: University of Chicago Press, 1996).

28. *Wall Street Journal,* May 11, 2004.

29. For a review essay, see Kevin J. O'Brien, "Collective Action in the Chinese Countryside," *China Journal* 48 (July 2002): 139–154.

30. Elizabeth J. Perry and Mark Selden, eds., *Chinese Society: Change, Conflict and Resistance* (London: Routledge, 2000), 17.

31. O'Brien, "Rightful Resistance," 42.

32. Perry, *Challenging the Mandate,* xxx.

33. See O'Brien and Li, *Rightful Resistance.*

34. James Q. Wilson, "The Strategy of Protest: Problems of Negro Civic Action," *Journal of Conflict Resolution* 3 (1961): 291–292.

35. Phyllis M. Frakt, "Mao's Concept of Representation," *American Journal of Political Science* 23,4 (1979): 690.

36. Richard M. Pfeffer, "Serving the People and Continuing the Revolution," *China Quarterly* 52 (1972): 621.

37. Diao Jiecheng, *Renmin xinfang shilue* (A brief history of people's letters and visits) (Beijing: Beijing xueyuan chubanshe, 1996), 59.

38. This principle was first stipulated by the State Council in "Renmin laixin laifang gongzuo de jiben jingyan (caogao)" (Basic experiences in handling people's letters and visits—A draft), in Diao Jiecheng, *Renmin xinfang shilue,* 364–369.

39. Calculated from monthly summaries of petition letters produced by Hunan Provinicial Xinfang Bureau, which the author collected at the Bureau, in Changsha, in 2002.

40. "Comrade Zhu Rongji's opening speech at the Fourth National Conference on Xinfang Work, 1996." This document was on file at the xinfang bureau of County H in Hunan Province. It was probably distributed to every xinfang bureau in China.

41. For research on imperial China, see Zhou Guangyuan, "Illusion and Reality in the Law of the Late Qing," *Modern China* 19,4 (1993: 427–456; Jonathan K. Ocko, "'I'll Take It All the Way to Beijing': Capital Appeals in the Qing," *Journal of Asian Studies* 47,2 (May 1988): 291–315; and William Alford, "Of Arsenic and Old Laws: Looking Anew at Criminal Justice in Late Imperial China," *California Law Review* 72 (1984): 1180–1255. For research on the Soviet Union, see Nicholas Lampert, *Whistle Blowing in the Soviet Union: Complaints and Abuses under State Socialism* (London: MacMillan, 1985).

42. See, for example, Wang Shaoguang, "The Rise of the Regions: Fiscal Reform and the Decline of Central State Capacity in China," in Andrew Walder, ed., *The Waning of the Communist State* (Berkeley: University of California Press,

1995), 87–113; Andrew Walder, "The Decline of Communist Power: Elements of a Theory of Institutional Change," *Theory and Society* 23,2 (1994): 297–323; Dali Yang, "Reform and the Restructuring of Central-Local Relations," in David S. G. Goodman and Gerald Segal, eds., *China Deconstructs: Politics, Trade, and Regionalism* (London: Routledge, 1994), 59–98; Richard Baum and Alexei Shevchenko, "The 'State of the State,'" in Merle Goldman and Roderick MacFarquhar, eds., *The Paradox of China's Post-Mao Reforms* (Cambridge, Mass.: Harvard University Press, 1999), 333–360.

43. O'Brien, "Rightful Resistance."

44. For example, the Shuifenhe city government in Heilongjiang Province stipulates: "when collective petitions to Beijing occur, [the responsible units] will be reduced 20 points for each petition; 10 points will be deducted for each collective petition to the provincial government; 5 points will be deducted for collective petitions to the city government; if the petitions are repeated, the points will be deducted twice." See Xu Zhiyong, Yao Yao, and Li Yingqiang, "Xianzheng shiyezhong de xinfang zhili" (On the management of xinfang from the perspective of constitutionalism) Gansu lilun xuekan (Gansu theory journal) 3 (2005): 15–20.

45. For an argument similar to Ding's on amphibiousness but in relation to people's congresses, see Kevin J. O'Brien, "Chinese People's Congresses and Legislative Embeddedness: Understanding Early Organizational Development," *Comparative Political Studies* 27,1 (April 1994): 80–109.

46. Ira Katznelson, "Structures and Configuration," in Mark Lichbach and Alan S. Zuckerman, eds., *Comparative Politics: Rationality, Culture, and Structure* (Cambridge: Cambridge University Press, 1997), 99.

3. Mass Frames and Worker Protest

Research for this project would not have been possible without the assistance of friends and colleagues in Beijing, Benxi, Chongqing, Datong, Harbin, Luoyang, Shanghai, Shenyang, and Zhengzhou. I am very grateful for their help and regret that they must remain anonymous here. I have also benefited from frequent visits to the library of the Universities Service Centre at the Chinese University of Hong Kong. For generous funding, I thank: Fulbright-Institute of International Education, the National Security Education Program, Beijing University, Harvard-Yenching Institute, the University of Hawaii, the University of California, Berkeley, the University of California Institute for Labor and Employment, the Urban China Research Network, Oxford University, the Higher Education Funding Council for England, and the British Academy.

1. William James, *Principles of Psychology,* vol. 2 (New York: Dover, 1950), 283–324.

2. Erving Goffman, *Frame Analysis: An Essay on the Organization of Experience* (Harmondsworth, England: Penguin Books, 1975), 2–3, 8–11.

3. Ibid., 21.

4. Gregory Gonos, "'Situation' versus 'Frame': The 'Interactionist' and the 'Structuralist' Analyses of Everyday Life," *American Sociological Review* 42,6 (December 1977): 854–867; Doug McAdam, *Political Process and the Development of Black Insurgency, 1930–1970* (Chicago: University of Chicago Press, 1982), 48–51.

5. Doug McAdam, John D. McCarthy, and Mayer N. Zald, eds., *Comparative Perspectives on Social Movements: Political Opportunities, Mobilizing Structures, and Cultural Framings* (Cambridge: Cambridge University Press, 1996), 6.

6. For example, William A. Gamson, Bruce Fireman, and Steven Rytina, *Encounters with Unjust Authority* (Homewood, Ill.: Dorsey Press, 1982); Bert Klandermans, "Mobilization and Participation: Social-Psychological Expansions of Resource Mobilization," *American Sociological Review* 49,5 (October 1984): 583–600; David A. Snow, Burke Rochford Jr., Steven K. Worden, and Robert D. Benford, "Frame Alignment Processes, Micromobilization, and Movement Participation," *American Sociological Review* 51,4 (August 1986): 464–481. See also the excellent review essay on the conceptualization of frames by John A. Noakes and Hank Johnston, "Frames of Protest: A Road Map to a Perspective," in Johnston and Noakes, eds., *Frames of Protest: Social Movements and the Framing Perspective* (Lanham, Md.: Rowman and Littlefield, 2005), 1–29.

7. James M. Jasper, *The Art of Moral Protest: Culture, Biography, and Creativity in Social Movements* (Chicago: University of Chicago Press, 1997), 85.

8. Doug McAdam, Sidney Tarrow, and Charles Tilly, *Dynamics of Contention* (Cambridge: Cambridge University Press, 2001), 25–27, 48.

9. This book received criticism from some for reading "like it was written by a committee that is not quite sure of its agenda." Pamela E. Oliver, "Mechanisms of Contention," *Mobilization* 8,1 (February 2003): 120.

10. This has been clearly exposed in Ruud Koopmans, "A Failed Revolution— But a Worthy Cause," *Mobilization* 8,1 (February 2003): 116–119.

11. Kevin J. O'Brien and Lianjiang Li, *Rightful Resistance in Rural China* (Cambridge: Cambridge University Press, 2006), 38.

12. Ching Kwan Lee, *Against the Law: Labor Protests in China's Rustbelt and Sunbelt* (Berkeley: University of California Press, 2007), 25–26, 114–120.

13. For a more detailed discussion of the contentious politics of Chinese laid-off workers of each region and of each regional political economy, see William Hurst, "Understanding Contentious Collective Action by Chinese Laid-Off Workers: the Importance of Regional Political Economy," *Studies in Comparative International Development* 39,2 (Summer 2004): 94–120.

14. Marc J. Blecher, "Hegemony and Workers' Politics in China," *China Quarterly* 170 (June 2002): 283–303.

15. Interviews, 45-year-old female laid-off fish warehouse worker; 47-year-old female laid-off chemical worker; and 49-year-old male laid-off sanitation worker; Shanghai, May 2002.

16. Interview, 37-year-old female laid-off textile worker, Shanghai, May 2002.

17. Ching Kwan Lee, "The 'Revenge of History': Collective Memories and Labor Protests in Northeastern China," *Ethnography* 1,2 (December 2000): 217–237; and Lee, "From the Specter of Mao to the Spirit of the Law: Labor Insurgency in China," *Theory and Society* 31,2 (2002): 189–228.

18. Interview, 58-year-old female retired miner, Benxi, November 2001.

19. Interview, 43-year-old male laid-off miner, Benxi, November 2000.

20. Interview, 47-year-old female laid-off chemical worker, Benxi, November 2000.

21. This is a reference to the title character—a rickshaw puller in Beijing in the early 1920s—in Lao She's tragic 1936 novel about brutal exploitation *Luotuo Xiangzi* (Camel Xiangzi).

22. Interview, 51-year-old male laid-off chemical worker, Beijing, July 2002.

23. Dorothy J. Solinger, "Labour Market Reform and the Plight of the Laid-Off Proletariat," *China Quarterly* 170 (June 2002): 304–326.

24. Interview, 44-year-old female laid-off textile worker, Chongqing, October 2001.

25. Interview, 41-year-old male laid-off coal miner, Datong, July 2002.

26. Interview, party secretary of a large state-owned enterprise, Luoyang, June 2002.

27. Xueguang Zhou, "Unorganized Interests and Collective Action in Communist China," *American Sociological Review* 58,1 (February 1993): 54–73. For a similar view of the countryside, see Daniel Kelliher, *Peasant Power in China: The Era of Rural Reform, 1979–1989* (New Haven, Conn.: Yale University Press, 1992).

28. Mario Luis Small, "Culture, Cohorts, and Social Organization Theory: Understanding Local Participation in a Latino Housing Project," *American Journal of Sociology* 108,1 (July 2002): 34.

29. Ira Katznelson, "Working Class Formation: Constructing Cases and Comparisons," in Ira Katznelson and Aristide R. Zolberg, eds., *Working Class Formation: Nineteenth-Century Patterns in Western Europe and the United States* (Princeton, N.J.: Princeton University Press, 1986), 17, 19.

30. On how this happened in pre-1949 Shanghai and why it helped keep the working class divided, see Elizabeth J. Perry, *Shanghai on Strike: The Politics of Chinese Labor* (Stanford, Calif.: Stanford University Press, 1993).

31. On the latter, see Ying Zhu and Malcolm Warner, "An Emerging Model of Employment Relations in China: A Divergent Path from the Japanese?" *International Business Review* 9,3 (2000): 345–361.

32. Robert Cliver, "'Red Silk': Labor, Capital, and the State in the Yangzi Delta Silk Industry, 1945–1960" (Ph.D. Diss., Harvard University, 2007).

33. Interview, 43-year-old male laid-off coal miner, Benxi, November 2000.

34. Interview, 42-year-old male laid-off machine plant worker, Benxi, November 2000.

35. Xu Xiaoqing and Liu Xiaonan, "Laodong jiuye chengguo xianzhe; zongliang yu jiegou maodun reng xian tuchu" (The results of labor re-employment are remarkable; but contradictions of scale and structure are still grave), in Cao,

Fang, and Zhang, eds., *2006 nian: Liaoning jingji shehui xingshi fenxi yu yuce* (2006: Analysis and Forecast of the shape of Liaoning's Economy and Society) (Beijing: Shehui kexue wenxian chubanshe, 2006), 250.

36. Interview, 33-year-old male laid-off warehouse worker, Shanghai, May 2002.

37. Interview, 40-year-old male laid-off warehouse worker, Shanghai, May 2002.

38. Interviews, 42-year-old male laid-off dock worker; 45-year-old male laid-off auto worker, Shanghai, May 2002.

39. Cathy Schneider, "Political Opportunities and Framing Puerto Rican Identity in New York City," in Johnston and Noakes, *Frames of Protest,* 163–181.

40. Ann Swidler, "Culture in Action: Symbols and Strategies," *American Sociological Review* 51,2 (April 1986): 273–286; Mayer N. Zald, "Culture, Ideology, and Strategic Framing," in McAdam, McCarthy, and Zald, *Comparative Perspectives,* 266–268.

41. Paul D. Almeida, "Opportunity Organizations and Threat-Induced Contention: Protest Waves in Authoritarian Settings," *American Journal of Sociology* 109,2 (September 2003): 352.

42. James B. Rule, *Theories of Civil Violence* (Berkeley: University of California Press, 1988), 188–191, 198; James M. Jasper, *The Art of Moral Protest: Culture, Biography, and Creativity in Social Movements* (Chicago: University of Chicago Press, 1997), 80–85.

43. See, for example: Mary Marx Ferree, "Resonance and Radicalism: Feminist Framing in the Abortion Debates of the United States and Germany," *American Journal of Sociology* 109,2 (September 2003): 304–344; Ellen Reese and Garnett Newcombe, "Income Rights, Mothers' Rights, or Workers' Rights? Collective Action Frames, Organizational Ideologies, and the American Welfare Rights Movement," *Social Problems* 50,2 (2003): 294–318.

44. Rory McVeigh, Daniel J. Meyers, and David Sikkink, "Corn, Klansmen, and Coolidge: Structure and Framing in Social Movements," *Social Forces* 83,2 (December 2004): 656.

45. Snow et al., "Frame Alignment Processes," 465.

46. McAdam, Tarrow, and Tilly, *Dynamics,* 48.

47. On the role of countermovements, see Joseph Luders, "Countermovements, the State, and the Intensity of Racial Contention in the American South," in Jack A. Goldstone, ed., *States, Parties, and Social Movements* (Cambridge: Cambridge University Press, 2003), 27–44.

48. McAdam, *Political Process,* 34–35, 48–49.

49. Ibid., 51.

50. Zhou, "Unorganized Interests," 59.

51. Hurst, "Understanding Contentious Collective Action," 105–106. Lee (*Against the Law,* 72) later also alluded to this in reference to the Northeast.

52. McVeigh, Meyers, and Sikkink, "Corn, Klansmen and Coolidge," 657–658.

4. Worker Leaders and Framing Factory-Based Resistance

Funding for this research was provided by the Research Council of Hong Kong. I am especially grateful to Kevin O'Brien, who so kindly invited me to the Berkeley conference and provided detailed suggestions for improving this chapter. My thanks also go to Sidney Tarrow, David Meyer, and other participants at the conference, who offered valuable comments.

1. E. J. Hobsbawm, *Primitive Rebels* (New York: Norton, 1959). Gustave Le Bon, *Crowd: A Study of the Popular Mind* (New York: Viking Press, 1960).
2. Edward Walsh, "Resource Mobilization and Citizen Protests in Communities around Three Mile Island," *Social Problems* 29 (October 1981): 1–21.
3. See Jack Goldstone and Elizabeth Perry, "Leadership Dynamics and Dynamics of Contention," in Ronald Aminzade et al., eds., *Silence and Voice in the Study of Contentious Politics* (New York: Cambridge University Press, 2001).
4. Sharon Erickson Nepstad and Clifford Bob, "When Do Leaders Matter? Hypotheses on Leadership Dynamics in Social Movements," *Mobilization* 11,1 (2006): 1–22.
5. See, for example, William Gamson, *Talking Politics* (New York: Cambridge University Press, 1992); Sidney Tarrow, *Power in Movement* (New York: Cambridge University Press, 1998); and "Part III Framing Process" (which includes five articles), in Doug McAdam, John McCarthy, and Mayer Zald, eds., *Comparative Perspectives on Social Movements* (New York: Cambridge University Press, 1996).
6. Charles Tilly, *The Contentious French* (Cambridge, Mass.: Belknap Press, 1986); Tilly, "Contentious Repertoires in Great Britain, 1758–1834," in Mark Traugott, ed., *Repertoires and Cycles of Collective Action* (Durham, N.C.: Duke University Press, 1995), 15–45; Tarrow, *Power in Movement*.
7. For discussions of framing and repertoires, see Charles Tilly and Sidney Tarrow, *Contentious Politics* (Boulder, Colo.: Paradigm, 2007).
8. Gamson, *Talking Politics*, 7.
9. Bert Klandermans, *The Social Psychology of Protest* (Oxford: Blackwell, 1997), 44.
10. Charles Tilly, *Popular Contention in Great Britain, 1758–1834* (Cambridge, Mass.: Harvard University Press, 1995), 41.
11. Tarrow, *Power in Movement*, 30.
12. A contentious gathering, according to Charles Tilly, is "an occasion in which ten or more persons outside the government gather in the same place and make a visible claim which, if realized, would affect the interests of some specific person(s) or group(s)," *From Mobilization to Revolution* (Reading, Mass.: Addison-Wesley, 1978), 275.
13. James Jasper, *The Art of Moral Protest* (Chicago: University of Chicago Press, 1997), 54–58.
14. Ibid., 57.

15. For a detailed account of antiprivatization resistance in these factories, see Feng Chen, "Privatization and Its Discontents in Chinese Factories," *China Quarterly* 185 (March 2006): 42–60.

16. For discussion of the influence of Maoist ideas on laid-off workers' thinking and claims, see Ching Kwan Lee, "The Revenge of History: Collective Memories and Labor Protests in Northeastern China," *Ethnography* 1,2 (2000): 217–237; William Hurst and Kevin J. O'Brien, "China's Contentious Pensioners," *China Quarterly* 170 (June 2002): 345–360; Feng Chen, "Industrial Restructuring and Workers' Resistance in China," *Modern China* 29,2 (April 2003): 237–262. Popular actions by other social groups are also framed using Maoist ideas. See Kevin J. O'Brien and Lianjiang Li, "Campaign Nostaligia in the Chinese Countryside," *Asian Survey* 39,2 (March–April 1999): 375–393; Elizabeth J. Perry, "To Rebel Is Justified—Cultural Revolution Influences on Contemporary Chinese Political Protest," in Kaw-Yee Law, ed., *The Chinese Cultural Revolution Reconsidered: Beyond Purge and Holocaust* (New York: Palgrave, 2003), 262–281; and Patricia Thornton, "Comrades and Collectives in Arms, Tax Resistance, Evasion, and Avoidance Strategies in Post-Mao China," in Peter Hays Gries and Stanley Rosen, eds., *State and Society in Twenty-First-Century China* (New York: RoutledgeCurzon, 2004), 87–104.

17. Tarrow, *Power in Movement.*

18. It is difficult to know how many labor leaders were Cultural Revolution activists. During my field work in Zhengzhou, Henan Province, I was told that some organizers of protests in other factories in the city also had been Cultural Revolution activists.

19. An engineer at the Zhengzhou Railway Bureau, Tang Qishan, was one of the most famous worker rebels during the Cultural Revolution. He became a member of the ninth and tenth Central Committee, as well as party secretary of Henan Province. He was sentenced to life imprisonment in 1979.

20. Interview, January 2004.

21. For more on worker nostalgia for Maoism, see Ching Kwan Lee, "The Labor Politics of Market Socialism," *Modern China* 24,1 (January 1998): 3–33. There are also many workers, however, who suffer from the "hegemony of the market and of the state." See Marc Blecher, "Hegemony and Workers' Politics in China," *China Quarterly* 170 (June 2002): 283–303.

22. Interview, August 2004.

23. Interview, January 2004.

24. Interview, January 2004.

25. The "three types of people" included those who (1) rose to power by following the Lin Biao and Jiang Qing cliques and participating in rebellion; (2) had strong factional tendencies; and (3) were involved in beating, smashing, and looting during the Cultural Revolution.

26. Interview, January 2004.

27. Interview, January 2004.

28. Interview, January 2004.
29. Interview, January 2004.
30. For "moral economy" protests by laid-off workers, see Hurst and O'Brien, "China's Contentious Pensioners," and Feng Chen, "Subsistence Crisis, Managerial Corruption, and Labor Protests in China," *China Journal* 44 (July 2000): 41–66. For claims related to downsizing, closures, bankruptcy, and privatization, see Chen, "Privatization and Its Discontents."
31. My fieldwork included other factories, where I found similar rhetoric. The worker leaders I interviewed also told similar stories about factories in Zhengzhou and neighboring cities, including Luoyang. During a large-scale demonstration in March 2002, workers carried a huge portrait of Mao; the scene was captured by a photo that was widely circulated on the internet.
32. On every anniversary of Mao's birthday since the mid-1990s, people have gathered in the largest square in Zhengzhou to lay flowers, sing songs, and distribute leaflets. At another square next to the Workers' Cultural Palace, there was a "debate corner," where debates occurred nearly every afternoon, joined by workers, retirees, and other residents. In a visit to this debate corner in the winter of 2004, I observed a fierce argument involving about 30 people, with a tiny minority defending market reforms and an overwhelming majority critical of current policies and nostalgic for the Maoist era. A few old men wore Mao badges.
33. Tarrow, *Power in Movement*.
34. Elizabeth J. Perry, "Shanghai's Strike Wave of 1957," *China Quarterly* 139 (March 1994): 1–27.
35. For worker rebellions during the Cultural Revolution, see Elizabeth J. Perry and Li Xun, *Proletarian Power: Shanghai in the Cultural Revolution* (Boulder, Colo.: Westview, 1997).
36. Interview, February 2003.
37. Leafleting beyond the factory and targeting political leaders is not tolerated. Mr. Z was arrested for disseminating leaflets that criticized Deng and Jiang.
38. Interview, January 2004.
39. For details of the labor struggle in this factory, see Chen, "Privatization and Its Discontents."
40. Interview, January 2004.
41. Interview, January 2004.
42. Interview, January 2004.
43. Cited in Zhu Xiaoyang, "Wudu falü he zixu chongjian: guoying qiye gaige de gean fenxi" (Misreading the law and the construction of order: A case of SOE reform), Shehui Kexue Zhanxian (Social science front) 3 (2005): 197–206.
44. Interview, January 2004.
45. Zhu Xiaoyang, "Misreading the Law."
46. Tilly and Tarrow, *Contentious Politics*, 21–23.

47. Worker rebellion in Henan during the Cultural Revolution led to the promotion of numerous workers to leadership positions and highlighted the primacy of the working class in the province. That was one of major reasons that Henan was defined by the post-Mao leadership as "an area most affected by the Cultural Revolution." It is said that over 95 percent of the party secretaries at various levels of government in Henan were purged in the early 1980s.

48. Lee, "'Revenge of History'"; Tong Xin, "Yanxu de shehuizhuyi wenhua chuantong: Yige guoyou qiye gongren jiti xingdong de gean fenxi" (Continuing the socialist cultural tradition: A case study of collective action in an enterprise), Shehuixue Yanjiu (Sociological research) 1 (2006): 59–76; Yu Jianrong, Zhongguo gongren zhuangkuang (The state of the Chinese working class) (Hong Kong: Minjing chubanshe, 2006).

49. See, for example, William Sewell, *Work and Revolution in France* (New York: Cambridge University Press, 1980); Marc Steinberg, *Fighting Words: Working Class Formation, Collective Action and Discourse in Early Nineteenth-Century England* (Ithaca, N.Y.: Cornell University Press, 1999); Koo Hagen, *Korean Workers: The Culture and Politics of Class Formation* (Ithaca, N.Y.: Cornell University Press, 2001).

50. For the concept of "diffuse support," see David Easton, *A Systems Analysis of Political Life* (New York: Wiley, 1965), 273–274. Also see Edward Muller and Thomas Jukam, "On the Meaning of Political Support," *American Political Science Review* 71 (September 1997): 1561–1595.

51. *Guangming ribao* (Guangming daily), August 13, 1999.

52. *Renmin ribao* (People's daily), May 1, 1996.

53. Kevin J. O'Brien and Lianjiang Li, *Rightful Resistance in Rural China* (New York: Cambridge University Press, 2006).

54. James Scott, *Weapons of the Weak: Everyday Forms of Peasant Resistance* (New Haven, Conn.: Yale University Press, 1985), 336.

55. Chinese workers are now increasingly able to frame their claims using a "rights discourse" derived from labor laws and regulations. On this, see Mary Gallagher, "'Use the Law as Your Weapon!' Institutional Change and Legal Mobilization in China," and Isabelle Thireau and Hua Lishan, "One Law, Two Interpretations: Mobilizing the Labor Law in Arbitration Committees and in Letters and Visits Bureaus," in Neil J. Diamant, Stanley B. Lubman, and Kevin J. O'Brien, eds., *Engaging the Law in China: State, Society, and Possibilities for Justice* (Stanford, Calif.: Stanford University Press, 2005), 54–83 and 84–103.

56. What the authorities fear most is "infiltration of foreign hostile forces" into labor agitation. Any attempt by Chinese workers to contact overseas political groups can have serious consequences. For example, one reason two worker leaders received prison sentences for organizing demonstrations in Liaoyang

was that they were said to have contacted the Chinese Democratic Party, a group now located in the United States.

57. On limitations of the labor struggle, see Ching Kwan Lee, "Pathways of Labor Insurgency," in Elizabeth Perry and Mark Selden, eds., *Chinese Society: Change, Conflict and Resistance* (London: Routledge, 2000), 41–60.

58. For a detailed description of the protest in Liaoyang, see "Paying the Price: Worker Unrest in Northeast China," hrw.org/reports/2002/chinalbr02/index.htm#TopOfPage (accessed June 6, 2007).

59. On the characteristics of protest leaders in the countryside, see Lianjiang Li and Kevin J. O'Brien, "Protest Leadership in Rural China," *China Quarterly* 193 (March 2008): 1–23.

60. For example, of the worker leaders I interviewed, four were once arrested for "causing disturbances." In addition, they were all labeled "leftovers of the Cultural Revolution."

61. Doug McAdam, *Political Process and the Development of Black Insurgency, 1930–1970* (Chicago: University of Chicago Press, 1982), 49–51.

5. Recruitment to Protestant House Churches

This chapter would not have been possible without the willingness of Protestants, Chinese and foreign, to discuss their activities. We gratefully acknowledge their assistance; comments on earlier versions by Dan Bays, Ken Foster, Tom Gold, and Fenggang Yang; and generous financial support from the Chiang Ching-Kuo Foundation, Harvard Yenching Institute, the Mustard Seed Foundation, and the Center for Chinese Studies at the University of California, Berkeley.

1. Luther P. Gerlach and Virginia H. Hine, *People, Power, Change* (Indianapolis: Bobbs-Merrill, 1970), 97.

2. On social movements, see Mario Diani, "Networks and Participation," in David A. Snow, Sarah A. Soule, and Hanspeter Kriesi, eds., *The Blackwell Companion to Social Movements* (New York: Oxford University Press, 2004), 339–359. On religious movements, see Gerlach and Hine, *People, Power, Change*, 88.

3. On new identities, see Florence Passy, "Social Networks Matter. But How?" in Mario Diani and Doug McAdam, eds., *Social Movements and Networks* (New York: Oxford University Press, 2003), 23. On trust, see Sharon Erickson Nepstad and Christian Smith, "Rethinking Recruitment to High-Risk/Cost Activism: The Case of Nicaragua Exchange," *Mobilization* 4,1 (1999): 26. For the application of pressure, see Doug McAdam, "Recruitment to High-Risk Activism: The Case of Freedom Summer," *American Journal of Sociology* 92,1 (1986): 68. On easing circulation of information, see Mario Diani, "Introduction: Social Movements, Contentious Actions, and Social Networks," in Diani and McAdam, *Social Movements and Networks*, 8. On "pull factors," see James A. Kitts, "Mobilizing in Black Boxes: Social Networks and Participation in Social

Movement Organizations," *Mobilization* 5,2 (2000): 241. On solidarity, see David Knoke and Nancy Wisely, "Social Movements," in David Knoke, ed., *Political Networks* (New York: Cambridge University Press, 1990), 68. On interpersonal rewards, see Rodney Stark and William Sims Bainbridge, "Networks of Faith: Interpersonal Bonds and Recruitment to Cults and Sects," *American Journal of Sociology* 85,6 (1980): 1394.

4. Hank Johnston and Carol Mueller, "Unobtrusive Practices of Contention in Leninist Regimes," *Sociological Perspectives* 44,3 (2001): 360–361.

5. Maryjane Osa, "Networks in Opposition: Linking Organizations through Activists in the Polish People's Republic," in Diani and McAdam, *Social Movements and Networks*, 78–79.

6. Karl-Dieter Opp and Christiane Gern, "Dissident Groups, Personal Networks, and Spontaneous Cooperation: The East German Revolution of 1989," *American Sociological Review* 58,5 (1993): 662, 674. Social connections have also been found to be crucial for recruitment to illegal organizations and subcultures with less mainstream messages. See Diani, "Networks and Participation," 350–351; Passy, "Social Networks Matter," 27–28.

7. Michael I. Harrison, "Sources of Recruitment to Catholic Pentecostalism," *Journal for the Scientific Study of Religion* 13,1 (1974): 57–58. See also Gerlach and Hine, *People, Power, Change*, 88.

8. Stark and Bainbridge, "Networks of Faith," 1377.

9. David A. Snow, Louis A. Zurcher Jr., and Sheldon Ekland-Olson, "Social Networks and Social Movements: A Microstructural Approach to Differential Recruitment," *American Sociological Review* 45,5 (1980): 787–801; Stark and Bainbridge, "Networks of Faith," 1376–1395.

10. See Gerlach and Hine, *People, Power, Change*, 82; John Lofland and Rodney Stark, "Becoming a World-Saver: A Theory of Conversion to a Deviant Perspective," *American Sociological Review* 30,6 (1965): 862–875; Snow et al., "Social Networks and Social Movements," 791.

11. Snow et al., "Social Networks and Social Movements," 790.

12. Stark and Bainbridge, "Networks of Faith," 1389. On movements more broadly, see Diani and McAdam, *Social Movements and Networks*.

13. For stranger recruitment by animal rights activists, see James M. Jasper and Jane D. Poulsen, "Recruiting Strangers and Friends: Moral Shocks and Social Networks in Animal Rights and Anti-nuclear Protests," *Social Problems* 42,4 (1995): 498–499. On Dutch peace activists who had prior links with about four-fifths of the movement's "mobilization potential" but also lacked ties with about one-fifth of those approached, see Bert Klandermans and Dirk Oegema, "Potentials, Networks, Motivations, and Barriers: Steps towards Participation in Social Movements," *American Sociological Review* 52,4 (1987): 525. For Hare Krishna recruitment, see E. Burke Rochford, "Recruitment Strategies, Ideology, and Organization in the Hare Krishna Movement," *Social Prob-*

lems 29,4 (1982): 399–410. On self-recruitment to the antiabortion movement, see Kristin Luker, *Abortion and the Politics of Motherhood* (Berkeley: University of California Press, 1984).

14. For animal rights activists, see Jasper and Poulsen, "Recruiting Strangers and Friends." On peace demonstrations, see Klandermans and Oegema, "Potentials, Networks, Motivations, and Barriers," 522. In a Hare Krishna sect, see Rochford, "Recruitment Strategies."

15. On mechanisms, see Hyojoung Kim and Peter S. Bearman, "The Structure and Dynamics of Movement Participation," *American Sociological Review* 62,1 (1997): 90; Kitts, "Mobilizing in Black Boxes"; Doug McAdam and Ronnelle Paulsen, "Specifying the Relationship between Social Ties and Activism," *American Journal of Sociology* 99,3 (1993): 640–667; Passy, "Social Networks Matter."

16. Tony Lambert, *China's Christian Millions* (Grand Rapids, Mich.: Monarch Books, 1999), 216.

17. Shu Jingxiang, "Guanyu Heilongjiangsheng tianzhujiao, jidujiao gaikuang jiqi jiaotu xinyang quxiang de diaocha fenxi" (Investigation and analysis of a survey of Catholicism and Protestantism in Heilongjiang Province and trends in the believers' faiths), Zongjiao yu Minzu (Religion and ethnic groups) 74,3 (2003): 115–116.

18. Jason Kindopp, "Fragmented yet Defiant: Protestant Resilience under Chinese Communist Party Rule," in Jason Kindopp and Carol Lee Hamrin, eds., *God and Caesar in China* (Washington, D.C.: Brookings Institution, 2004), 124; Stephen Wang, *The Long Road to Freedom* (Kent, England: Sovereign World, 2002), 85.

19. Richard C. Bush Jr., *Religion in Communist China* (New York: Abingdon Press, 1970), 204, 211, 232; Guowuyuan zongjiaoju cailiao weiyuanhui (State Council Religious Affairs Bureau Materials Committee), "Jidutu juhuichu gaikuang" (Situation of Christian meeting places), Heilongjiang Provincial Archives, Harbin 159-2-155, 1955, 16–38.

20. Ka-lun Leung, *Gaige kaifang yilai de zhongguo nongcun jiaohui* (The rural churches of mainland China since 1978) (Hong Kong: Alliance Bible Seminary, 1999), 81.

21. For new converts recruited by unregistered churches during the Cultural Revolution, see Tony Lambert, *The Resurrection of the Chinese Church* (Wheaton, Ill.: Harold Shaw, 1994), 18–21, 80; Heilongjiang Provincial Gazette, *Heilongjiang shengzhi, zongjiaozhi* (Heilongjiang provincial history, religious history) (Harbin, Heilongjiang: Heilongjiang People's Press, 1999), 301. House churches generally seek to avoid detection, but some are "half-public, half-underground," or known to local authorities, say, the neighborhood residents' committee or the local police station, but not TSPM officials. Interviews, Beijing, August 2003; Harbin, November 2003. See also May M. C. Cheng,

"House Church Movements and Religious Freedom in China," *China: An International Journal* 1,1 (2003): 34–35; Alan Hunter and Kim-Kwong Chan, *Protestantism in Contemporary China* (New York: Cambridge University Press, 1993), 192.

22. See Donald E. MacInnis, *Religion in China Today* (Maryknoll, N.Y.: Orbis Books, 1989), 10–11, 32.

23. Since the 1990s, governments from the municipal level up have issued a stream of regulations that codify what constitutes "normal" (*zhengchang*) religious activities. See Guojia Zongjiao Shiwuju Zhengce Faguisi (National Religious Affairs Bureau Policy and Regulations Office), *Quanguo zongjiao xingzheng fagui guizhang huibian* (Collection of national religious administrative rules and regulations) (Beijing: Religious Cultures Press, 2000). But even the latest national regulations in March 2005 are sufficiently vague that cadres have considerable flexibility in how to implement them. See Anthony Lam, "A Commentary on the Regulations of Religious Affairs," *Tripod* 25,136 (Spring 2005), www.hsstudyc.org.hk (accessed August 19, 2006).

24. MacInnis, *Religion in China Today,* 8–26, 18. This policy statement was ambiguous on the legality of home gatherings. It declared that these meetings "in principle . . . should not be allowed, yet this prohibition should not be too rigidly enforced." Instead, "more appropriate arrangements"—such as registration or worship in a registered site—"should be made" (18). This ambiguity was reduced somewhat in 1994, when the National Religious Affairs Bureau issued study materials stating that registration does not apply to home meetings of a few family members and neighbors. See Cheng, "House Church Movements," 26. Since, however, home meetings typically recruit new members and the Religious Affairs Bureau requires that it be informed of all religious growth, the spirit of the ordinance still implies that home meetings should register with the TSPM.

25. See Jonathan Chao and Rosanna Chong, *Dangdai zhongguo jidujiao fazhanshi 1949–1997* (A history of Christianity in socialist China, 1949–1997) (Taipei: CMI, 1997), 278. Registration as a means to control churches was discussed in an interview in Harbin, November 2002. On requirements for meeting locations, participants, and leaders, see Zhonggong Zhongyang Wenxian (Comprehensive Study Group of the Documents Office of the Chinese Communist Party Central Committee), *Xinshiqi zongjiao gongzuo wenxian xuanbian* (Selected religious work documents of the new period) (Beijing: Religious Cultures Press, 2003), 222–225.

26. For the number of TSPM churches and meeting sites nationwide, see Xuezeng Gong, *Shehuizhuyi yu zongjiao* (Socialism and religion) (Beijing: Religious Cultures Press, 2003), 238. The number of registered churches in Harbin is drawn from interviews, Harbin, November 2003. In 1983, the crowd at a TSPM Christmas service in Harbin separated Kevin O'Brien from his wife, who was later lifted up off the packed floor and swayed with the congregation as they sung!

27. Hunter and Chan, *Protestantism in Contemporary China*, 84; Tetsunao Yama-mori and Kim-Kwong Chan, *Witnesses to Power* (Waynesboro, Ga.: Paternoster, 2000), 69.

28. Lydia Lee, *A Living Sacrifice* (Kent, England: Sovereign World, 2001), 239; also Ka-lun Leung, *Gaige kaifang*, 361–363. One interviewee (Shanghai, February 2003) also explained: "Who is the king of the church? Jesus. Who is the head of the TSPM? Ding Guangxun."

29. See MacInnis, *Religion in China Today*, 18. Rejection of registered churches as "false" was discussed in an interview, Wenzhou, February 2003; also Hunter and Chan, *Protestantism in Contemporary China*, 81.

30. Jason Kindopp, "The Politics of Protestantism in Contemporary China: State Control, Civil Society, and Social Movement in a Single Party-State" (Ph.D. diss., Georgetown University, 2004), 259–260.

31. Interview, Beijing, August 2003. Small, unregistered churches are also easy to set up, can be led by an unordained or enthusiastic believer, and can be located nearly anywhere. See Hunter and Chan, *Protestantism in Contemporary China*, 82; also Carsten Vala, "Training 'Patriotic' and Unregistered Protestant Church Leaders; Unintended Outcomes of State Policy for TSPM Leadership Training," in Yoshiko Ashiwa and David Wank, eds., *Making Religion, Making the State: The Politics of Religion in Contemporary China* (Stanford, Calif.: Stanford University Press, forthcoming).

32. Kindopp, "Politics of Protestantism," 372.

33. For believers feeling free to relate their experiences openly to an entire congregation, see Hunter and Chan, *Protestantism in Contemporary China*, 195. For the impersonal quality of TSPM services, see Richard Madsen, "Chinese Christianity, Indigenization and Conflict," in Elizabeth J. Perry and Mark Selden, eds., *Chinese Society*, 2nd ed. (New York: Routledge, 2003), 274.

34. Jason Kindopp, "Policy Dilemmas in China's Church-State Relations: An Introduction," in Kindopp and Hamrin, *God and Caesar in China*, 20, n. 3; Tony Lambert, "How Many Christians in China?" *China Insight Newsletter*, August–September 2005, www.omf.org.uk (accessed April 4, 2006); Fenggang Yang, "Lost in the Market, Saved at McDonald's: Conversion to Christianity in Urban China," *Journal for the Scientific Study of Religion* 44,4 (2005): 427.

35. On persistent official underestimation of Protestants, see Kindopp, "Politics of Protestantism," 3. On TSPM pastors failing to keep membership rolls, see Yang, "Lost in the Market," 426. Information on believers who worship in both above- and below-ground churches is drawn from an interview, Harbin, November 2002, and Hunter and Chan, *Protestantism in Contemporary China*, 87. On the clandestine nature of many unregistered churches, see Tony Lambert, "Counting Christians in China: A Cautionary Report," *International Bulletin of Missionary Research* 27,1 (2003): 6–10.

36. Chen Yun, "Guanyu gaodu zhongshi zongjiao shentou wenti de xin" (Letter about the issue of paying great attention to religious infiltration), letter to party secretary Jiang Zemin, April 4, 1990. Jiang then shared the letter with

other party officials. See Zhonggong Zhongyang Wenxian, *Xinshiqi zongjiao gongzuo wenxian xuanbian*, 177.

37. According to a top official of the Chinese Catholic Patriotic Association, it was in part the "continual troublemaking" of unregistered Protestants that led to the registration regulations. See Chao and Chong, *Dangdai zhongguo*, 652–653. The 2005 national Regulations on Religious Affairs also prohibit such preaching. See Kim-Kwong Chan and Eric Carlson, *Religious Freedom in China: Policy, Administration, and Regulation* (Santa Barbara, Calif.: Institute for the Study of American Religion, 2005), 84. Local-level regulations found in Guojia Zongjiao Shiwuju, *Quanguo zongjiao xingzheng fagui guizhang huibian*.

38. See Elizabeth Kendal, "China: Crackdown on House-Churches," Assist News Service, February 23, 2004, www.assistnews.net (accessed July 13, 2004).

39. In the city of Nanjing, Jiangsu Province, after implementing registration measures, cadres reported halving the religious growth rate from 10,000 Protestants a year to less than 5,000 a year. Jiacai Zhou, *Zongjiao gongzuo tansuo* (Exploration of religious work) (Beijing: Religious Cultures Press, 2002), 130–131.

40. See Ministry of Public Security, "Notice on Various Issues Regarding Identifying and Banning of Cultic Organizations," reprinted in *Chinese Law and Government* 36,2 (March–April 2003): 22–38.

41. Interview, Beijing, April 2003.

42. Interview, Shenyang, November 2003.

43. On this elsewhere, see Jasper and Poulsen, "Recruiting Strangers and Friends," 494.

44. Gerlach and Hine, *People, Power, Change*, 92; Knoke and Wisely, "Social Movements," 70; Miller McPherson, Lynn Smith-Lovin, and James M. Cook, "Birds of a Feather: Homophily in Social Networks," *Annual Review of Sociology* 27 (2001): 415–444.

45. Interviews, Changchun, October 2003; Shenyang, November 2003; Beijing, October 2003. For rural women spreading Christianity via a food stall, see Carl Lawrence, *The Church in China* (Minneapolis: Bethany House, 1985), 86–87.

46. Interview, Beijing, October 2003.

47. Snow et al., "Social Networks and Social Movements," 799; also Fred Kniss and Gene Burns, "Religious Movements," in Snow, Soule, and Kriesi, *Blackwell Companion*, 694–751. On flexible strategies, see Gerlach and Hine, *People, Power, Change*, 95.

48. Rochford, "Recruitment Strategies," 400, 408.

49. Interview, Dalian, November 2003.

50. Recruitment efforts by Mormon missionaries gained an average of one new member per thousand households. See Stark and Bainbridge, "Networks of

Faith," 1386. On American Pentecostals, see Gerlach and Hine, *People, Power, Change*, 82.

51. Interview, Beijing, October 2003. Though itinerant evangelism is still common, it was even more widespread in the late 1970s and early 1980s before rural authorities revived religious affairs supervision. See Lambert, *China's Christian Millions*, 69, 163, 171–172.

52. Interview, Dalian, November 2003.

53. Interview, Beijing, October 2003.

54. For reports of rural "faith healings," see Lambert, *Resurrection of the Chinese Church*, 147, 165; Yamamori and Chan, *Witnesses to Power*, 9–10, 45–47. For the Religious Affairs Bureau director's observation, see Jiacai Zhou, *Zongjiao gongzuo tansuo*, 135.

55. On itinerant evangelists downplaying doctrine, see Ka-lun Leung, *Gaige kaifang*. For deemphasis of theological rigor, see Kindopp, "Fragmented Yet Defiant," 135.

56. These are not "demonstration events" in the sense that Snow and Machalek use the term—public displays such as baptisms and speaking in tongues that act as status confirmation rituals—but efforts to legitimize an evangelist's message to nonbelievers. See David A. Snow and Richard Machalek, "The Sociology of Conversion," *Annual Review of Sociology* 10 (1984): 171–173.

57. On the rapid spread of tales of healing, see Chao and Chong, *Dangdai zhongguo*, 282; Lambert, *China's Christian Millions*, 112–119. In Latin America and Africa, a belief in faith healing has made Pentecostalism popular (in Mexico, for example) and reshaped mainline movements such as Lutheranism (in Tanzania, for example), particularly in communities that lack access to health care, have robust oral traditions, and are populated by rural residents or recent migrants. See Amanda Porterfield, *Healing in the History of Christianity* (New York: Oxford University Press, 2005), 174; David Martin, *Tongues of Fire: The Explosion of Protestantism in Latin America* (Cambridge, Mass: Blackwell, 1990), 165–167; Frieder Ludwig, *Church and State in Tanzania: Aspects of a Changing Relationship, 1961–1994* (Boston: Brill, 1999), 184, 186.

58. James Jasper, *The Art of Moral Protest* (Chicago: University of Chicago Press, 1997), 76–77, 172–74; Jasper and Poulsen, "Recruiting Strangers and Friends"; Gerlach and Hine, *People, Power, Change*, 88.

59. Interview, Changchun, November 2003.

60. Snow et al., "Social Networks and Social Movements," 790.

61. This recruiting technique works best with students who are from other cities or the countryside, and who live in dorms. Most local students go home to their families every weekend and do not have time to participate in follow-up activities that complete conversion. Interview, Changchun, November 2003.

62. Observation, Harbin, December 2002.

63. Yang, "Lost in the Market," 425, 438.

64. Rodney Stark, "How New Religions Succeed: A Theoretical Model," in David G. Bromley and Philip E. Hammond, eds., *The Future of New Religious Movements* (Macon, Ga.: Mercer University Press, 1987), 21.

65. Interview, Harbin, April 2003.

66. For unregistered church growth in Heilongjiang, see Lambert, *China's Christian Millions*, 217. On Henan, see Lambert, *Resurrection of the Chinese Church*, 149–150.

67. Lambert, *China's Christian Millions*, 165–166.

68. William A. Gamson, "Safe Spaces and Social Movements," *Perspectives on Social Problems* 8 (1996): 27; Francesca Polletta, "'Free Spaces' in Collective Action," *Theory and Society* 28 (1999): 7; William H. Sewell Jr., "Space in Contentious Politics," in Ronald Aminzade et al., eds., *Silence and Voice in the Study of Contentious Politics* (New York: Cambridge University Press, 2001), 69–70.

69. Klandermans and Oegema, "Potentials, Networks, Motivations, and Barriers," 520; Jasper and Poulsen, "Recruiting Strangers," 499.

70. On "subcultural 'worlds' [that] exist relatively peacefully amid the folds of the parent culture," see Rick Fantasia and Eric L. Hirsch, "Culture in Rebellion: The Appropriation and Transformation of the Veil in the Algerian Revolution," in Hank Johnston and Bert Klandermans, eds., *Social Movements and Culture* (Minneapolis: University of Minnesota Press, 1995), 157.

71. This is true for both unregistered and TSPM proselytizers. One elderly believer startled his fellow bus passengers by exhorting them to "believe in Jesus Christ" as he provided a tour of Harbin's TSPM meeting points (observation, November 2002).

72. Gamson, "Safe Spaces," 27; also Fantasia and Hirsch, "Culture in Rebellion," 156–157. Even when they are uncertain how safe a space is, some proselytizers are unafraid to test the limits of the permissible. These zealous evangelists feel impelled to recruit strangers, even in remote and politically sensitive border regions where authorities are wary of any religious activity. A few unregistered Protestants, for instance, have traveled far beyond their social networks to reach Tibetans in western China and Uighurs in the northwest. Here, they have worked one-on-one with local residents to learn the language while cultivating recruits by teaching simple Bible lessons. On detection, a number of these evangelists have overstepped what they can get away with and have been imprisoned. Interviews, Harbin, January and April 2003.

73. The TSPM Protestants also appropriate public spaces for evangelism. In a southern coastal city, TSPM church members evangelized strangers at four McDonald's restaurants over a period of four years. Interview, Guangzhou, January 2003; see also Yang, "Lost in the Market."

74. Polletta, "'Free Spaces.'"

75. On policing, see Sewell, "Space in Contentious Politics," 68–70. On "havens," see Eric L. Hirsch, "Protest Movements and Urban Theory," in Ray Hutchison, ed., *Urban Sociology in Transition* (Greenwich, Conn.: JAI Press, 1993), 159–180.

76. See Fantasia and Hirsch, "Culture in Rebellion," 157; Johnston and Mueller, "Unobtrusive Practices," 359–360; Gamson, "Safe Spaces"; Kevin J. O'Brien and Lianjiang Li, *Rightful Resistance in Rural China* (New York: Cambridge University Press, 2006), chap. 1; James Scott, *Domination and the Arts of Resistance* (New Haven, Conn.: Yale University Press, 1990).

77. Gamson, "Safe Spaces," 29. For discussions of the role spatial and ecological factors play in religious recruitment in the United States, see Harrison, "Sources of Recruitment"; Rochford, "Recruitment Strategies"; Snow et al., "Social Networks and Social Movements"; Yuting Wang and Fenggang Yang, "More than Evangelical and Ethnic: The Ecological Factor in Chinese Conversion to Christianity in the United States," *Sociology of Religion* 67,2 (2006): 179–192.

78. Jasper and Poulsen, "Recruiting Strangers," 494; Luker, *Abortion,* 150.

79. Diani, "Introduction," 8; Diani, "Networks and Participation," 352; Debra Friedman and Doug McAdam, "Collective Identity and Activism: Networks, Choices, and the Life of a Social Movement," in Aldon D. Morris and Carol McClurg Mueller, eds., *Frontiers in Social Movement Theory* (New Haven, Conn.: Yale University Press, 1992), 161.

80. Passy, "Social Networks Matter," 23.

81. Jasper, *Art of Moral Protest,* 76.

82. Kitts, "Mobilizing in Black Boxes," 241.

83. See Jasper and Poulsen, "Recruiting Strangers," 494.

84. Interviews, Harbin, March 2003 and May 2006; Shanghai, February 2003. In 1998, leaders of major house church networks issued an appeal to the party-state to end attacks on their churches because the "Chinese house church is the channel through which God's blessings come to China." See Lambert, *China's Christian Millions,* 56–57.

85. One interviewee described her training at an underground Bible school as occurring at a "guerrilla base." Interview, Harbin, March 2003. For examples of rural and urban unregistered seminaries, see David Aikman, *Jesus in Beijing* (Washington, D.C.: Regnery, 2003), 120–129. On unregistered church networks, see Tony Lambert, "House-Church Networks—An Overview," pts. 1–3, *Global Chinese Ministries Newsletter* (Littleton, Colo.: Overseas Missionary Fellowship International), March–May 2006.

86. Jasper and Poulsen, "Recruiting Strangers," 508; also McAdam, "Recruitment to High-Risk Activism," 67; Opp and Gern, "Dissident Groups," 677.

87. See also Jasper and Poulsen, "Recruiting Strangers," 494.

6. Contention in Cyberspace

An earlier version of this chapter was presented at the "Contentious Politics" workshop, Columbia University, October 23, 2006. I thank the participants there and at the Berkeley conference for their helpful comments, especially Jeff Goodwin, David Meyer, Rachel

Stern, Sidney Tarrow, Charles Tilly, and King-To Yeung. Special thanks are due to Kevin O'Brien for inviting me to join this project and providing thorough and constructive critique.

1. Radical communication routinely happens in Chinese cyberspace, but not all of it involves claims making, a central feature of contentious politics. See Charles Tilly and Sidney Tarrow, *Contentious Politics* (Boulder, Colo.: Paradigm, 2007).

2. Esbjörn Ståhle and Terho Uimonen, eds., *Electronic Mail on China*, 2 vols. (Stockholm: Strifter utgivna av Föreningen för Orientaliska Studier, 22, 1989), xxxv. This work provides a rich sample of numerous email and newsgroup items produced during and immediately after the student movement in 1989.

3. The first email was sent from China to a German address by Qian Tianbai through the Chinese Academic Network. See the internet timeline at the website of cnnic.net.cn. (accessed June, 5 2007).

4. Ernest J. Wilson III, *The Information Revolution and Developing Countries* (Cambridge, Mass.: MIT Press, 2004).

5. Jack Linchuan Qiu, "Virtual Censorship in China: Keeping the Gate between the Cyberspaces," *International Journal of Communications Law and Policy* 4 (Winter 1999–2000): 1–25.

6. Guobin Yang, "The Internet and the Rise of a Transnational Chinese Cultural Sphere," *Media, Culture and Society* 25,4 (2003): 469–490.

7. Wu Xiaolong, "The Challenges and Strategies Facing News Web Sites: An Interview with Min Dahong of the Institute of News and Communication of the Chinese Academy of Social Sciences." Zhejiang Online, June 30, 1999, at zjonline.com.cn/conf99/news/002.htm (accessed October 14, 2003).

8. This forum, later renamed Strengthening the Nation Forum, remains popular to this day.

9. Xueguang Zhou, "Unorganized Interests and Collective Action in Communist China," *American Sociological Review* 58,1 (1993): 54–73.

10. These are sometimes called "internet incidents" (*wangluo shijian*) in Chinese media, just as the term "mass incidents" (*qunti shijian*) is used to refer to popular protests.

11. There are replications of violent street tactics in cyberspace. Thus in lieu of sit-ins in public spaces, there are virtual sit-ins; instead of destroying public properties or seizing and occupying public spaces, there are hacking of websites, email bombing, and various forms of electronic disturbance. These virtual tactics are commonly used in the worldwide antiglobalization movement. In China, cybernationalists have hacked websites of foreign governments and business corporations, but generally speaking, internet contention in Chinese cyberspace assumes less radical forms. For discussions of hacktivism in China, see Dorothy E. Denning, "Activism, Hacktivism, and Cyber-

terrorism: The Internet as a Tool for Influencing Foreign Policy," in John Arquilla and David Ronfeldt, eds., *Networks and Netwars: The Future of Terror, Crime, and Militancy* (Santa Monica: Calif.: RAND, 2001): 239–288.

12. Mark Poster, *The Mode of Information: Poststructuralism and Social Context* (Chicago: University of Chicago Press, 1990).

13. Alberto Melucci, *Challenging Codes: Collective Action in the Information Age* (Cambridge: Cambridge University Press, 1996).

14. For example, the five-chapter, 25-article Computer Information Network and Internet Security, Protection and Management Regulations were promulgated by the Ministry of Public Security on December 30, 1997, outlining the duties and responsibilities of China's internet service providers. Regulations specifically targeting BBSs were announced in November 2000, stipulating that users are responsible for the information they release; that they cannot release information harmful to national interests; and that BBSs should follow a licensing procedure. In 2003, the State Broadcasting, Cinema, and Television Administration issued regulations for the control of content dissemination.

15. OpenNet Initiative, "Internet Filtering in China in 2004–2005: A Country Study," April 14, 2005, opennetinitiative.net/studies/china/ONI_China_Country_Study.pdf (accessed May 24, 2005).

16. Elizabeth J. Perry and Mark Selden, Introduction, Perry and Selden, eds., *Chinese Society: Change, Conflict and Resistance*, 2nd ed. (London: RoutledgeCurzon, 2003), 8.

17. On rural struggles, see Thomas Bernstein and Xiaobo Lü, *Taxation without Representation in Contemporary Rural China* (Cambridge: Cambridge University Press, 2003), and Kevin J. O'Brien and Lianjiang Li, *Rightful Resistance in Rural China* (Cambridge: Cambridge University Press, 2006). On worker protests, see Ching Kwan Lee, *Against the Law: Labor Protests in China's Rustbelt and Sunbelt* (Berkeley: University of California Press, 2007).

18. Kevin J. O'Brien, "Collective Action in the Chinese Countryside," *China Journal* 48 (2002): 144.

19. On neonationalism in China, see Peter H. Gries, *China's New Nationalism: Pride, Politics, and Diplomacy* (Berkeley: University of California Press, 2004).

20. For example, postings about Falun Gong have cropped up in public BBSs from time to time. They are immediately deleted and the website management may come under police investigation.

21. Geremie R. Barme and Gloria Davies, "Have We Been Noticed Yet? Intellectual Contestation and the Chinese Web," in Edward Gu and Merle Goldman, eds., *Chinese Intellectuals between State and Market* (London: RoutledgeCurzon, 2004), 75–108.

22. Michel Hockx, "Links with the Past: Mainland China's Online Literary Communities and Their Antecedents," *Journal of Contemporary China* 13,38 (2004): 105–127.

23. Yongming Zhou, "Living on the Cyber Border," *Current Anthropology* 46 (2005): 779–803.

24. Haiqing Yu, "Talking, Linking, Clicking: The Politics of AIDS and SARS in Urban China," *Positions* 15,1 (2007): 35–63.

25. Erving Goffman, *The Presentation of Self in Everyday Life* (New York: Anchor Books, 1959).

26. Barbara Mittler, *A Newspaper for China? Power, Identity, and Change in Shanghai's News Media, 1872–1912* (Cambridge, Mass.: Harvard University Asia Center, 2004), 420.

27. Michael Schudson, *The Power of News* (Cambridge, Mass.: Harvard University Press, 1995): 212.

28. See cnnic.net.cn.

29. The QGLT (http://202.99.23.237/cgi-bbs/ChangeBrd?to=14) boasted 30,000 registered user names in May 2000, with an average of 1,000 posts daily. As of April 2, 2003, the online community of which QGLT is a part had 196,402 registered users. The discussions on QGLT are mostly about current affairs. The forum opens on a limited basis, from 10 a.m. to 10 p.m. daily, and has computer filters and full-time hosts to monitor posts.

30. This finding is supported by internet survey results showing that compared with newspapers, television, and the radio, the internet is perceived as more conducive to expressing personal views. See Guo Liang and Bu Wei, "Hulianwang shiyong zhuangkuang ji yingxiang de diaocha baogao" (Investigative report on internet use and its impact), Chinese Academy of Social Sciences and Center for Social Development, April 2001, chinace.org/ce/itre/ (accessed April 2, 2003).

31. Postings by "suisheng yousi guoqiren," November 3, 1999; by "Guiyuan," November 7, 1999; by "Changren," November 15, 1999; and by "Zuishang bushuo, xinlixiang!" April 8, 2000. "Suisheng yousi guoqiren," the transliteration of the user name of the person who posted the first of these messages, means "a state enterprise employee who, though alive, is like dead." Many user names are humorous and expressive. These postings were among 289 postings archived by the BBS management that addressed issues concerning QGLT. The original URL was http://202.99.23.237/cgi-bbs/elite_list?typeid=14&whichfile=12 (accessed on December 10, 2000). Many of these posts are no longer available online but are part of my personal collection of downloaded files.

32. Posting by "Changren," January 19, 2000.

33. Manuel Castells, *The Internet Galaxy: Reflections on the Internet, Business, and Society* (Oxford: Oxford University Press, 2003).

34. Luther P. Gerlach, "The Structures of Social Movements: Environmental Activism and Its Opponents," in John Arquilla and David Ronfeldt, eds., *Networks and Netwars: The Future of Terror, Crime, and Militancy* (Santa Monica, Calif.: RAND, 2001): 289–310.

35. Steven M. Schneider and Kirsten A. Foot, "Crisis Communication and New Media: The Web after September 11," in Philip N. Howard and Steve Jones, eds., *Society Online: The Internet in Context* (Thousand Oaks, Calif.: Sage, 2004): 141.

36. Crossposting is an effective way to link newsgroups into social networks. See Marc A. Smith, "Invisible Crowds in Cyberspace: Measuring and Mapping the Social Structure of USENET," in Marc Smith and Peter Kollock, eds., *Communities in Cyberspace* (London: Routledge, 1999): 195–219.

37. At cnnic.net.cn.

38. See, for example, Francesca Polletta, *It Was Like a Fever: Storytelling in Protest and Politics* (Chicago: University of Chicago Press, 2006).

39. Charles Tilly, "Contentious Conversation," *Social Research* 65,3 (1998): 491–510. In a similar vein, see, Marc W. Steinberg, "The Talk and Back Talk of Collection Action: A Dialogic Analysis of Repertoires of Discourses among Nineteenth-Century English Cotton Spinners," *American Journal of Sociology* 105,3 (1999): 736–780.

40. Conor O'Clery, "Beijing Students Mourn Victim of Hushed-Up Rape," *Irish Times,* May 26, 2000.

41. For example, Paul Eckert, "Students Protest: March and Vigil Take Place Days before Political Anniversary," ABCNEWS_com Student Murder Prompts Rare Protest.htm, May 24, 2000, and Elisabeth Rosenthal, "Killing of Beijing Student Sets Off Protests," *New York Times,* May 25, 2000, A11.

42. For a description of the data collected for this study, see Guobin Yang, "The Internet and Civil Society in China: A Preliminary Assessment," *Journal of Contemporary China* 12,36 (August 2003): 453–475.

43. One reason for covering up the murder was that with the June 4 anniversary of the 1989 protests approaching, the authorities were concerned about student unrest. The details in this and the following paragraphs were reported in several widely circulated messages and confirmed by reports in the Western media. Some of the original messages posted to BBSs are still available in online archives. See http://cn.netor.com/m/memorial.asp?BID=2309 and www.mitbbs.com/digest/digest14/digest14.html. I have reconstructed the timeline on the basis of these messages.

44. Tilly, "Contentious Conversation," 495.

45. Ibid., 508.

46. Hua Sheng, "Perspective on Free Speech in China: Big Character Posters in China: A Historical Survey," *Journal of Asian Law* 4,2 (1990): 234–256.

47. Posting by "jinni," May 23, 2000, Triangle forum.

48. See http://qqf_19.homechinaren.com/www/c1/w31.htm.

49. The message was posted by users in the following order: "cind," May 23, 2000, 02:29, Tsinghua University BBS; "Rocktor," May 23, 2000, 08:40, Tsinghua University BBS; "onlooker," May 23, 2000, 08:55, Triangle forum.

50. Posting by "Young," May 23, 2000, Triangle forum. Ten photos of the scene

described in the posting can be viewed at http://mem.netor.com/m/ photos/adindex.asp?BoardID=2309 (accessed February 29, 2008).

51. Robert Benford and S. A. Hunt, "Dramaturgy and Social Movements: The Social Construction and Communication of Power," in S. M. Lyman, ed., *Social Movements: Critiques, Concepts, Case-Studies* (New York: New York University Press, 1995).

52. Doug McAdam and Dieter Rucht, "The Cross-national Diffusion of Movement Ideas," *Annals of the American Academy of Political and Social Science* 528 (1993): 56–74.

53. The first BBS in China was opened at Tsinghua University in August 1995.

54. Its BBS regulations contained seven chapters and 42 articles, far more detailed than the regulations promulgated by the Ministry of Public Security mentioned earlier.

55. This is revealed in a posting titled "The QGLT is trying to block news about the case in Peking University. This is futile! Discussions in all other bulletin boards are about this case." "Wo zhetou sizhou!" QGLT, May 24, 2000.

56. Northrop Frye calls such rhetoric "inarticulateness that uses one word . . . for the whole rhetorical ornament of the sentence, including adjectives, adverbs, epithets, and punctuation." Sometimes, Frye continues, "words disappear altogether, and we are back to a primitive language of screams and gestures and sighs" (p. 328). Northrop Frye, *The Anatomy of Criticism: Four Essays* (Princeton: Princeton University Press, 1957).

57. Posting by "I am anonymous," May 27, 2000, original posting on file with the author.

58. Steinberg, "Talk and Back Talk of Collection Action," 770.

59. O'Brien and Li, *Rightful Resistance in Rural China.*

60. On continuity in the repertoire of contention, see Elizabeth Perry, "'To Rebel Is Justified': Cultural Revolution Influences on Contemporary Chinese Protest," in Kam-yee Law, ed., *Beyond Purge and Holocaust: The Chinese Cultural Revolution Reconsidered* (New York: Palgrave, 2003): 262–281.

61. Sociologist Gary Fine treats a social movement as "a bundle of narratives." See Gary Alan Fine, "Public Narration and Group Culture: Discerning Discourse in Social Movements," in Hank Johnston and Bert Klandermans, eds., *Social Movements and Culture* (Minneapolis: University of Minnesota Press, 1995): 128.

62. On the dramatic elements of protest in modern China, see Joseph W. Esherick and Jeffrey N. Wasserstrom, "Acting Out Democracy: Political Theater in Modern China," *Journal of Asian Studies* 49,4 (1990): 835–865.

63. Among the few works that examine movement outcomes in China, O'Brien and Li look at three types of outcomes: policy implementation, effects on activists, and effects on the community. See their *Rightful Resistance in Rural China.*

64. On the boomerang effect, see Margaret Keck and Kathryn Sikkink, *Activists beyond Borders: Advocacy Networks in International Politics* (Ithaca, N.Y.: Cornell

University Press, 1998). On externalization of contention, see Sidney Tarrow, *The New Transnational Activism* (Cambridge: Cambridge University Press, 2005). Media internationalization significantly affected the student movement in 1989. See Craig Calhoun, *Neither Gods nor Emperors: Students and the Struggle for Democracy in China* (Berkeley: University of California Press, 1994).

65. For example, O'Clery, "Beijing Students Mourn Victim"; Rosenthal, "Killing of Beijing Student."

7. Environmental Campaigns

The authors wish to thank Kevin J. O'Brien, Rachel Stern, and two anonymous reviewers for their comments and suggestions. We thank the 2003 Research and Exchanges Board for financial support for this research.

1. For the purposes of this essay, civil society is defined as a society in which membership in social organizations is "both voluntary and overlapping" and individuals join social organizations only out of their own interests. For this definition, see Ernest Gellner, *Conditions of Liberty: Civil Society and Its Rivals* (London: Penguin Books, 1994); John A. Hall, *Civil Society: Theory, History, Comparison* (Cambridge: Polity Press, 1995), 15.

2. The focus of this chapter is Chinese grassroots ENGOs. There are yet two other types of organizations active on the environmental scene in China: government-organized NGOs (GONGOs) and international NGOs. On the former in China, see Fengshi Wu, "New Partners or Old Brothers? GONGOs in International Environmental Advocacy in China," *China Environmental Series* 5 (2002): 45–58; Fengshi Wu, "Environmental GONGO Autonomy: Unintended Consequences of State Strategies in China," *Good Society* 12 (2003): 35–45. We do not address the entire environmental movement, which also includes "not-in-my-backyard" contention. In today's China, pollution protests are particularly numerous. See Jun Jing, "Environmental Protests in Rural China," in Elizabeth J. Perry and Mark Selden, eds., *Chinese Society: Change, Conflict and Resistance* (London: Routledge, 2003). Tong divides the environmental movement in China into two categories: ideology driven and pollution induced. See Yanqi Tong, "Environmental Movements in Transitional Societies: A Comparative Study of Taiwan and China," *Comparative Politics* 37 (2005): 167–188.

3. For example, Elizabeth Knup, "ENGOs in China: An Overview," *China Environment Series* 4 (1997): 9–15; Anna Brettell, "Environmental Nongovernmental Organizations in the People's Republic of China: Innocents in a Co-opted Environmental Movement?" *Journal of Pacific Asia* 6 (2000): 27–56; Peter Ho, "Greening without Conflict? Environmentalism, NGOs and Civil Society in China," *Development and Change* 32 (2001): 893–921; Nick Young, "Introduction: Searching for Civil Society," in Young, ed., *250 Chinese NGOs: Civil*

Society in the Making (Hong Kong: China Development Brief): 9–19; Elizabeth Economy, *The River Runs Black: The Environmental Challenge to China's Future* (Ithaca, N.Y.: Cornell University Press, 2004); Guobin Yang, "Weaving a Green Web: The Internet and Environmental Activism in China," *China Environment Series* 6 (2003): 89–93; Guobin Yang, "ENGOs and Institutional Dynamics in China," *China Quarterly* 181 (2005): 46–66; Jonathan Schwartz, "ENGOs in China: Roles and Limits," *Pacific Affairs* 77 (2004): 28–50; Jiang Ru, "ENGOs in China: The Interplay of State Controls, Agency Interests and NGO Strategies" (Ph.D. diss., Stanford University, 2004); Phillip Stalley and Dongning Yang, "An Emerging Environmental Movement in China?" *China Quarterly* 186 (2006): 333–356; Jennifer Turner and Kenji Otsuka, *Reaching across the Water: International Cooperation Promoting Sustainable River Basin Governance in China* (Washington, D.C.: Woodrow Wilson International Center for Scholars, 2006); and *China Information* 21 (2007), special issue on environmental NGOs.

4. For example, Economy, *River Runs Black*.

5. Tony Saich, "Negotiating the State: The Development of Social Organizations in China," *China Quarterly* 163 (2000): 124–141.

6. Brettell, "Environmental Non-governmental Organizations"; Ho, "Greening without Conflict?" Ru, "ENGOs in China."

7. For those who use the term "civil society," see Martin K. Whyte, "Urban China: A Civil Society in the Making?" in Arthur L. Rosenbaum, ed., *State and Society in China: The Consequences of Reform* (Boulder, Colo.: Westview, 1999), 77–141. For those who prefer "corporatism," see Jonathan Unger and Anita Chan, "Corporatism in China: A Developmental State in an East Asian Context," in Barrett L. McCormick and Jonathan Unger, eds., *China after Socialism* (Armonk, N.Y.: Sharpe, 1996); Dorothy J. Solinger, "Urban Entrepreneurs and the State: The Merger of State and Society," in Rosenbaum, *State and Society in China*, 121–140; Jonathan Unger, "Bridges: Private Business, the Chinese Government and the Rise of New Associations," *China Quarterly* 147 (1996): 795–819. For reviews of this debate, see Yijiang Ding, "Corporatism and Civil Society in China: An Overview of the Debate in Recent Years," *China Information* 12 (1998): 44–67.

8. Saich, "Negotiating the State," 124–141.

9. See Ho, "Greening without Conflict?"

10. Theda Skocpol, *States and Social Revolutions: A Comparative Analysis of France, Russia, and China* (Cambridge: Cambridge University Press, 1979).

11. Joel S. Migdal, Atul Kohli, and Vivienne Shue, *State Power and Social Forces: Domination and Transformation in the Third World* (Cambridge: Cambridge University Press, 1994); Joel S. Migdal, *State in Society: Studying How States and Societies Transform and Constitute One Another* (Cambridge: Cambridge University Press, 2001); Michael Mann, *Sources of Social Power*, vol. 2 (Cambridge: Cambridge University Press, 1993).

12. Dingxin Zhao, *The Power of Tiananmen: State-Society Relations and the 1989 Beijing Student Movement* (Chicago: University of Chicago Press, 2001); Dingxin

Zhao, *Shehui yu zhengzhi yundong jiangyi* (Social and political movement) (Beijing: Shehui kexue wenxian chubanshe, 2006).

13. The peak of the Three Gorges Dam controversy took place before 1989. Since this chapter concerns the environmental movement centering on ENGOs, which emerged in post-1989 China, this controversy is not addressed. As was not the case in the three campaigns we will discuss, objection to the Three Gorges Dam was chiefly voiced by a handful of members of the Chinese People's Political Consultative Conference and did not involve mobilization of civil society actors.

14. A report based on the survey can be found at the website of the All-China Environmental Federation, www.acef.com.cn (accessed June 10, 2007).

15. Hongyan Lu, "Bamboo Sprouts after the Rain: The History of University Student Environmental Associations in China," *China Environment Series* 6 (2003): 55–66.

16. Yang, "Weaving a Green Web," 89–93.

17. Field research for this study was conducted in Beijing, Heilongjiang, Yunnan, and Jiangsu provinces from April to August 2004. During this period, Yanfei Sun interviewed ENGO members and participated in their activities. Follow-up interviews were conducted in December 2005 and January 2006. The study is based on an analysis of these interviews and ethnographic data, as well as newspaper reports, data collected from websites, and newsletters, annual reports, and other documents produced by ENGOs. For more details about the campaign for the snub-nosed monkey, see Ru, "ENGOs in China," 186–209; Economy, *River Runs Black*, 149–156; and Xiaohui Shen, *Xueshan Xunmeng* (Seeking dreams in the snowcapped mountains) (Shenyang: Shenyang chubanshe, 1998). On the campaign to conserve the Tibetan antelope, see Ru, "ENGOs in China," 210–247, and Economy, *River Runs Black*, 153–156. Information about the Chinese ENGOs' efforts to save the Tibetan antelope was also derived from interviews conducted in 2003, supplemented by media reports, Friends of Nature newsletters, and the website of Shanghai tongmeng, a website established by environmental volunteers with the chief purpose of collecting and distributing information about the protection of Tibetan antelope, which provides the most comprehensive information in Chinese: www.green2008.com/zjzl/index.asp (accessed December 12, 2003), and the website of the Tibetan Antelope Information Center, www.taic.org (accessed December 12, 2003).

18. Sources for the Nujiang campaign were interviews conducted from December 2005 to January 2006, media reports, and a number of websites, including: www.chinariver.org (accessed February 1, 2006), www.nujiang.ngo.cn, www.chinarivers.ngo.cn, (accessed February 1, 2006), and www.xys.org (accessed February 1, 2006).

19. Although the Chinese media are controlled by the state, environment-related news falls in a grey zone. On the relationship between the media and the environmental movement, see Bo Wen, "Greening the Chinese Media,"

China Environment Series 2 (1998): 39–44; Kanping Hu, "Harmony and Diversity: The Relationship between Environmental Journalists and Green NGOs in China," in Jennifer Tuner and Fengshi Wu, eds., *Green NGO and Environmental Journalist Forum* (Washington, D.C.: Woodrow Wilson Center, 2002), available at www.wilsoncenter.org/cef (accessed December 12, 2003); Kanping Hu and Xiaogang Yu, "Bridge over Troubled Waters: The Role of the News Media in Promoting Public Participation in River Basin Managements and Environmental Protection in China," in Jennifer L. Turner and Kenji Otsuka, eds., *Promoting Sustainable River Basin Governance: Crafting Japan-U.S. Water Partnership in China* (Tokyo: Institute for Developing Economies, 2005), 125–141; Craig Calhoun and Guobin Yang, "Media, Civil Society, and the Rise of a Green Public Sphere in China," *China Information* 21 (2007): 211–236.

20. The West Working Committee was established in 1992. Its original mission was to tap mineral resources in Zhiduo County to develop the local economy. Sonam Dorje shifted its focus to fighting poaching of Tibetan antelope.

21. The four officials of the Brigade were asked to return to Zhiduo County. Ru, "ENGOs in China," 210–247, provides a rich account of the Brigade's history.

22. Michael Palmer, "Environmental Regulation in the People's Republic of China," *China Quarterly* 156 (1998): 788–808; Xiaoying Ma and Leonard Ortolano, *Environmental Regulation in China: Institutions, Enforcement, and Compliance* (Lanham, Md.: Rowman and Littlefield, 2000).

23. Zhao, *Power of Tiananmen.*

24. Doug McAdam, Sidney Tarrow, and Charles Tilly, *Dynamics of Contention* (Cambridge: Cambridge University Press, 2001). For use of these terms in a Chinese context, see Kevin J. O'Brien and Lianjiang Li, *Rightful Resistance in Rural China* (Cambridge: Cambridge University Press, 2006), chap. 3.

25. O'Brien and Li, *Rightful Resistance.*

26. Zhao, *Power of Tiananmen;* Zhao, *Shehui yu zhengzhi yundong jiangyi.*

27. On the campaign against the construction of the Yangliuhu dam near Dujiangyan in Sichuan Province, see Yiyi Lu, *Environmental Civil Society and Governance in China,* Chatham House Asia Program Briefing Paper, August 1–8, 2005, available at http://www.chathamhouse.org.uk/files3268 _china160805.pdf (accessed February 1, 2006); Hu and Yu, "Bridge over Troubled Waters," 125–141; Andrew C. Mertha and William R. Lowry, "Unbuilt Dams: Seminal Events and Policy Change in China, Australia, and the United States," *Comparative Politics* 39 (2006): 1–20; Andrew C. Mertha, *Water Warriors: Political Pluralization in China's Hydropower Policy* (Ithaca, N.Y.: Cornell University Press, 2008). On the campaign against dam building on Mugecuo Lake in Sichuan Province, see Hu and Yu, "Bridge over Troubled Waters." On the campaign against the Nujiang dam project, see "China Facing a Flood of Environmental Protests of Dam Policy," *Taipei Times,* December 17, 2004, 9; "Chinese Project Pits Environmentalists against Development Plans," *New York Times,* January 3, 2005; "Seeking a Public Voice on China's

'Angry River,'" *New York Times,* December 26, 2005; Mertha and Lowry, "Unbuilt Dams"; Mertha, *Water Warriors.*

28. The NDRC is a macro-economic regulatory department of the State Council. Its mandate is to develop national economic strategies, long-term as well as annual economic plans, and to report on the national economy and social development to the National People's Congress.

29. That ENGOs sought help from foreign NGOs to stop the Nujiang dam project gave the prodam side a good excuse to lambaste them. See Zhang Boting (pen name Shuibo), "Hydropower Development in China: Be Aware of the Anti-dam Organizations Creating Barriers by Raising Diplomatic Questions," www.xys.org/dajia/nujiang.html (accessed February 1, 2006).

30. These bold moves by Yu Xiaogang and his organization greatly irritated the Yunnan provincial government, which ordered a thorough investigation of his organization, pressed partner agencies to dissociate themselves from Green Watershed, and barred Yu from leaving China by confiscating his passport.

31. In January 2005, a debate on the human-nature relationship swept over China in the wake of the Asian tsunami. The debate was sparked by He Zuoxiu's pointed criticism of the view that humans should revere nature, expressed in an interview with *Huanqiu* (The globe) magazine. Among environmentalists, Wang Yongchen was the first to respond with an article, "Revering Nature Is Not Anti-Science," the next day. Fang Zhouzi's acerbic refutation of Wang, "Revering Nature IS Anti-Science," incurred many rejoinders from environmentalists and their league, followed by another round of rebuttals from the opposing camp.

32. See www.xys.org/dajia/nujiang.html (accessed February 1, 2006).

33. See "Liang Yuanshi shangshu Hu Wen cu Nujiang gongcheng fugong" (Two academicians petition Hu Jintao and Wen Jiabao about resuming the Nujiang project), Wenhui po (Hong Kong), September 11, 2005.

34. "Nujiang shuidian wancheng huanping shencha" (Nujiang hydropower project completed its environmental impact assessment inspection), Wenhui po January 11, 2006.

35. Abigail Jahiel, "The Organization of Environmental Protection in China," *China Quarterly* 156 (1998): 757–787; Economy, *River Runs Black.*

36. In 2004 the Yuanmingyuan Park administration embarked on a 30-million-yuan project to cover the park's lake beds with plastic sheets, which were supposed to prevent water seepage. However, the project never underwent the required environmental impact assessment, and experts and environmentalists blasted the scheme for its damage to the ecosystem. The dispute reached a climax in April 2005, when SEPA held a public hearing on the project. More than 120 people, including staff members from the Yuanmingyuan administrative office, ENGO representatives, and experts from research institutes, attended the hearing. It ended with SEPA ordering most of the plastic membrane covering removed. The Yuanmingyuan case was widely covered

by the media. Two influential websites, people.com.cn and news.xinhuanet
.com, broadcast the public hearing live on April 13, 2005.

37. Jahiel, "The Organization of Environmental Protection"; Economy, *River Runs Black;* Schwartz, "ENGOs in China."

38. Economy, *River Runs Black,* 148.

39. The text of the letter is available at the website of Friends of Nature, www .fon.org.cn (accessed February 1, 2006).

40. Nick Young, "Public Enquiries Draw SEPA and Green NGOs Closer Together," *China Development Brief,* April 22, 2005, www.chinadevelopmentbrief .com/node/72 (accessed February 1, 2006).

41. C. Wright Mills, *The Power Elite* (Oxford: Oxford University Press, 1956); G. William Domhoff, *The Powers That Be: Processes of Ruling Class Domination in America* (New York: Random House, 1978).

42. Theda Skocpol, "Bringing the State Back In: Strategies of Analysis in Current Research," in Peter Evans, Dietrich Rueschemeyer, and Theda Skocpol, eds., *Bringing the State Back In* (Cambridge: Cambridge University Press, 1985), 3–37.

43. Mann, *Sources of Social Power,* vol. 2.

44. Doug McAdam, *Political Process and the Development of Black Insurgency, 1930–1970* (Chicago: University of Chicago Press, 1982); Hanspeterl Kriesi, Ruud Koopmans, Jan Willem Duyvendak, and Marco G. Giugni, *The Politics of New Social Movements in Western Europe: A Comparative Analysis* (Minneapolis: University of Minnesota Press, 1995).

45. David S. Meyer, "Protest and Political Opportunities," *American Sociological Review* 30 (2004): 125–145; David S. Meyer and Debra C. Minkoff, "Conceptualizing Political Opportunity," *Social Forces* 82 (2004): 1457–1492; O'Brien and Li, *Rightful Resistance;* also Fayong Shi and Yongshun Cai, "Disaggregating the State: Networks and Collective Resistance in Shanghai," *China Quarterly* 186 (2006): 314–332.

46. Zhao, *Power of Tiananmen.*

47. Lewis A. Coser, *The Functions of Social Conflict* (Glencoe, Ill.: Free Press, 1956); William Kornhauser, *The Politics of Mass Society* (New York: Free Press, 1959); Zhao, *Power of Tiananmen;* Zhao, *Shehui yu zhengzhi yundong jiangyi.*

8. Disruptive Collective Action in the Reform Era

1. Jae Ho Chung, Hongyi Lai, and Ming Xia, "Mounting Challenges to Governance in China: Surveying Collective Protestors, Religious Sects and Criminal Organizations," *China Journal* 56 (July 2006): 1–31.

2. Chen Jinsheng, *Quntixingshijian yanjiu baogao* (Research report on instances of collective action) (Beijing: Qunzhong chubanshe, 2004), 12.

3. He Zuowen, "Zhengque renshi he chuli woguo xianjieduan de liyi guanxi maodun" (Properly handling conflict in our country), *Kexue shehui zhuyi* (Scientific socialism) 2 (2005): 8–11.

4. Sidney Tarrow, *Power in Movement* (New York: Cambridge University Press, 1994), 108.

5. Frances Piven and Richard Cloward, "Collective Protest: A Critique of Resource-Mobilization Theory," in Stanford Lyman, ed., *Social Movements: Critique, Concepts, Case-Studies* (New York: New York University Press, 1995), 137–167.

6. See Marco Giugni, "Was It Worth the Effort? The Outcomes and Consequences of Social Movements," *Annual Review of Sociology* 98 (1998): 371–93.

7. William Gamson, *The Strategy of Social Protest* (Belmont, Calif.: Wadsworth, 1990), 81; Steven Barkan, "Legal Control of the Southern Civil Rights Movement," *American Sociological Review* 49 (1984): 552–565.

8. Tarrow, *Power in Movement*, 104.

9. William Gamson, "The Success of the Unruly," in Doug McAdam and David A. Snow, eds., *Social Movements* (Los Angeles: Roxbury, 1997), 357–364.

10. Donatella della Porta, "Protest, Protesters, and Protest Policing: Public Discourses in Italy and Germany from the 1960s to the 1980s," in Marco Giugni, Doug McAdam, and Charles Tilly, eds., *How Social Movements Matter* (Minneapolis: University of Minnesota Press, 1999), 66–96.

11. For a discussion of tactical escalation in the Chinese context, see Kevin J. O'Brien and Lianjiang Li, *Rightful Resistance in Rural China* (New York: Cambridge University Press, 2006), chap. 4.

12. For example, see Jerry Hough and Merle Fainsod, *How the Soviet Union Is Governed* (Cambridge, Mass.: Harvard University Press, 1990). See Tianjian Shi, *Political Participation in Beijing* (Cambridge, Mass.: Harvard University Press, 1997).

13. The State Planning Commission, "Woguo shehui wending genzong diaocha" (A follow-up investigation of social stability in our country), Guanli shijie (Management world) 5 (1999): 169–178.

14. Minxin Pei, "Citizens v. Mandarins: Administrative Litigation in China," *China Quarterly* 152 (December 1997): 832–862.

15. National Statistical Bureau, Zhongguo tongji nianjian 2003 (*Chinese Statistical Yearbook 2003*) (Beijing: Zhongguo tongji chubanshe, 2004), 834.

16. The 31.3 percent won by citizens included: (1) courts' revoking administrative conduct (14.9 percent); plaintiffs' withdrawal after government agencies corrected their conduct (12.9 percent); state agencies' fulfillment of their responsibilities as required by the courts (2.5 percent); and courts' changing the conduct of state agencies (0.9 percent). Wu Jing, "Mingaoguan, baixing weihe ying de duole" (Administrative litigations: Why have the people won more cases?), Renmin ribao (People's daily), 19 February 2003.

17. Stanley B. Lubman, *Bird in a Cage: Legal Reform in China after Mao* (Stanford, Calif.: Stanford University Press, 1999).

18. Kevin J. O'Brien and Lianjiang Li, "Suing the Local State: Administrative Litigation in Rural China," *China Journal* 51 (January 2004): 53–74; Randall

Peerenboom, *China's Long March toward Rule of Law* (New York: Cambridge University Press, 2002), chap. 9; Yuen Yuen Tang, "When Peasants Sue *En Masse*," *China: An International Journal* 3 (2005): 24–49.

19. Hu Kui, "2003 nian Zhongguo zhaoyu xinfang hongfeng" (China witnessed floods of petitions in 2003), Heilongjiang gongren bao (Heilongjiang workers), December 17, 2003.

20. Qiao Yunxia, Hu Lianli, and Wang Junjie, "Zhongguo xinwen yulun jiandu xianzhuang diaocha fenxi" (A survey and analysis of media exposure in China), Xinwen yu chuanbo yanjiu (News and communication studies) 4 (2002): 21–28.

21. Benjamin L. Liebman, "Watchdog or Demagogue? The Media in the Chinese Legal System," *Columbia Law Review* 105,1 (January 2005): 1–157.

22. Shi Tan, "'Jiaodian fangtan': yulunjiandu shinian yiyi" (Focus: Ten years of practice), Fenghuang zhoukan (Phoenix weekly), September 30, 2004; Li Xiaoping, "Focus (*Jiaodian Fangtan*) and the Changes in the Chinese Television History," *Journal of Contemporary China* 11,30 (2002): 17–34.

23. Yongshun Cai, "Managed Participation in China," *Political Science Quarterly* 119,3 (2004): 425–451; Laura Luehrmann, "Facing Citizen Complaints in China, 1951–1996," *Asian Survey* 43,5 (2003): 845–66; Carl Minzner, "Xinfang: An Alternative to the Formal Chinese Judicial System," *Stanford Journal of International Law* 42,1 (2006): 103–179.

24. Lu Xin, Lu Xueyi, and Chan Tianlun, eds., *2001 Zhongguo shehui xingshi fenxi yu yuce* (2001: An analysis of Chinese society and some predictions) (Beijing: Shehui kexue wenxian chubanshe, 2001), 31.

25. Inga Markovits, "Law and *Glasnost:* Some Thoughts about the Future of Judicial Review under Socialism," *Law and Society Review* 23 (Spring 1989): 399–447.

26. Xi Chen, "Between Defiance and Obedience: Protest Opportunism in China," in Elizabeth J. Perry and Merle Goldman, eds., *Grassroots Political Reform in Contemporary China* (Cambridge, Mass.: Harvard University Press, 2007), 253–281.

27. Zhao Ling, "Guonei shoufeng xinfang baogao huo gaoceng zhongshi" (The first report on petition receives serious attention from the top level), Nanfang zhoumo (Southern weekend), November 4, 2004, 4.

28. Hu Kui, "2003 nian."

29. Zhu Cuixia, "Beijing Dongzhuang: Jijiang xiaoshi de shangfangcun" (Dongzhuang of Beijing: A disappearing village of complainants), Xinwen zhoukan (Newsweekly) 5 (2002): 22–27.

30. Yu Jianrong, "Zhongguo xinfang zhidu pipan" (Criticisms of the petition system in China), Zhongguo gaige (China reform) 2 (2005): 26–28.

31. Holly McCammon, "'Out of the Parlors and into the Streets': The Changing Tactical Repertoire of the U.S. Women's Suffrage Movements," *Social Forces* 81 (March 2003): 787–818.

32. O'Brien and Li, *Rightful Resistance*, chap. 4.

33. Howard French, "Riots in Shanghai Suburb as Pollution Protest Heats Up," *New York Times*, July 19, 2005.

34. Chen Jinsheng, *Quntixingshijian yanjiu baogao* (Research report on instances of collective action) (Beijing: Qunzhong chubanshe, 2004), 59–60.

35. O'Brien and Li, *Rightful Resistance*, 27–30.

36. The data used for this chapter were mainly collected from Chinese sources, including newspapers, magazines, and court reports. A very small portion were collected from foreign newspapers, mainly the *New York Times* and *Washington Post*. A basic criterion for inclusion was information about the outcome (i.e., whether or not the protesters' demands were met and how the government dealt with the participants).

37. *Zhongguo Jingji shibao* (China economic times), June 20, 2005, 3.

38. *Qiaobao* (News about overseas Chinese), December 16, 2005, 2.

39. See the website of the Hengshan government, hengshan.gov.cn/news/show .aspx?id=966&cid=35 (accessed March 2, 2005).

40. Edward Cody, "For Chinese, Peasant Revolt Is Rare Victory," *Washington Post*, June 13, 2005, 10.

41. O'Brien and Li, *Rightful Resistance*.

42. Chen, "Between Defiance and Obedience."

43. Wu Sha, "Dali jiaqiang quntixing tufa shijian chuzhi gongzuo" (Doing a good job of handling instances of collective action), Gongan yanjiu (Research on public security) 12 (2004): 48–53.

44. "Li Shuguo zai qunshi zhengfa gongzuo huiyi shang de jianhua" (Talk by Li Shuguo at the meeting of the city political and legal issues), at the website of the Bureau of Justice of Changchun city. http://www.cc148.com/ndex.asp (accessed February 26, 2004). gwwy.99081.com/Article_Print.asp? ArticleID= 5413 (accessed February 22, 2004).

45. John Chan, "Mass Protests in China Point to Sharp Social Tensions," socialistviewpoint.org/nov_04/nov_04_27.html (accessed June 12, 2004); William Hurst and Kevin J. O'Brien, "China's Contentious Pensioners," *China Quarterly* 170 (June 2002): 345–360.

46. Frances Fox Piven and Richard Cloward, *Poor People's Movements: Why They Succeeded, How They Fail* (New York: Vintage, 1977).

47. For example, in Zhunyi, Guizhou Province, 460 taxi drivers collectively sued the city government over its regulations on the duration of licenses but lost. In Hangzhou, Zhejiang, in 2001, 688 drivers lodged a collective lawsuit against the city government over mounting fees for licenses, but they lost in both a first trial and a retrial. *Renmin ribao* (People's daily), September 27, 2001, 2.

48. They damaged those taxis that refused to cooperate and even beat the drivers. Tang Jianguang, "Ningxia yinchuan chuzuche tingyun fengbo" (The incident of the taxi drivers' strike in Yinchuan, Ningxia), *Xinwen zhoukan* (Newsweekly), September 8, 2004, 11–13.

49. Marco Giugni, "How Social Movements Matter: Past Research, Present Problems, Future Developments," in Marco Giugni, Doug McAdam, and Charles Tilly, eds., *How Social Movements Matter* (Minneapolis: University of Minnesota Press, 1999), xiii–xxxiii.
50. Gamson, *Strategy of Social Protest.*
51. Kevin J. O'Brien and Lianjiang Li, "Selective Policy Implementation in Rural China," *Comparative Politics* 31,2 (January 1999): 167–186.
52. Kevin J. O'Brien, "Collective Action in the Chinese Countryside," *China Journal* 48 (July 2002): 139–154.
53. Tarrow, *Power in Movement,* 97.
54. *Yan'an ribao* (Yan'an Daily), March 27, 2006, 1.
55. *South China Morning Post,* March 3, 2006, 8.
56. O'Brien and Li, *Rightful Resistance,* 33.
57. *Nanfang ribao* (Nanfang daily), July 27, 2000, 1.
58. Charles Tilly, *From Mobilization to Revolution* (New York: Random House, 1978), 114; Tarrow, *Power in Movement.* Karl-Dieter Opp and Wolfgang Ruehl, "Repression, Micromobilization and Political Protest," *Social Forces* 69,2 (1990): 521–547.
59. O'Brien and Li, *Rightful Resistance,* 105.
60. See, for examples, Lianjiang Li and Kevin J. O'Brien, "Protest Leadership in Rural China," *China Quarterly* 193 (March 2008): 1–23; Ying Xing, *Dahe yimin shangfang de gushi* (The experience of Dahe migrants' petitions) (Beijing: Sanlian chubanshe, 2001).
61. In China, see O'Brien and Li, *Rightful Resistance,* chap. 2.
62. Doug McAdam, *Political Process and the Develoment of Black Insurgency, 1930–1970* (Chicago: University of Chicago Press, 1990), xi.
63. O'Brien and Li, *Rightful Resistance,* chap. 2.
64. Piven and Cloward, "Collective Protest."
65. *Fazhi ribao* (Legal daily), July 3, 2000, 3.
66. Editorial Group, *Goujian shehuizhuyi hexie shehui dacankao* (Reference materials on the building of a socialist harmonious society) (Beijing: Hongqi chubanshe, 2005), 102.
67. Seven party and government officials of Daye were accused of inciting the demonstrations and were given party and administrative discipline. *Chutian dushi bao* (Chutian Urban Daily), February 25, 2006, 2.
68. Su Quanshui et al., "Guangxi nongcun shehui wending jizhi yu duice yanjiu" (Research on the mechanisms of maintaining social stability in Guangxi), at the website of Guangxi Provincial Government, gx-info.gov.cn/chenguo/2003–10.asp (accessed August 15, 2004).
69. James Jasper, *The Art of Moral Protest: Culture, Biography, and Creativity in Social Movements* (Chicago: University of Chicago Press, 1997), 234.
70. For a review, see David Meyer and Debra Minkoff, "Conceptualizing Political Opportunity," *Social Forces* 82,4 (2004): 1457–1492.

71. O'Brien and Li, *Rightful Resistance,* chap. 2.

72. Maria Edin, "State Capacity and Local Agent Control in China: CCP Cadre Management from a Township Perspective," *China Quarterly* 173 (March 2003): 35–72.

73. Sidney Tarrow, "States and Opportunities: The Political Structuring of Social Movements," in Doug McAdam, John McCarthy, and Mayer Zald, eds., *Comparative Perspectives on Social Movements* (New York: Cambridge University Press, 1998), 41–61.

74. William Gamson and David Meyer, "Framing Political Opportunity," in McAdam, McCarthy, and Zald, *Comparative Perspectives on Social Movements,* 275–290.

75. Yongshun Cai, "Local Governments and the Suppression of Popular Resistance in China," *China Quarterly* 193 (March 2008): 24–42.

9. Manufacturing Dissent in Transnational China

I gratefully thank Kevin O'Brien, Sidney Tarrow, and the other conference participants for their insightful comments and suggestions on earlier drafts of this chapter.

1. The website is located at (http://www.tuidang.epochtimes.com); the technological means to circumvent China's domestic firewall was provided by DynaWeb (Dongtai Wangluo) and Ultrareach Internet (Wujie Wangluo), two United States–based software companies hired by *Epoch Times* to make their proxy services available to Chinese users.

2. See Dynamic Internet Technology, "Report on Internet Circumvention Technologies and Renunciations from the Chinese Communist Party" (June 2005), www.dit-inc.us/report/9p200505/9preport.php (accessed July 5, 2007). On its website, Dynaweb lists *Epoch Times* as one of its clients, along with the Voice of America, Radio Free Asia, and Human Rights in China.

3. Han Fudong, "Jingwai wangzhan zaoyao Meng Weizai tuidang zhenxiang" (The real story of the overseas website fabricating rumors of Meng Weizai's resignation from the Party), Fenghuang Zhoukan (Hong Kong), February 28, 2005, www.phoenixtv.com/phoenixtv/72931714371944448/20050228/510382 .shtml (accessed July 5, 2007).

4. Nailene Chou Wiest, "Bitter Battle over Cadre's Loyalties Waged in Cyberspace," *South China Morning Post,* December 14, 2004, 8.

5. Hai Tao, "Zhenjia Meng Weizai tuidang fengbo he hubo jingwai" (The overseas tempest and contradictory reports concerning the true and false resignation of Meng Weizai), Voice of America broadcast (Hong Kong), December 12, 2004.

6. "The Jiuping—the Epoch Times New Years' Gift to the People of China," *Epoch Times,* December 24, 2004, www.theepochtimes.com/news/4-12-24/25193 .html (accessed July 5, 2007).

7. Wiest, "Bitter Battle," 8.

8. Han Fudong, "Jia Meng Weizai."

9. Yi Ping, "Washington D.C. Rally Celebrates 12 Million CCP Resignations," *Epoch Times,* July 26, 2006, www.theepochtimes.com/news/6-7-26/44283 .html) (accessed July 5, 2007); Brian Marple, "Hundreds Rally to Commemorate 5,000,000 Quitting Communism in China," *Epoch Times,* October 16, 2005, www.theepochtimes.com/news/5-10-16/33401.html) (accessed July 5, 2007); Ye Shuxing, "One Thousand March in Support of 4 Million Withdrawals from the CCP," *Epoch Times,* September 1, 2005, www.theepochtimes.com/ news/5-9-1/31843.html (accessed July 5, 2007).

10. Daniel W. Drezner, "Can 200,000 Chinese Ex-Communists Be Wrong?" (March 15, 2005), www.danieldrezner.com/archives/001940.html (accessed July 5, 2007).

11. Sidney Tarrow, *The New Transnational Activism* (New York: Cambridge University Press, 2005).

12. W. Lance Bennett, "Communicating Global Activism: Strengths and Vulnerabilities of Networked Politics," *Information, Communication and Society* 6,2 (2003): 143–168.

13. Patricia M. Thornton, "The New Cybersects: Resistance and Repression in the Reform Era," in Elizabeth J. Perry and Mark Selden, eds., *Chinese Society: Change, Conflict and Resistance,* 2nd ed. (London: Routledge, 2003), 147–170.

14. Margaret E. Keck and Karen Sikkink, *Activists beyond Borders: Advocacy Networks in International Politics* (Ithaca, N.Y.: Cornell University Press, 1998).

15. On the role of credibility in establishing frame resonance, see Robert D. Benford and David A. Snow, "Framing Processes and Social Movements: An Overview and Assessment," *Annual Review of Sociology* 26 (2000): 619–621.

16. Clifford Bob, *The Marketing of Rebellion: Insurgents, Media, and International Activism* (Cambridge: Cambridge University Press, 2006).

17. Serguei Alex Oushakine, "The Terrifying Mimicry of Samizdat," *Public Culture* 13,2 (2001): 191–214.

18. Kevin J. O'Brien and Lianjiang Li, *Rightful Resistance in Rural China* (New York: Cambridge University Press, 2006).

19. On the processes of "certification" and "decertification," see Doug McAdam, Sidney Tarrow, and Charles Tilly, *Dynamics of Contention* (Cambridge: Cambridge University Press, 2001), particularly chaps. 5 and 7.

20. Stanley D. Brunn and Charles D. Cottle, "Small States and Cyberboosterism," *Geographical Review* 18,2 (April 1997): 240–258.

21. Edward S. Herman and Noam Chomsky, *Manufacturing Consent: The Political Economy of the Mass Media* (1988; reprint, New York: Pantheon, 2002).

22. Tarrow, *New Transnational Activism,* 3–5.

23. Mario Diani, "Social Movement Networks: Virtual and Real," in Frank Webster, ed., *Culture and Politics in the Information Age: A New Politics* (London: Routledge, 2001), 117–128.

24. Manuel Castells, *The Rise of Network Society* (Malden, Mass.: Blackwell, 1996): 469.

25. Jessica Lipnack and Jeffrey Stamps, "Creating Another America: the Power and Joy of Networking," in David Corten and Rudi Klaus, eds., *People-Centered Development: Contributions toward Theory and Planning Framework* (West Hartford, Conn.: Kumarian, 1984), 294, 296.

26. Keck and Sikkink, *Activists beyond Borders,* 12–13, 18.

27. Thornton, "New Cybersects," 148–149.

28. He Hanhun, "Xiejiao de zhidu jingjixue fenxi" (An economic analysis of the heretical sect system), Kexue yu wushenlun (Science and atheism) 15,6 (2003); Lu Yunfeng, "Entrepreneurial Logics and the Evolution of Falun Gong," *Journal for the Scientific Study of Religion* 44,2 (2005): 173–185.

29. N. J. Demerath III, Peter Dobkin Hall, Terry Schmitt, and Rhys H. Williams, eds., *Sacred Companies: Organizational Aspects of Religion and Religious Aspects of Organizations* (Oxford: Oxford University Press, 1998); Hank Johnston, "The Marketed Social Movement: A Case Study of the Rapid Growth of TM," *Pacific Sociological Review* 23,3 (July 1980): 333–354.

30. See Sun Wanning, "Media and the Chinese Diaspora: Community, Consumption, and Transnational Imagination," *Journal of Chinese Overseas* 1,1 (May 2005): 65–83.

31. Keck and Sikkink, *Activists beyond Borders,* 200.

32. David Hess and Brian Martin, "Repression, Backfire and the Theory of Transformative Events," *Mobilization* 11,2 (2006): 249–267.

33. Ting Jen-chieh, *Shehui fenhua yu zongjiao zhidu yanbian: Dangdai Taiwan xinxing zongjiao xianxiang de shehuixue kaocha* (Social differentiation and the evolution of religious systems: A sociological investigation of the phenomenon of new religions in contemporary Taiwan) (Taipei: Lianjing, 2004): 313–316, 386; Howard Chua-eoan and Donald Shapiro, "The Buddhist Martha," *Time,* January 20, 1997.

34. Supreme Master Ching Hai International Association, "The Quan Yin Method Frequently Asked Questions," last modified May 29, 1998, www.godsdirectcontact.org/eng/faq.txt (accessed July 5, 2007).

35. Research Directorate, Canadian Immigration and Refugee Board (Ottawa), Response to Information Request Report, "China: Meditation Practice Called "Kuan Yin Famen," CHN36385.E8 February 2001, www.irb-cisr.gc.ca/en/research/rir/ (accessed July 5, 2007); BBC Summary of World Broadcasts, "Human Rights Sources Say China Begins Suppression of Buddhist Sect," September 9, 2000, Lexis-Nexis.

36. BBC Summary of World Broadcasts, "China-Banned Buddhist Group Holds Hong Kong Rally," May 6, 2000, LexisNexis.

37. "Believe That You Are Really Great!" in Supreme Master Ching Hai Ocean of Love Tour: Experience the Divine, www.godsdirectcontact.org/lovetour/29-Sr11.htm (accessed July 5, 2007).

38. "An Old Farmer's Auspicious Retreat," www.godsdirectcontact.org/eng/news/148/mw2.htm (accessed July 5, 2007).

39. "Information on Vegetarianism Is Welcome in Mainland China," www.godsdirectcontact.org/incoming/pub/enews185/ (accessed July 5, 2007).

40. Steve Friess, "The Internet: Podcast Dissidents," *Newsweek*, October 9, 2006, 10.

41. "A Dedication of Love: Report from Mainland China," www.godsdirectcontact.us/sm21/enews/www/101/m-20.htm (accessed July 5, 2007).

42. The texts in question were "Dada and Lala," "A New Noah's Ark," and "Biography of Babaji."

43. Wuhan gong'an nianjian bianji bu [Wuhan Public Security Yearbook Editorial Board], Wuhan gong'an nianjian [Wuhan Public Security Yearbook] (Beijing: Zhongguo Renmin Gong'an Daxue Chubanshe, 2003), 93–94.

44. "Cash and the Campaign: Clinton Faces a Tide of Revelations about His Political Fund-raising," *Maclean's*, Toronto ed., January 13, 1997, 32–34.

45. Carey Goldberg, "In the Eye of a Political Storm, a Peaceful Ashram," *New York Times*, December 19, 1996, 14.

46. Donald J. Liddick, Jr., "Campaign Fund-Raising Abuses and Money Laundering in Recent U.S. Elections: Criminal Networks in Action," *Crime, Law and Social Change* 34 (2000): 129–132.

47. William Clairborne, "Behind Clinton Fund Donations, Sect with a Flamboyant Leader," *Washington Post*, December 19, 1995, A6; Miranda Ewell, "'Messiah' Sent Thousands to Clinton; Sect Gains Unfavorable Attention," *Times-Picayune*, December 22, 1996, A24; Gordon Young, "God, Inc.: Inner Peace Isn't the Only Thing Supreme Master Ching Hai Is Selling Bay Area Disciples," *San Francisco Weekly*, May 22, 1996; Rafer Guzman, "Immaterial Girl: Part Buddha, Part Madonna, Supreme Master Ching Hai Promises Immediate Enlightenment to San Jose's Asian Immigrants," *San Jose Mercury*, March 28–April 3, 1996.

48. Liddick, "Campaign Fund-Raising," 129–132.

49. Yin Xin, "*Zhong Gong*'de fazhan he renxing fankang" (The development and tenacious resistance of Zhong Gong), Qianshao (Outpost) (October 2000): 35–36.

50. Thornton, "New Cybersects," 147–170.

51. See "Road of Enterprise: Brief Introduction about Tianhua (Kilin) Group," www.speakout.com/forum_view.asp?Forum=China&MID=82261&mMID=82261 (accessed July 5, 2007); Chen Zong, "Zhong Gong bei dacheng xiejiao canzhao pohuai" (China Gong is attacked as a heretical sect and destroyed), Qianshao, June 2000, 32.

52. Agence France Presse Report, "HK Group Says China about to Ban Zhonggong Group," January 31, 2000, Foreign Broadcast Information Service, FBIS-CHI-2000–0205.

53. US Newswire, "'Campaign to Free Master Zhang Hongbao' to Hold Press Conference Dec. 20," December 19, 2000, Lexis-Nexis.

54. Executive Office of China Shadow Government, "The First Public Announcement by China Shadow Government," August 9, 2003, www.world-chinese.com/Eng/DispNews.asp?ID=8899 (accessed July 5, 2007).

55. Marshall Allen, "Zhang Preliminary Hearing Begins," *Pasadena Star-News,* December 9, 2003, Lexis-Nexis.

56. Associated Press, "China Detains American, New Zealander Belonging to Exiled Dissident Group," May 26, 2003, Lexis-Nexis.

57. China Support Network, "CSN Declares No Confidence in Peng Ming," May 29, 2003, http://chinasupport.net/site.htm?page=news64 (accessed July 5, 2007).

58. John Kusumi, "Zhang Hongbao, Qi Gong Master, Chinese Dissident, and Lightning Rod for Controversy Dies at Age 52," China Support Network, September 10, 2006, http://chinasupport.net/site.htm?page=buzz09100601 (accessed July 5, 2007).

59. "Dissident Accused of Terrorism Jailed for Life," *South China Morning Post,* October 14, 2005, 5.

60. Kusumi, "Zhang Hongbao."

61. See Wen Hua, "Possibly Murdered Qigong Master Disclosed CCP Military Secrets," *Epoch Times,* September 7, 2006, www.theepochtimes.com/news/6–9–7/45723.html (accessed July 5, 2007).

62. Zhang Weiqing and Gong Qiao, *Falun Gong chuangshiren Li Hongzhi pingzhuan* (A biography of Li Hongzhi, founder of Falun Gong) (Taipei: Business Weekly Press, 1999), 53.

63. Lu Yunfeng, "Entrepreneurial Logics," 175.

64. James Tong, "An Organizational Analysis of the Falun Gong: Structure, Communications, Financing," *China Quarterly* 171 (September 2002): 636–660.

65. Ibid., 651.

66. Yuezhi Zhao, "Falun Gong, Identity, and the Struggle over Meaning inside and outside China," in Nick Couldry and James Curran, eds., *Contesting Media Power: Alternative Media in a Networked Society* (Lanham, Md.: Rowman and Littlefield, 2003), 213.

67. "The Battle between the Chinese Government and the Falun Gong," *Chinese Law and Government* 32,5 (September–October 1999): 87–90.

68. Zhao, "Falun Gong," 209–224.

69. Agence-France Presse, "Largest Demonstration Since Tiananmen in Beijing," Foreign Broadcast Information Service, FBIS-CHI-1999-0425, April 25, 1999.

70. For detailed analysis of the Liu Qi and Xia Deren cases, see Mark J. Leavy, "Discrediting Human Rights Abuse as an 'Act of State': A Case Study on the Repression of the Falun Gong in China and Commentary on International Human Rights Law in U.S. Courts," *Rutgers Law Journal* 35 (2004): 749–842.

71. Mei Duzhi, "How China's Government Is Attempting to Control Chinese Media in America," *China Brief,* November 21, 2001, www.jamestown.org/

publications_details.php?volume_id=17&&issue_id=638 (accessed July 5, 2007). Mei Duzhi is affiliated with several Falun Gong organizations.

72. John Leicester, "TV Hijackings, Email Attacks: China's Government, Falun Gong Battle for a Hazy Concept—Truth," Associated Press On-Line, April 13, 2002, LexisNexis; Zhao, "Falun Gong."

73. Susan V. Lawrence, "Falun Gong Uses Free Speech as a Sword," *Far Eastern Economic Review* 167,15, April 15, 2004, 26–29.

74. Vanessa Hua, "Dissident Media Linked to Falun Gong: Chinese Language Print, Broadcast Outlets in U.S. Are Making Waves," *San Francisco Chronicle,* December 18, 2005, A34.

75. Karlyn Barker and Lena H. Sun, "Falun Gong Activist Defiant after Arrest," *Washington Post,* April 22, 2006, A5.

76. "U.S. Finds No Evidence of Alleged Concentration Camp in China—Repression of Falun Gong, Reports of Organ Harvesting Still Worry Officials," *Washington File,* April 16, 2006; Mike Steketee, "The Price Is Rights," *Australian,* April 1, 2006.

77. Jim Bronskill, "China Accused of Organ Harvest: Falun Gong Prisoners Targeted, Report Says," *Gazette* (Montreal), July 7, 2006, A10.

78. Paul Mooney, "Activist Harry Wu Challenges Organ Harvesting Claims; Scale of Conspiracy Alleged by Falun Gong 'Impossible,'" *South China Morning Post,* August 9, 2006, 7.

79. Wu Hongda [Harry Wu], "Wo duiyu Falun Gong meiti baogao Sujiatun jizhongying wenti de renzhi ji qi jingli" (My knowledge of the problem of Falun Gong media reports regarding Sujiatun concentration camp and other experiences), Guancha (Observe), July 18, 2006, www.observechina.net/info/artshow.asp?ID=39862 (accessed July 5, 2007).

80. Zhang Yu and Zhen Baihe, "Organ Harvesting Exists—There Is No Doubt," *Epoch Times,* September 27, 2006, www.theepochtimes.com/news/6–9–27/46418.html (accessed July 5, 2007).

81. Jiao Guobiao, "Tupo dalu de wangluo fengsuo" (Break through the mainland's internet blockade) Pingguo ribao (Apple daily), May 8, 2006, www.ncn.org/asp/zwginfo/daKAY.asp?ID=68602&ad=5/8/2006 (accessed July 5, 2007).

82. Jonathan Bach and David Stark, "Link, Search, Interact: The Co-evolution of NGOs and Interactive Technology," *Theory, Culture and Society* 21,3 (2004): 101–111.

83. John D. Clark and Nuno Themundo, "The Age of Protest: Internet-Based 'Dot Causes' and the Anti-Globalization Movement," in John D. Clark, ed., *Globalizing Civic Engagement: Civil Society and Transnational Action* (London: Earthscan, 2003), 109–126. Clifford Bob, *The Marketing of Rebellion,* 8.

84. Calvert W. Jones, "Online Impression Management: Case Studies of Activist Web Sites and Their Credibility-Enhancing Tactics during the Kosovo Crisis," paper presented at the conference "Safety and Security in a Networked

World," the Oxford Internet Institute, Oxford University, September 8–10, 2005.

85. Emphasis added. Kathleen Stewart, "Conspiracy Theory's Worlds," *Paranoia within Reason* (Chicago: University of Chicago Press, 1999), 18.

86. John Downing, *Radical Media: Rebellious Communication and Social Movements* (Thousand Oaks, Calif.: Sage, 2001), 278.

87. On a Microsoft-funded letter-writing campaign that included letters by citizens who were deceased, see Simon English, "Back from the Grave to Boost Microsoft Case," *Daily Telegraph* (London), August 24, 2001, 35.

88. On a purported alliance of consumer advocacy groups that was in fact heavily funded by Verizon Communications and AT&T, see Dionne Searcey, "Consumer Groups Tied to Industry; Some Advocacy Lobbyists for Cable Users Are Backed by Telecoms, Report Says," *Wall Street Journal*, March 28, 2006, B4.

89. For a Moldovan example, see "Disinformation: Old and New Information Tricks," *Economist*, August 5, 2006, Lexis-Nexis.

90. Thomas P. Lyon and John W. Maxwell, "Astroturf: Group Lobbying and Corporate Strategy," *Journal of Economics and Management Strategy* 13,4 (Winter 2004): 561–597.

91. Charles Tilly, "Social Movements and National Politics," in Charles Bright and Sandra Harding, eds., *State-Making and Social Movements* (Ann Arbor: University of Michigan Press, 1984), 311–313.

10. Permanent Rebellion?

1. Thomas Taylor Meadows, *The Chinese and Their Rebellions* (London: Smith, Elder, 1856), 25.

2. Ibid.

3. Franz Michael, *The Taiping Rebellion* (Seattle: University of Washington Press, 1966); Jen Yu-wen, *The Taiping Revolutionary Movement* (New Haven, Conn.: Yale University Press, 1973).

4. Roderick MacFarquhar and Michael Schoenhals, *Mao's Last Revolution* (Cambridge, Mass.: Harvard University Press, 2006); Harry Harding, *China's Second Revolution: Reform after Mao* (Washington, D.C.: Brookings Institution, 1987).

5. Elizabeth J. Perry and Mark Selden, eds., *Chinese Society: Change, Conflict and Resistance* (London: Routledge, 2002), 16.

6. Thomas P. Bernstein and Xiaobo Lü, *Taxation without Representation in Contemporary Rural China* (Cambridge: Cambridge University Press, 2003), 163.

7. Daniel L. Overmyer, *Folk Buddhist Religion: Dissenting Sects in Late Traditional China* (Cambridge, Mass.: Harvard University Press, 1976); Susan Naquin, *Millenarian Rebellion in China* (New Haven, Conn.: Yale University Press, 1976).

8. Prasenjit Duara, *Sovereignty and Authenticity: Manchukuo and the East Asian Modern* (Lanham, Md.: Rowman and Littlefield, 2003), chap. 3.

9. David Strand, *Rickshaw Beijing: City People and Politics in the 1920s* (Berkeley: University of California Press, 1989).

10. Jonathan K. Ocko, "I'll Take It All the Way to Beijing: Capital Appeals in the Qing," *Journal of Asian Studies* 47,2 (May 1988): 291–315.

11. Paul A. Cohen, *History in Three Keys: The Boxers as Event, Experience and Myth* (New York: Columbia University Press, 1997): 106–107.

12. Elizabeth J. Perry, *Rebels and Revolutionaries in North China, 1845–1945* (Stanford, Calif.: Stanford University Press, 1980); and Joseph W. Esherick, *The Origins of the Boxer Uprising* (Berkeley: University of California Press, 1987).

13. For an overview of the pioneering works on Chinese rebellion and revolution, see Frederic Wakeman Jr., "Rebellion and Revolution: The Study of Popular Movements in Chinese History," *Journal of Asian Studies* 36,2 (February 1977): 201–237.

14. Charles O. Hucker, *The Ming Dynasty: Its Origins and Evolving Institutions* (Ann Arbor: University of Michigan Center for Chinese Studies, 1978).

15. Philip A. Kuhn, *Rebellion and Its Enemies in Late Imperial China: Militarization and Social Structure, 1796–1864* (Cambridge, Mass.: Harvard University Press, 1970).

16. For a critical review, see Frederic Wakeman Jr., "The Civil Society and Public Sphere Debate: Western Reflections on Chinese Political Culture." *Modern China* 19,2 (April 1993): 108–138.

17. Chalmers A. Johnson, *Peasant Nationalism and Communist Power: The Emergence of Revolutionary China* (Stanford: Stanford University Press, 1962).

18. Mark Selden, *China in Revolution: The Yenan Way Revisited* (Armonk, N.Y.: Sharpe, 1995); Tetsuya Kataoka, *Resistance and Revolution in China: The Communists and the Second United Front* (Berkeley: University of California Press, 1974); Suzanne Pepper, *Civil War in China: The Political Struggle, 1945–49* (Berkeley: University of California Press, 1978).

19. Kenneth Lieberthal, *Governing China: From Revolution through Reform* (New York: Norton, 2004); William L. Parish and Martin K. Whyte, *Village and Family in Contemporary China* (Chicago: University of Chicago Press, 1978); Martin King Whyte and William L. Parish, *Urban Life in Contemporary China* (Chicago: University of Chicago Press, 1984).

20. Elizabeth J. Perry, *Challenging the Mandate of Heaven: Social Protest and State Power in China* (Armonk, N.Y.: Sharpe, 2002).

21. Elizabeth J. Perry, "Shanghai's Strike Wave of 1957," *China Quarterly* 137 (March 1994): 1–27.

22. Sebstian Heilmann, "The Social Context of Mobilization in China: Factions, Work Units and Activists during the 1976 April Fifth Movement," *China Information* 8,3 (Winter 1993–94): 18.

23. Tyrene White, *China's Longest Campaign: Birth Planning in the People's Republic, 1949–2005* (Ithaca, N.Y.: Cornell University Press, 2005).

24. Elizabeth J. Perry, *Shanghai on Strike: The Politics of Chinese Labor* (Stanford, Calif.: Stanford University Press, 1993).

25. Jeffrey N. Wasserstrom, *Student Protests in Twentieth-Century China: The View from Shanghai* (Stanford, Calif. : Stanford University Press, 1991).

26. The scholarly literature on this topic is vast. For a useful review, see Ian Johnson, "The Death and Life of China's Civil Society," *Perspectives on Politics* 1,3 (September 2003): 551–554.

27. Chen Yung-fa, *Making Revolution: The Communist Movement in Eastern and Central China, 1937–1945* (Berkeley: University of California Press, 1986); Kathleen Hartford and Steven M. Goldstein, eds., *Single Sparks: China's Rural Revolutions* (Armonk, N.Y.: Sharpe, 1989).

28. Kevin J. O'Brien and Lianjiang Li, "Campaign Nostalgia in the Chinese Countryside," *Asian Survey* 39,3 (May–June 1999): 375–393; Elizabeth J. Perry, "'To Rebel Is Justified': Cultural Revolution Influences on Contemporary Chinese Protest," in Kam-yee Law, ed., *Beyond Purge and Holocaust: The Chinese Cultural Revolution Reconsidered* (New York: Palgrave, 2003).

29. Elizabeth J. Perry and Li Xun, *Proletarian Power: Shanghai in the Cultural Revolution* (Boulder, Colo.: Westview, 1997).

30. Merle Goldman, *From Comrade to Citizen: The Struggle for Political Rights in China* (Cambridge, Mass.: Harvard University Press, 2005).

31. Liang Heng and Judith Shapiro, *Son of the Revolution* (New York: Vintage Books, 1983); Gao Yuan, *Born Red: A Chronicle of the Cultural Revolution* (Stanford, Calif.: Stanford University Press, 1987).

32. Dorothy J. Solinger, *Contesting Citizenship in Urban China* (Berkeley: University of California Press, 1999).

33. Elizabeth J. Perry, "Studying Chinese Politics: Farewell to Revolution?" *China Journal* 57 (January 2007): 1–22.

34. Shanthi Kalathil and Taylor Boas, "Internet Control in Authoritarian Regimes: China, Cuba, and the Counterrevolution," 21 (July 2001): 1–21, Carnegie Endowment for International Peace Working Papers.

35. Victor H. Li, *Law without Lawyers* (Stanford, Calif.: Stanford University Press, 1977).

36. Yu Jianrong, *Zhongguo nongmin de kangzheng* (Peasant resistance in China) (Hong Kong: Mirror Books, 2007); Neil J. Diamant, Stanley B. Lubman, and Kevin J. O'Brien, eds., *Engaging the Law in China: State, Society, and Possibilities for Justice* (Stanford, Calif.: Stanford University Press, 2005).

37. The guidelines (in Chinese) can be found on the website of the All-China Lawyers Association, www.acla.org.cn (accessed May 25, 2007).

38. Marie-Claire Bergere, *Sun Yat-sen* (Stanford, Calif.: Stanford University Press, 1998); Maurice Meisner, *Li Ta-chao and the Origins of Chinese Marxism* (Cambridge, Mass.: Harvard University Press, 1967); Lee Feigon, *Chen Duxiu, Founder of the Chinese Communist Party* (Princeton, N.J.: Princeton University Press, 1983).

39. John Foran, ed., *Theorizing Revolutions* (New York: Routledge, 1997).

40. Meadows, *Chinese*, 27.

41. Kevin J. O'Brien and Lianjiang Li, *Rightful Resistance in Rural China* (New York: Cambridge University Press, 2006); Ching Kwan Lee, *Against the Law:*

Labor Protests in China's Rustbelt and Sunbelt (Berkeley: University of California Press, 2007).

42. O'Brien and Li, *Rightful Resistance,* chap. 2.
43. Bernstein and Lü, *Taxation without Representation.*
44. Peter Ho, *Institutions in Transition: Land Ownership, Property Rights and Social Conflict in China* (New York: Oxford University Press, 2005).
45. Meadows, *Chinese,* 27.
46. Andrew J. Nathan, "Authoritarian Resilience," *Journal of Democracy* 14,1 (2003): 13.

Contributors

Yongshun Cai is Assistant Professor in the Division of Social Science at Hong Kong University of Science and Technology. He is the author of *State and Laid-Off Workers in Reform China: The Silence and Collective Action of the Retrenched* (2005) as well as articles on rural and urban China.

Feng Chen is Professor of Political Science at Hong Kong Baptist University. His current research focuses on Chinese labor politics. His work has appeared in *China Quarterly, China Journal, Modern China, Communist and Post-communist Studies,* and other journals.

Xi Chen is Assistant Professor of Political Science at Louisiana State University. His most recent publication appeared in a volume edited by Elizabeth Perry and Merle Goldman, *Grassroots Political Reform in Contemporary China* (2007).

William Hurst is Assistant Professor of Government at the University of Texas at Austin. His research focuses on Chinese urban and labor politics, and has appeared in *China Information, China Quarterly,* and *Studies in Comparative International Development.*

Kevin J. O'Brien is Alann P. Bedford Professor of Asian Studies, and Professor of Political Science at the University of California, Berkeley. His latest books are *Rightful Resistance in Rural China* (2006) (with Lianjiang Li) and *Engaging the Law in China: State, Society, and Possibilities for Justice* (2005) (with Neil J. Diamant and Stanley B. Lubman).

Elizabeth J. Perry is Henry Rosovsky Professor of Government at Harvard University. Her most recent books include *Patrolling the Revolution:*

Worker Militias, Citizenship and the Modern Chinese State (2006) and *Grass-roots Political Reform in Contemporary China* (2007).

Rachel E. Stern is a Ph.D. candidate in Political Science at the University of California, Berkeley. She has published articles in *Mobilization, Asian Survey* and *Current Anthropology*. Her dissertation focuses on lawyers and environmental litigation in China.

Yanfei Sun is a Ph.D. candidate in Sociology at the University of Chicago. Her dissertation focuses on religious growth in China at the county level.

Sidney Tarrow is Maxwell M. Upson Professor of Government and Professor of Sociology at Cornell University. His most recent books are *The New Transnational Activism* (2005) and *Contentious Politics* (2006) (with Charles Tilly).

Patricia M. Thornton is Associate Professor of Political Science at Trinity College in Hartford, Connecticut. She is currently teaching International Studies at Portland State University. Her most recent publications include *Disciplining the State: Virtue, Violence and State-Making in Modern China* (2007) and *Identity Matters: How Ethnic and Sectarian Allegiances Both Prevent and Promote Collective Violence* (2007) (with James L. Peacock and Patrick B. Inman).

Carsten T. Vala is Assistant Professor of Political Science at Loyola College in Maryland. He is the author of a chapter in Yoshiko Ashiwa and David Wank, eds., *Making Religion, Making the State: The Politics of Religion in Contemporary China* (forthcoming). His dissertation focuses on Protestantism in contemporary China.

Teresa Wright is Professor of Political Science at California State University, Long Beach. Her research focuses on comparative social movements and democratization in East Asia. Her publications include *The Perils of Protest: State Repression and Student Activism in China and Taiwan* (2001), as well as articles in *Comparative Politics, China Quarterly,* and *Asian Survey*.

Guobin Yang is Associate Professor in Asian and Middle Eastern Cultures, Barnard College, and an affiliated faculty member in the Department of Sociology, Columbia University. His research focuses on social